# YOUTH:
## Divergent Perspectives

# YOUTH:
## Divergent Perspectives

Edited by
**Peter K. Manning**
Departments of Sociology and Psychiatry
Michigan State University
East Lansing, Michigan 48823

**John Wiley and Sons, Inc.**
New York   London   Sydney   Toronto

**Library of Congress Cataloging in Publication Data:**

Manning, Peter K.     comp.
  Youth divergent perspectives.

  Includes bibliographical references.
  CONTENTS: Bell, D. Sensibility in the 60's.—
Douglas, J. D. The growing importance of youth and of college students in American Society.—Laqueur, W. Reflections of youth movements. [etc.]
  1. Student movements—United States. 2. College students—United States—Attitudes. 3. Youth. I. Title.

LA229.M33     378.1′98′10973     72-11793
ISBN 0-471-56758-2

Printed in the United States of America

10-9 8 7 6 5 4 3 2 1

# Preface

My experience in collecting and editing these articles is described best in Tom Cottle's aphoristic remark, "To write about youth means confronting one's prior and future selves and generations and, even more, one's single self properly bound, trapped and free, in the single growing point of now." I am now, accurately speaking, marginal between youth and some sort of murky early adulthood. Having rushed, in a sense, through what others were able to experience as youth, I find I spend a lot of time trying to pin down where I stand in the unrolling of the generations. It's easiest when I'm with my children or with my parents; it's most difficult when I'm with my students. These articles struck chords with me, and perhaps they even allowed me the luxury of shifting back and forth in time, and of simply enjoying not having to wonder where I stood chronologically.

**Peter K. Manning**
East Lansing, Michigan, 1971

v

# A Note to the Instructor

Any good textbook reflects something of the author's self and his vision of the field. By definition, then, a good textbook in sociology is not likely to be a fully rounded treatment covering the great diversity within the field. In this note, I explain what this book is and what it is not intended to do.

The selections are written mostly by male, elite academic observers—men deeply involved, personally and occupationally, in the subject and actuality of youth. The experiences (what might be called the "glaringly obvious" facets of the experiences) of the white middle-class college student are vital to this collection. The decision to provide the book with this focus was not an attempt to slight other, equally significant experiential patterns of the minorities, of noncollege youth, or of the "youthful" who are neither young nor collegiate. The selections reflect the analysis of observers writing about youth in the late 1960s and early 1970s who were primarily concerned with the white, middle-class student. Within the context of these kinds of writings, I chose the ones with style and clarity, and I attempted to select articles that underscored the interdigitation of sensibilities and structure. Finally, the practical editorial considerations of depth, balance, and size were weighed.

The timeliness of the topic—youth—is the great advantage and the disadvantage of this type of book. Many of these pieces reflect a concern with the militant outbursts and demonstrations on campuses in the late 1960s, just prior to the axial events culminating in murder at Kent State and Jackson State in the spring of 1970. Questions of morality are raised, implicitly and explicitly: Are the youth of today really good or really bad? It seems to me that these kinds of moral questions, as I explain in the first few pages of my introductory essay, are almost chronically a part of the relationships between generations in a complex society. As new generations appear to replace their progenitors, invidious comparisons seem inevitable. Competition for power and authority gives rise to moral arguments and justifications for or against the present state of affairs. This process of competition, threat, justification and attack seems almost universal and ahistorical, but the particulars of the arguments, as they occur in the United States in the period roughly circumscribed by the 1960s, are certainly time and place bound.

In its immersion in the concrete facts of a given epoch, the existential perspective possesses strength. It turns attention to feelings and symbols that affect men in given life situations, but attempts to derive what is patterned or transsituational. The framework is not itself created by participants, but it is constructed by sensitive observers who seek systematically to illuminate human experience. I hope that this book will provide a sense of self-understanding for students and teachers. Rational thought and analysis can be a therapeutic experience and, for those of us who experienced the events of the last five years, such catharsis is doubtless welcome.

**P. K. M.**

# Contents

ix

Contents

# INTRODUCTORY ESSAY

I have to be incredibly *there*, man. Whatever I do, I do a lot, and whatever it is, it's a damn sight better than being bored . . .

Yeah, I know I might be going too fast . . . Man, I'd rather have ten years of superhypermost than live to be seventy by sitting in some goddam chair watching TV. Right now is where you are, how can you wait.[1]

Janis Joplin

Modern Culture began as an effort to annihilate the contemplative mode of experience by emphasizing *immediacy, impact, simultaneity,* and *sensation.* It is today at the point of breaking up all fixed points of reference in formal genres (Bell, 1965, p. 220).

One of the most controversial and interesting subjects of recent years is certainly American youth, and they continue to elicit a rich variety of often intense reactions. Although sociologists have occasionally ventured an objective definition of youth, one that they argue is free of the contamination of sociocultural and historical context, they have thus far been unsuccessful. The youth resemble a screen on which others project their fears, hopes, and fantasies. These reactions to what is taken to be youth are themselves useful and interesting sociological phenomena. As the young are more differentiated with regard to their experiences, their perspectives, and hopes for the future, it is less accurate to generally refer to "the youthful subculture" the "generation gap," or even the "younger generation." Youth may be better seen as a group of people, primarily those excluded from the constraints of adult commitments, who espouse the same symbols and perspectives. These perspectives and symbols, as is pointed out below, are often highly situational, and can be examined only on selected occasions. The highly variable behavior of youth in this society gives rise to the fractionated reactions of sophisticated observers. If a single generalization can be made concerning the nature of

---

[1] In Lydon, 1971, p. 90.

1

the reactions, it is that the pattern of response is *ambivalent*, stimulating hatred, fear, and envy simultaneously with feelings of love, respect, and admiration. To adults, as some writers have suggested (Berger, 1970; Friedenberg, 1962), the young symbolize the passage of time, the recession of their vitality, and the threat of the new and demanding authority of peers. Adolescent relationships, characterized by a deep sense of honor, personal commitment, spontaneity, and passion, may represent to adults personal qualities they desire, have compromised, or never developed (Friedenberg, 1962). Adult ambivalence is more than reciprocated by adolescents. A sense of disappointment with adults punctuates much adolescent social commentary, and is mixed, on occasion, with fear. On the other hand, a number of scholars have launched bitter and angry attacks against the young and youthful behavior. Most notorious of these is perhaps Lewis Feuer, whose massive scholarship in *The Conflict of Generations* (1968) was intended to discredit youth movements as oedipal fantasies. He was joined in this attack by another psychoanalytically oriented commentator, Bruno Bettelheim. One of the more creative attempts to place the young within an interpretive framework was John Aldridge's *In the Country of the Young* (1970): but his tone was also often strident and harsh:[2]

> Certainly, young people have radically influenced, where they have not positively dictated, our views on just about every significant issue confronting us in this age. We have been told by them what we had better think about race relations, foreign policy, the problems of backward nations, the war in Vietnam, the poor and underprivileged, the industrial, military, and educational hierarchies, marriage, sex, drugs, nudity, perversion, obscenity, and pornography. They have created the prevailing fashions in manners, morals, dress, and personal hygiene (or the lack of it), and have even given us new standards of physical attractiveness based, it would seem, on some new mutation in facial and body types which has made their very persons structurally and physiognomically different from our own. They seem, for example, to be the first generation which has succeeded in democratizing the human body and evolving a corporate type or norm of female beauty and male handsomeness. Extreme variations in size, shape, and symmetry have been largely eradicated among them. The face or figure whose beauty is absolutely individual and unmistakable has given way to a generalized young-class style which may be appealing but is also highly forgettable. The ideal of good looks represented by the early Ingrid Bergman and Gary Cooper has disappeared so completely that when one sees those beautiful people on the Late Show, they seem like last survivors of some extinct superrace, as well as sad reminders of an age when a person could

[2] Interested readers should compare the imagery in this quote with Friedenberg's brilliant essay, "The Image of the Adolescent Minority," (1963) where Friedenberg attempts an explanation for the emotion generated by the young among their critics.

be considered attractive after twenty-five. The new body style for men is neither tall nor short, fat nor thin. Classic Arrow Collar features have been replaced by the androgynous medieval squire or hairy simian look, ugliness now supposedly being suggestive of ferocious sexual vitality. Among male hippies this notion has been carried to the point where hair—usually of exactly the right color and texture—is worn like a public growth covering indiscriminately head, face, groin, and armpits, so that the entire person becomes a sex organ. For young women the latest fashion in face is a sort of fixed kewpie-doll vapidity. Cheeks are softly plump miniature babies' bottoms; eyes are like decorated Alfa Romeo headlights; and bodies appear to be transplants from promisingly contoured ten-year-old boys. Even the thighs exposed by miniskirts no longer seem to be the sexy upper parts of legs but interchangeable items of mannequin decor, purchased like wigs at boutiques (Aldridge, 1970, pp. xiv-xv).

The intellectuals have, in some senses, chosen sides, selected weapons and begun to write.

This collection includes a variety of selections that are representative, I think, of the best opinion and sociological analysis in recent years. The purpose of this collection is to make available these divergent perspectives on youth within a relatively neutral framework. The focus is issues and concepts, as well as opinion and evaluation. It is my opinion that the themes in the book are quite repetitive and surprisingly consistent, in spite of *differing interpretations of the observed facts.*

In the following section, some of the themes of the selections are explicit. The framework employed is existential sociology,[3] a sociology that shows great promise as a means of understanding the often confusing and inchoate events of our times. The principal focus is twofold: what is the nature of American social order, and how does it generate and pattern certain basic feelings, or sensibilities.

## Youth: Sensibilities and Structures

The threat of modern society is that its very strength, its rationality and efficiency, and bureaucratically based social organization, will run away from the underpinnings of human feelings that legitimate society. In other words, we are in danger of reducing man to a strictly rational functionary, demanding complete subservience, rationality, and compulsive productivity, while expecting him to ignore the perceived lack of opportunity for the expression of common human emotions such as love, fear, hate, lust, and compassion. The young pinpoint the dilemma of the "abstract society" (Zijderveld, 1971)

[3] Examples of sociological work in this tradition are Jack D. Douglas, ed. 1970a and 1970b. See also the provocative work of Peter Berger (with Luckman) 1966, 1969, and Zijderveld, 1971.

3

for they must be incorporated and mobilized in order to quite literally man the technological apparatus, and their feelings and desires must be channeled and directed by the institutional framework in which they are to live the one life they have. The young, the focus of this collection, reflect certain *structural* problems of modern societies, and they raise to the foreground the underlying *sensibility* of modern societies. This section of the introduction is an attempt to integrate and introduce these two features of modern society, structure and sensibility, as they are illustrated by the behavior and attitudes of the young.

Perceptive social observers, at least since the time of the Greeks, have seen social life as a mixture or synthesis of the objective and the subjective. Some have made distinctions between motives and opportunities (compare Merton, 1957 with Cloward and Olin, 1960); some have drawn a line between attitudes and feelings and values (Thomas and Znaniecki, 1927), some between culture and society, and still others between systems and actions (Parsons, 1951; Znaniecki, 1965). What is at issue here is the fit between individual feelings and attitudes and social order, or a pattern of social life that is seen as continuous, external to the individual, and almost absolute in its character. Structure has attained the status of a nearly universally employed gloss or sensitizing concept referring to any enduring social relationship, be it between lovers, friends, husband and wife, and among the Lions, Catholics, Democrats or nation-states. In this tradition, a distinction will be drawn between structure and sensibilities. Let us first delineate the meaning we wish to assign to the concept of structure.

Structures may be depicted as clusters of symbols such as those associated with the Catholic Church: the Mass, the symbols of the hierarchy of religious authority, and the components of the Christian liturgy, for example. However, structures do not simply exist, perpetuated through time by apathy, conformity, and blind obedience. They must be intentionally constructed or interpreted by members of society; members must indicate the meaning of social objects and communicate that meaning to others. Others in the same concrete situations must in turn confirm or disconfirm the indicated meanings. By so doing, actors may be able to work out or construct a situated social order that will permit concerted behavior (see Douglas, ed., 1970a, p. 16). An adequate sociological analysis, as Weber pointed out, must clarify our understanding of conduct at the level of *meaningful* action. That is, we must be able to move from generalized descriptions of patterns to concrete meanings, what people feel, think, and do when they take each other into account. In this case, we are interested in the general relationship of the youth to the social order.

Unfortunately, sociology has not been of a single mind in its approach to the relationships between sensibilities and structures (It has not been of a single mind in its approach to many things). Social psychologists, especially those of the gestaltist, person-perception, Freudian, and "humanistic" per-

4

suasions have addressed the problem of mood, feeling, and emotion in social life. However, they have tended to restrict their concerns to artificial or contrived laboratory experimental situations that recently have received major criticism for many perspectives (Freidman, 1967; Rosenthal, 1966), or they have published clinical or case studies that have not been convincing to sociologists who look for pattern and continuity of empirical data bearing groups and larger social units: some of the most fascinating work on phenomenological aspects of feeling, such as pain and body meanings, are unsatisfying for their methodological or sociological naivete.

Many sociologists have developed models of social organization and structure that ignore the inner feelings of men and the attribution of sentiment or emotion to social objects. This is true even of those within the Meadian symbolic interactionist tradition that is most closely associated with attempts at understanding the ways in which symbols and the meanings and attitudes they elicit alter the pattern of human action.[4]

Sociologists have demonstrated that as societies develop toward a configuration that is called more "modern," they become more specialized and functionally specific. These societies contain radically differentiated private worlds, each with its own set of assumptions, jargon, ideologies, roles, and statuses (academic disciplines provide a familiar example). Evidence mounts that one of the primary features of modern societies is that these changes in the scale and quantity of social relations, and the requirements of participation in social hierarchies, tend to create a *malaise* growing from a sense of disarticulation between private feelings and moods and these structures. (Marx touched these themes, but his main concern was with relationships between the work role and other roles and between personal feelings and work requirements. His analysis requires extention for its problem is more diffuse, pervasive, and generic). Few sociologists have satisfactorily explicated the implications of increased societal complexity upon sensibilities associated with the process (for an exception to this, see Faunce, 1968). We can broadly conclude that sociologists have tended to overlook the moods and feelings of men. However, to depict society solely as a structure is to impale the moods of man upon a dulled wooden splinter.

Man's sensibilities, his feelings, moods, desires, and sentiments, especially as they are expressed in language, are shaped by and literally embedded in social structure. However, the relationships between social structure (as a

[4] A leading symbolic interactionist complained (personal communication) that compiling an outstanding collection of articles representative of symbolic interactionism, ". . . entailed hour after futile hour of quest for something significant on the unconscious or the nonrational." Although these topics may appear to be more extreme in their focus, the generally inadequate treatment of emotion in Meadian (and his followers') thought has been acknowledged in Manis and Metzer, eds., 1972 and in Lyman and Scott, *Sociology of the Absurd,* 1970.

5

pattern of social rules and culture and as a heritage of meanings, practices, and physical artifacts) and language are extremely complex. If man's sensibilities grow from his sense of a clear connection with the past and with tradition, they may be reaffirmed, clarified, and strengthened through ritual and conventionalized meanings. If, on the other hand, they are suffused with a search for novelty, new experience, and centered on the personality, then the unique and the novel become the criteria for judgement of adequacy of meaning. The vital connection between the individual and his culture becomes increasingly less predictable as a society moves toward a modern form. This detachment of standardized or routinely given meaning from behavior in time may give rise to a generally shared perception that culture has little relation to social life. Consequently, social objects have a high probability of being defined as "meaningless," or "absurd." In a society in which emotions are channeled by means of traditional modes of social control (gossip, face-to-face-interaction, neighborhood censorship) and shared myths and rituals, the private worlds of people are closely and deeply integrated with the world order in which they live. Their very existence symbolizes the order itself in the sense that they have a role in the cosmology of the society. The private emotions are integrated with the structures and the public symbolization of the collective purpose. On the other hand, in a society such as ours where the institutions have become abstractions governed by technological elites and cynically symbolized by the mass media, where each institution has attained a degree of functional autonomy from the others and where cultural pluralism reigns, emotions are no longer channeled through the legitimate social structures with taken-for-granted ease and nonconcern. Institutions tend to generate their own rationales and cultural mandates, quite apart from the needs of the people they are expected to serve. Consequently and simultaneously, the individual is thrown back on his own resources, private meanings, and personal interpretations of events. The glue that holds feeling and sentiment to social action becomes strained and fragile. The great growing edge of change in modern society lies in the interstices of structures where cultural forms and symbols are no longer adequate to express the meanings that experience has for the participants.

The growth of society—in numbers of people, intensity of interaction, complexity of role relationships, and the demands of the industrial order—has produced a characteristic sensibility in modern man. And this modern man or "post-modern man" is detected first in youthful patterns of adjustment of biography to history.

The speed of change in modern society, some call it a shock (Toffler, 1970), undercuts traditional bases of judgement, extends rationality as a substitute for previously taken for granted cultural axioms, and heightens the importance of (1) individual interpretations of events, (2) of the self as the center of meaning, and (3) of feelings as prime factor in orientation of events. The past thus grows increasingly less relevant and remote; the future takes on a problematic quality. The present becomes *the present*, the immediate, knowable, the empirical. Man feels thus a sense of *disconnectedness* with those clusters of symbols that bind him to the moral unit that is society. He is further immersed in the very complexity and potential satiety that the present provides—he may be, in fact, flooded with imagery as Lifton suggests in the selection below. Those structures that do exist, a product of the technology and rational bureaucratism, are seen as fearful and threatening because they limit, reduce, constrain, and otherwise coerce the freedom of the modern man. In the Bell and Lifton selections we discover the dilemma of the modern man, perhaps epitomized by the modern youth. He is eager for meaning and for the construction of existential truths in the face of cultural traditions; yet this very freedom extracts a high price—anxiety, dread, and self-doubt. The quest for identity and for meaning can, of course, overwhelm the individual with his own sense of freedom, a condition Durkheim called anomie. The young, striving to avoid the weight of tradition, to separate themselves from arbitrary meanings, and provided with little recognized significance aside from their attributed idealistic moral sensibilities, have transformed this culturally defined liability, this absence of learning, traditional wisdom, and ascription to convention, into their principal source of dignity. This residual moral function may therefore constitute the grounds of the young's concern with idealism, with truth, and with hypocrisy as Laqueur, Cottle, Nisbet and Lifton herein correctly see. Once the young preempt the high ground, and possess symbolic control of morality, they may, as Lifton warns, "substitute experience for history." He terms this quest the search for a "new history" that will obviate the presence of biological or nuclear death, and will provide for symbolic immortality, a sense of living forever.

A new personality style emerges from the disjunction of cultural and social structure and the rise of the existential quest and rapid alteration in institutions: *The Protean Man*, he who is open to experience, who is relatively uncommitted to a moral or political philosophy, and who is constantly searching for the creation and recreation of meaning. The Protean style, called *Consciousness III*, by Reich (1970), *Other-Direction* by Riesman (1956), and *The Seeker* by Keniston (1969), is a personality style of postmodern man. This style illustrates the sensibility associated with the young in our society. The Consciousness Three man is the man we might call "adolescent": one who seeks to liberate himself, who posits the absolute value of every self, who rejects concepts of excellence and competitive merit, who emphasizes honesty, who rejects impersonal role relationships, who feels a deep sense of personal responsibility for events, and who is open to any and all experience (Reich, 1970, Chapter 9). This movement and style, Bell concludes, warrants the conclusion that the sensibilities of the 1960s are those traditionally associated with the adolescent.

This personality style, the source of a great capacity for change in politics, in art, and in social relations, although gratifying to many, also generates many psychological burdens, as Cottle (below) and Keniston, speaking of a collegiate "seeker," points out:

> Along with the focus on the present and on "existential" values goes a very great tolerance for experimentation. Youth is increasingly defined (by youth itself) as a time for exploration, trial and error, and deliberate efforts to enlarge, change or expand personality. Experimentation in the interest of deliberate self-change is seen as essential to pursuit of meaning. Convinced that meaning is not found but created, members of the counterculture consider their own personalities the prime vehicles for the creation of significance. Since significance emerges from the self, it is only by transforming the self that significance can be achieved. In a kind of deliberate, self-conscious and intentional identity-formation, apparently unconnected activities and experiences find their rationale. Self-exploration, psychotherapy, sexual experimentation, travel, "encounter groups," a reverence for nature, and "sensitivity training" are tools in the pursuit of meaning—along with drug use (Keniston, 1968).

When the past is consciously faded into a mere background for the present, the loss of generational models and continuity may create significant strain for the young. For they then become the seers of the future. Margaret Mead (below) argues forcefully that the young are best capable of sensing the future, a future for which past experience has little relevance. If this is so, the dilemma of the young may be excruciating; they may take the role of transmitting the future to their parents, much as parents once transmitted the past to their children. The role reversal and the new content may bring even further dislocation for young who are barely able to discern a difference between self as child and as adult.

When the asymmetry of the role relations crumbles, the alignment of self with the future becomes increasingly problematic. To what can I become committed, if at all? What roles are meaningful to pour oneself into? Cottle, in the selection below, expands on this theme.

> What complicates these matters seven more is that our customs and rituals often cannot keep up with or comprehend the consequences of our changing sensations and private trials. Society seems to have no place for ambivalence and the indecision it yields. Often it is as if the social casings, the social roles into which we are obliged to fit our personal intrusiveness, our "real" selves, perhaps, cannot accommodate the presence of all our feelings, especially the anger. And how unfair this is, not just for youth, since all these other feelings have as much right to be seen and heard as the ones

for which the social customs and rituals were originally conceived (Cottle, 1971, p. 342).

These same ambivalences are noted by Riesman in his essay here. For some women, perhaps, incipient feelings of freedom will be overwhelming. Riesman advises against rejecting a challenging career requiring graduate or professional education because the problems of the present appear so urgent and demanding of attention. He quite accurately sees the challenges that lie before the educated woman, challenges for which she has growing cultural support. She may lack the personal experience or resources to accurately judge these personal dilemmas. Personal choices show dramatically the interrelationship of external constraints and individual feelings.

## *The Drug Experience*

The primary example of the modern sensibilities of the young is the psychedelic drug culture, for there, mood and meaning dominate. The drug culture, an established part of the repertoire of experience of a considerable segment of the young since its flowering in the early 1960s in the Bay Area (as chronicled by Tom Wolfe in *Electric Kool Aid Acid Test* (1968), contains many of the themes manifested by the present youth culture.

When discussing "drug culture," it is unwise to attempt any global description—the cultural associations that lead to use, the generalized cultural meanings associated with use, the identities imputed to the user, and the role of the user vary by the drugs involved. The greatest degree of overlap is found among those who seek enlightenment, mind expansion, and more intense personal experiences through the use of LSD, mescaline, psilocybin and marijuana. (Even here, as Carey (1968) and Goode (1970) suggest, there are differences among users in the meanings attributed to the drug experience.) We are concerned with description of the symbolic themes generated by the psychedelic or mind-altering drugs (especially LSD and marijuana), not those associated with "hard" drugs or amphetamines. Marijuana use is symbolic of a range of other matters of taste, politics, feelings, and life-style; marijuana, like prohibition, is a status issue (Gusfield, 1963; Goode, 1970; Kaplan, 1970). Rather than being a subculture, users of marijuana are a collection of people who share some conceptions of taste, morality, and attitude displayed in symbolism; they constitute not a subculture, but a *status aggregate*, or status aggregates (Stone and Form, 1953). Displaying these symbols may become the basis for a claim of status honor but more commonly display becomes an end in itself—expressive symbolism.

The symbolism of marijuana use represents the shifting of modalities of experience—the alteration of the perception of the locus of control as being "within" to seeing it as being "without." There is a close fit between the symbols, meanings, and experiences associated with the effects of these drugs

9

and the everyday experiences sought by many young. In the situation of use, the separation of the "mind" and the "body" are not taken as normal, but a state to be avoided, and a sense of concrete wholeness is sought. It is this sense of wholeness that is the essence of the experience of being high. The experience of smoking casts one's self with others "out there," while the self retains a sense of partial being in the body. It is a form of socially constructed madness. It diffuses the self, but it recreates it in the context of other trusting selves. When this superordinate self-consciousness appears, there is nothing (as Laing points out) between it and me or us and them; there is no is, only being. Being in this submerged, moody situation actualizes feelings as the locus of social bonding. As such, the ties of the marijuana user to other users are above all found in the situation of use itself. In this situation, the self is created, in part because one is high. The salient self is not found in the economic transactions that only produce the means for the self-of-the-mood, nor in the correlated political and social attitudes of users. Neither access nor attitude provide sufficient difference between users and nonusers—the high does. It is precisely in the experience that the user locates his being.

In drug use, the prime experience is the experience of use itself, where instead of having meanings and roles ascribed by others in an impersonal fashion, the *being is doing*. Keniston has noted that young drug users often experience a fusion fantasy in which many have a semiconscious concept of almost mystical union with nature, with their own inner lives, or with other people—of communication that requires no words.

> *A . . . frequent characteristic of alienated students is a fantasy of fusion and merger, which contrasts sharply with their current feelings of estrangement.* Many have a semiconscious concept of almost mystical union with nature, with their own inner lives, or with other people—of communication that requires no words, of the kind of oneness with nature, people, or the world that has always characterized intense religious experience. For a student with unusual impatience with the boundaries that separate the self from the not-self, the powerful hallucinogens are especially attractive, for they can profoundly alter the boundaries of body and self. This change in boundaries is by no means always pleasant, and one of the most common sources of panic during drug experiences is the feeling of being "trapped" in an isolated, barricaded subjectivity. But at other times, the hallucinogens do produce feelings of being in unusually direct contact, even fusion, with others (Keniston, 1968).

Quite a number of themes are illustrated in this single statement. The centrality of *shared experience* is underscored; the *non-verbal elements* of relationships, generalized much beyond the drug use situation itself are critical; and the *subjective qualities* of the relationship are also implied. However, the characteristics are not only attitudinal—emphasis on developing, emergent meanings of the situation (the present) further blurs the time and space dimensions of human relationships. The private, inner experience in the present is primary, with no intervening words to differentiate, analyze, or separate person from experience. In the situation of use, differences among people are radically equalized—no hierarchy exists. There is no central authority, no externally enforced social roles. This radical equality permits the spontaneous development of pure sociability. A member of The Grateful Dead, a San Francisco rock group, describes one of the early "acid tests" where LSD created a new, fresh, exhilarating mood of creation at author Ken Kesey's house.

When it was moving right, you could dig that there was something that it was getting toward, something like ordered chaos, or some region of chaos. The Test would start off and then there would be chaos. Everybody would be high and flashing and going through insane changes during which everything would be demolished, man, and spilled and broken and affected, and after that, another thing would happen, maybe smoothing out the chaos, then another, and it'd go all night til morning.

Just people being there, and being responsive. Like, there were microphones all over. If you were wandering around there would be a mike you could talk into. And there would be somebody somewhere else in the building at the end of some wire with a tape recorder and a mixing board and earphones listening in on the mikes and all of a sudden something would come in and he'd turn it up because it seemed appropriate at that moment.

What you said might come out a minute later on a tape loop in some other part of the place. So there would be this odd interchange going on, electroneural connections of weird sorts. And it was people, just people, doing it all. Kesey would be writing messages about what he was seeing on an opaque projector and they'd be projected up on the wall, and someone would comment about it on a mike somewhere and that would be singing out of a speaker somewhere else.

And we'd be playing, or, when we were playing we were playing. When we weren't, we'd be doing other stuff. There were no sets, sometimes we'd get up and play for ten minutes and all freak out and split. We'd just do it however it would happen. It wasn't a gig, it was the Acid Tests where anything was OK. Thousands of people, man, all helplessly stoned, all finding themselves in a roomful of other thousands of people, none of whom any of them were afraid of. It was magic, far out, beautiful magic (Lydon, 1971, pp. 120–121).

In a broad sense, youth are the focal point of these changes and permutations in sensibility. Certainly, to some degree, the search for alternative modes of expression is not exclusively the concern of the young, but also those espousing the *norms* of youthfulness—spontaneity, irresponsibility, hedonism —which, as Berger (1970) notes, are a reflection of the subterranean values of the larger adult society. The cultural changes of the last 10 years are signified not only by the emergence of the norms of youthfulness, epitomized in the Protean style, and in their public espousal by a young excessively exposed by the mass media, but are demonstrated in the degree to which the norms of youth—the youthful style—pervade modern art, music, literature, dissent, and dress and, indeed, appear to have suffused throughout the entire culture. They have attained the status of a minority theme in pluralistic society.

## Politics: The Public Experience

If the "culture," or symbolism of the drug status aggregate(s) represents the consummation of the implications of a change in consciousness in the *private sphere*, the development of the politics of youth has been a correlate in the *public sphere*. Explanations of student political activism offered so facilely in the past, which rest simply on features of all industrialized nations, explain too much. Such generalizations as, "The generational conflict is worldwide" ignores the very different meanings that "generations," "age," and "conflict" have in different cultures. Highly industrialized societies, those with a complex division of labor, high productivity, high per capita income, education, and stable, rationally organized bureaucratic governments have experienced notable student political activity since World War II. It is, however, the rise of American student protest, much in evidence since the Free Speech Movement in Berkeley in 1964, that occasioned greatest interest and attention.

Laquer, in terms designed to reduce our cultural and historical myopia, describes vividly some characteristics of past student movements, charting their violence and the degree of involvement of faculty, and identifies a set of persistent themes in the German youth movement recently manifested in America:

> The politics and culture of youth movements have always been a reflection of the Zeitgeist, a hodgepodge, often, of mutually exclusive ideas. A Proto-Nazi wrote about the unending and fruitless discussions of German youth movements in 1920: "Look at those Freideutsche leaders and their intellec-tual leap-frogging from Dostoevsky to Chuang-tse, Count Keyserling, Spengler, Buddha, Jesus, Landauer, Lenin, and whichever literary Jew happens to be fashionable to the moment. Of their own substance they have little or nothing." There was, let's face it, more than a grain of truth in this criticism; a list of the main formative intellectual influences on the Ameri-can movement would look even more incongruous. But what was essential about the German youth movement, at least in its first phase, was not its

"intellectual leap-frogging" and confused politics but something else entirely. The movement represented an unpolitical form of opposition to a civilization that had little to offer the young generation, a protest against the lack of vitality, warmth, emotion, and ideals in German society. (Hoelderlin: "I can conceive of no people more dismembered . . . You see workmen but no human beings, thinkers but no human beings, priests but no human beings, masters and servants, youth and staid people, but no human beings . . .)." It wanted to develop qualities of sincerity, decency, open-mindedness, to free its members from petty egoism and careerism, to oppose artificial conventions, snobbery, and affectation. Its basic character was formless and intangible, its authentic and deepest experience difficult to describe and perhaps impossible to analyze: the experience of marching together, of participating in common struggles, of forming lasting friendships. There was, of course, much romantic exaltation as well, but although it is easier to ridicule the extravagances of this state of mind than to do it justice, the temptation should be resisted: experiences of such depth are very serious matters indeed.

Douglas shows in tabular form (below) the growth in number of people under 25 and the number of students enrolled in higher education in the United States. It is argued in detail by Moller (1968) that demographic changes, that is, an upsurge in the size of the proportion of the population under 25, have important effects on the growth of student movements. As both Laqueur and Lipset discuss, and as elaborated by Flacks, student movements emerge in periods of growth in numbers of students and where the general political atmosphere is one of change, reorientation, and disruption. In the United States, as Lipset, Flacks and Nisbet agree, the Vietnam war and the race issue precipitated the upsurge of student activism after 1964. It is the university environment where, as Lifton says, "symbolic fathers and sons encounter each other." There are broader social trends, and the characteristics of the university are joined: the university prolongs adolescence while demanding that the young search out and commit themselves to meaningful, that is, occupational, roles. Further, education ideally assaults conventional thought and suggests the power of abstraction and idealized thinking; it simultaneously isolates and joins students together in an interacting, dense, moral community; it provides a rich ground for recruitment; and it has espoused an imagery of acceptance and tolerance of a range of political beliefs and actions (summarized from Lipset, below). All these features, of course, have always been true to a degree in the better universities. It is the combination of *structure* and *event* in unique ways with the trends of the larger political system and the dynamics of family life that create the conditions under which a student collectivity emphasizing political activism blooms.

Flacks, in a series of studies and essays, has clearly substantiated his argument that the relationships between parents and activist children are not those of alienation and disaffection, but of shared political and social values. His argument supports a *generational cause,* one of continuity of values among the intelligentsia and their children.

> In part, the disaffection of these youth is a direct consequence of the values and impulses their parents transmitted to them. The new generation had been raised in an atmosphere that encouraged personal autonomy and individuality. Implicitly and explicitly it had been taught to be skeptical about the intrinsic value of money making and status and to be skeptical about the claims of established authority. It incorporated new definitions of sex roles. Having seen their parents share authority and functions more or less equally in the family, and having been taught to value aesthetic and intellectual activity, these were boys who did not understand masculinity to mean physical toughness and dominance, and girls who did not understand femininity to mean passivity and domesticity. Moreover, they were young people—young people for whom the established means of social control were found to be relatively ineffective (and here they were particularly different from the older generation). Growing up with economic security in families of fairly secure status, the normal incentives of the system—status and income—were of relatively minor importance, and indeed many of their parents encouraged them to feel that such incentives ought to be disdained (Flacks, 1970, p. 49).

Flacks asserts that the structural conditions of modern society are such that the future will be filled with conflict.

> The emergence of the student movement in the sixties, then, signifies a more fundamental social change and is not simply a species of "generational conflict." The convergence of certain social structural and cultural trends has produced a new class, the intelligentsia, and, despite the apparent material security of many in this class, its trajectory is toward revolutionary opposition to capitalism. This is because, first, capitalism cannot readily absorb the cultural aspirations of this group—aspirations that fundamentally have to do with the abolition of alienated labor and the achievement of democratic community. Second, the incorporation of this group is made more difficult by the concrete fact of racism and imperialism—facts which turn the vocations of the intelligentsia into cogs in the machinery of repression rather than means for self-fulfillment and general enlightenment. Third, the numerical size of this group and the concentration of much of it in universities make concerted oppositional political action extremely feasible. Finally, the liberal default has hastened the self-consciousness of students and other members of this class, exacerbated their alienation from the political system and made autonomous oppositional politics a more immediate imperative for them. Thus, a stratum, which under certain conditions might have accepted a modernizing role within the system, has instead responded to the events of this past decade by adopting an increasingly revolutionary posture (Flacks, 1970, p. 50).

Nisbet, however, argues forcefully that the movement is not in fact ideological, but is rather a set of situational and expedient responses that merely provides a rationale for the usual student propensities to excess, to emotionalism, to exaggeration, and to impulsive behavior. Nisbet and others do not see the present youth scene as rooted in *malaise* or repression, the decline of tradition, or in police brutality (although this doubtless plays a proximal role in many riots).

The aim of the student movement, in part, is to create a parallel or *alternative* set of interpretations of social events, especially crisis-like events affecting large numbers of persons. Once these interpretations become widely diffused and acceptable as legitimate counterthemes, the conventional wisdom is more easily seen as an arbitrary construction shored up by the authority of the segments of the society in power. The primary weapon in this assault upon and explicit questioning of dominant institutions has been face-to-face confrontation taking the form of guerilla theater, mime troupes, demonstrations, and other forms of explicit affrontery. The immediacy and directness of these tactics has served to shock the body politic, but other subtle forms of ridicule and satire, such as those incorporated in the style and lyrical content of rock music, have also done much to alter modern sensibility. Daniel Bell, in the title page quote, argues that this assaultive process, when examined in the broad context of the arts, and music and politics in the conventional sense, has in effect all but destroyed the contemplative mode of existence. In the most obvious of these challenges, we see only the iceberg of those forces and behaviors that hasten the fragmentalization of the already strained social worlds in which we live. But to fractionate the moral hegemony of the dominant society is but one step, a partial accomplishment. As Zijderveld (1971) argues, following Durkheim, man is *homo duplex,* requiring both external, collective symbols and traditional patterns, and private, affect-laden, social worlds. Simmel pointed out that it is through social relationships that man obtains the capacity to see himself both as an insider, a group member, and an outsider, an individual with special interpretations and experiences known only to him. Many interpretations of radical politics and demonstrational activity have seen them as attempts to integrate the exterior symbolic order that seems increasingly unresponsive to personal needs with the quest for identity that has been allocated to the youth. In this sense, politics and private experiences (the drug scene) come full circle and mesh in the identity-making inherent in confrontational politics.[5]

The recreation of meaning under a new ideological framework, something Nisbet feels is lacking, would infuse the movement with enormous potential for extensive change. Until that time, as Flacks notes, the political movement

[5] See Aldridge, 1970, Chapter 10, for a one-sided, but stimulating discussion of the contrast between public and private demeanor of students.

will remain on campuses, under a "hothouse," while the broader cultural change inspired by and emanating from the youth will diffuse in ever-expanding circles creating a major cultural and life-style change.

## The Scope of the Book

Not only are there a number of sociological approaches that one may adopt in order to analyze the young; the *variety* of youthful behavior in this society is, in fact, very wide. In this pluralistic society, with its many cultural, political and religious traditions, its frontier qualities of violence, individualism, and self-righteousness, and the resultant heterogeneity of its rules and their meanings, there are many kinds and types of American youth.

Because this volume is meant to only highlight issues and themes, it operates with practical limitations. It is admittedly modest and narrow in scope. It contains principally the perspectives of sensitive social observers concerned with trends and developments among the white, middle-class, collegiate youth. Why have these segments of the society been the object of such attention in the last five to 10 years? Why are the various observers so passionate in their arguments? The seven to 10 million people who came of age (literally, through the granting of the 18-year-old vote and lowering of drinking and age of majority in many states) in the period of the late 1960s through the early 1970s, are of *dramatic* interest. Courted by the media and commercial interests, hassled by the police, object of public anger and disgust, altogether an enigma to many, youth represent the *future* in a nation committed overmuch to the future. Youth represent the dilemmas of *growing old*, caught as they are between their own sexual and social needs and the social constraints of a society that increasingly demands extended educational exposure. In the torment of youth, how many people see a microcosm of *"civilized man,"* he who accommodates passion to order, excitement to routine, today to tomorrow? The public activities of activist youth represent yet another reason underlying the nature and amount of response of recent years. Flacks (1971) and others see the youth as the "new opposition," while Keniston (1971) sees the "liberated generation." To Flacks, the position of the young in the social structure, that is, its relationship to the means of production as emergent and potential participants in the labor force, is *strategic*. If the young in a post-capitalist society question such fundamental ideas as work and striving, the fiction underlying the control of the dominant classes may be fully exposed. From this perspective, the college-educated segment of the population (Flacks is careful to point out that he sees these trends as effecting the broad spectrum of the educational strata, not simply "the young") represents an important focus because of their potential for creating and fomenting major structural changes in American society. An element assumed in this argument is that social structure, as we have suggested, is a problematic, fluid, ever-changing

16

set of negotiated realities. Granted that the fundamental reality for the Marxists, neo-Marxists, and new advocates such as Flacks is the *economic reality*, it must be altered in some fashion. To these scholars, postcapitalist abundance and overproduction will create a condition where the white collar classes and service elements of the economy will control resources and power (rather than the "working classes"). What is little explored, and why this book takes aim at both sensibilities and structures, is the extent to which the everyday world of persons is composed, defined, built up, and maintained not by such reified fictions as the "economic system" or the "political system," but by sequential decisions and assumptions guiding the practical paths to goals that actors carve out of their existential situations. In this sense then, shocks to the everyday world of large segments of the population that we discussed above are revolutionary in a significant sense. They begin to delegitimate assumptions about order, continuity, civility, and honor that weld men and man. Activist youth, mounting these challenges to the phenomenological structures of experience, are significant foci of concern for sociologists, and as Berger and others have noted, they provide role models for high school and younger youth beginning to ask profound questions about their own futures. On both dramatic and potential-for-change criteria, the focus of this book may be defended. This focus, in turn, precludes equal attention to the very real differences in the process of growing up brown, black and/or poor, or extremely wealthy. In some respects, it partially ignores the majority of collegians, those conventional students who have always failed to capture the imagination and attention of their professors. Except in so far as these categories of people are discussed by implication or contrast, they will not appear in the following selections.

The book cannot contain all the substantive disagreements now brewing, all the issues and controversies now of concern, nor can all the activities of the selected segment of youth be discussed. Like most sociology, this collection is at least to some degree a classification, categorization, and glossing of the challenging and marvelous complexity of the social world. The selections I include were chosen because they fit my own notions of appropriateness, once I had decided that they met the following criteria. First, they were chosen for their *style*, the extent to which writers were able to capture, in an orderly way, their own experiences, as young, with the young, or in opposition to them. Second, the selections were chosen for their *clarity* and *perspective*. It was important to include essays that adopted a particular stand, made that position clear, and argued persuasively for it. Finally, the essays were chosen to illustrate and analyze in an abstract way types of everyday experiences that many of the readers of the book will recognize. In other words, this collection is meant to clarify the social world of the reader, to expand his experience, and to focus his attention on some existing facets of the present.

## An Overview of Contents

The book is introduced by an essay by Daniel Bell describing the cultural and artistic sensibilities of the 1960s; it explicates some of the very complex relationships existing between culture, society and the prevailing feelings or moods of creative people.[6] Since creative people mirror in many ways broad social trends, and certainly profoundly affect the young—the most important consumers of mass art in American society—the arts are an important index of the society's sense of itself. In the article following Bell's, Jack Douglas clearly sets forth a set of the most important facts about the number, concentration, and subjective importance of college youth in American society. This introductory section thus describes a portion of the American mood and social organization—the structural context of American society and some of the salient social psychological consequences of life within that reality.

Three areas of controversy are identified for more extended treatment in this book: the sources and consequences of student politics; the viability of the educational ambience of the modern university; and the nature and meanings of generational ties. Each of the sections contains two to four selections.

In the section on student *politics*, its history, sources, meanings, and implications are discussed. The selections by Laqueur, an historian, and Lipset, a leading political sociologist, place youth and their politics within an historical and comparative (cross-national) context. In the selections by Flacks and Nisbet, a particular moral and political position is adopted concerning the existence, meanings, and causes of the "student revolution." Richard Flacks, a cofounder of the Students for a Democratic Society, cautiously, yet hopefully explicates the possibilities of a worldwide cultural and social revolution transcending age and generational differences. Nisbet, on the other hand, views the entire student rebellion, youth movement, and associated cultural phenomena (the counterculture) as moribund, destroyed by its own lack of belief, commitment, self-concern and its political naiveté.

In the *education* section, Cottle and Reisman assess two of the most critical issues on the campus: the education of women, and the meanings of education for radical and disaffected students. In contrast, in his essay, Becker suggests that most students are more concerned with making a living and learning a few useful skills (political, romantic, social) than with political activism (see also Lipset, p. 00).

In the section on *generational ties*, the impact of the generations on each other under radically changing social conditions, is suggested by Lifton, Cottle, and Mead. The essence of the generational relationship is the asymmetry of the roles: the attributed wisdom and authority of the elders, com-

[6] For a readable tracing of the development of this pattern, see Nuttall (1968).

plemented by a pattern of deference and subordination on the part of the young. In accepting this equation, the young gain sustenance and support, and a sense of identity, a placement in social time and space. Thus, culturally based knowledge needed for facing the repetitive challenges life represents to that group is recreated in a new generation. There is evidence, argue Cottle and Lifton, that suggests a number of forces have begun to rend asunder this previously established asymmetry of roles. The sense of imminent death, and the threat to human survival itself represented by the potential of nuclear war and ecological pollution, seem to undercut so profoundly the continuous quality of human life on which traditional family ties rest that society may be searching for alternative modes of socialization. In the extreme, Lifton fears, the young may feel so disconnected from the past that they will substitute the present for the lessons of history. Margaret Mead, in the final essay, argues that these same conditions argue strongly for a reversal of the traditional asymmetry; she envisions the young in the role of teachers. As Crosby, Stills, Nash, and Young sing, ". . . teach your parents well. . . ."

## LIST OF REFERENCES CITED

ALDRIDGE, JOHN W., 1970
*In the Country of the Young.* New York: Harper & Row.

BELL, DANIEL, 1965
"The Disjunction of Culture and Social Structure: Some Notes on the Meaning of Social Reality," *Daedalus* 94 (Winter), 208–222.

BERGER, BENNETT, 1970
*Looking for America.* Englewood Cliffs, N.J. Prentice-Hall.

BERGER, PETER, 1969
*The Sacred Canopy.* New York: Doubleday.

BERGER, PETER AND THOMAS LUCKMANN, 1966
*The Social Construction of Reality.* New York: Doubleday.

CAREY, J., 1968
*The Drug Scene.* Englewood Cliffs, N.J.: Prentice-Hall.

CLOWARD, R. AND L. OHLIN, 1960
*Delinquency and Opportunity.* Glencoe: The Free Press.

DOUGLAS, JACK, 1970A
*Deviance and Respectability.* New York: Basic Books.

——————————, 1970B
*Understanding Everyday Life.* Chicago: Aldine.

EISENSTADT, S. N., 1962
*From Generation to Generation.* New York: The Free Press.

FAUNCE, W. A., 1968
*Problems of Industrial Society.* New York: McGraw-Hill.

FEUER, LEWIS, 1968
*The Conflict of Generations.* New York: Basic Books.

FLACKS, RICHARD, 1971
*Youth and Social Change.* Chicago: Markham.

FREIDMAN, N., 1967
*The Social Nature of Psychological Research.* New York: Basic Books.

FREIDENBERG, EDGAR Z., 1963
"The Image of the Adolescent Minority, *Dissent* **10** (Spring), 149–158.

———————————————, 1962
*The Vanishing Adolescent.* New York: Dell Laurel editions.

GOODE, E., 1970
*The Marijuana Smokers.* New York: Basic Books.

GUSFIELD, J., 1963
*Symbolic Crusade.* Urbana: University of Illinois Press.

KAPLAN, J., 1970
*Marijuana: The New Prohibition.* Cleveland: World Publishers.

KENISTON, KENNETH, 1968–1969
"Heads and Seekers: Drugs on Campus, Counter-Cultures and American Socity," *The American Scholar,* **38** (Winter).

———————————————, 1971
*Youth and Dissent: The Rise of a New Opposition.* New York: Harcourt, Brace, Jovanovich.

LIFTON, ROBERT J., 1970
*History and Human Survival.* New York: Random House.

LUCKMANN, THOMAS, 1968
*The Invisible Religion.* New York: Macmillan.

LYDON, MICHAEL, 1971
*Rock Folk: Portraits from the Rock N'Roll Pantheon.* New York: Dial Press.

LYMAN, STANFORD AND MARVIN SCOTT, 1970
*Sociology of the Absurd.* New York: Appleton-Century-Crofts.

MANIS, J. AND B. MELTZER, EDS., 1972
*Symbolic Interaction.* Boston: Allyn and Bacon.

MERTON, ROBERT, 1957
*Social Theory and Social Structure.* Revised and enlarged edition. New York: Free Press.

MOLLER, H., 1968
"Youth as a Force in the Modern World," *Comparative Studies of Society and History,* **X** (April, 237–260.

NUTTALL, JEFF, 1968
*Bomb Culture.* London: MacGibbon and Kee, Ltd.

PARSONS, TALCOTT, 1951
*The Social System.* Glencoe: The Free Press.

REICH, CHARLES, 1970
*The Greening of America.* New York: Random House.

RIESMAN, DAVID, NATHAN GLAZER, AND REUEL DENNEY, 1956
*The Lonely Crowd.* New York: Doubleday Anchor Books.

ROSENTHAL, R., 1967
*Experimental Effects in Behavioral Research.* New York: Appleton-Century-Crofts.

ROSZAK, THEODORE, 1969
*The Making of the Counter-Culture.* New York: Doubleday.

STONE, G. AND W. H. FORM, 1953
"Instabilities in Status: The Problem of Hierarchy in the Community Study of Status Arrangements." *ASR,* **18** (April) 149–162.

THOMAS, W. I. AND F. ZNANIECKI, 1927
*The Polish Peasant.* 2 vols. New York: A. A. Knopf.

TOFFLER, ALVIN, 1970
*Future Shock.* New York: Random House.

WOLFE, TOM, 1969
*The Electric Kool Aid Acid Test.* New York: Bantam Books.

ZNANIECKI, F., 1965
*Social Relations and Social Roles.* San Francisco: Chandler Publishing Company.

ZIJDERVELD, A. C., 1971
*The Abstract Society.* New York: Doubleday Anchor Books.

# SECTION I

# The American Mood and Social Order

In the development of sociology, Durkheim's exposition of the "objective" nature of society was fundamental in establishing the paradigm of sociological thought. It was his contention that social order was external and constraining on the individual; that it persisted through time and generations, and that it exercised an influence in the daily lives of men. In *Suicide* (1897), Durkheim claimed that values and norms were social facts and resided in the collective conscience, or the collective will. This classic exercise was instrumental in the development of a sociology which followed the natural science model of positivistic investigation. That is, it conceptualized the nature of social facts to be parallel to other objectively discovered facts, permitting the use of statistical investigation, experimental technique, and the scientific paraphernalia previously reserved exclusively for the physical and biological sciences. Durkheim did not ignore the "subjective" aspect of social order, but they were of lesser significance to him.

A recent critique of Durkheim by Jack Douglas (1967), discredits Durkheim's claim that an external order does exist, and in fact demonstrates that Durkheim was aware of and used his own knowledge of the way meaning is established in everyday interaction to abstract his notion of society. By objectifying society, he removed it from the confused attempts of men to deal with their perceived social worlds. If there is one fact that existential sociologists including Douglas and others have established, it is that the social structure is never established once and for all, but rather events and situations are attributed meaning in a moment to moment fashion. Things in the world have no essential meaning and may be radically transformed, as for example when the rock group The Who destroys their equipment before an audience, changing the event from a concert to a political commentary.

Nevertheless, Durkheim asked a classic question, how do men become

22

entangled in a social order? And the contrary question, how do they disengage themselves or come to feel disengaged? We return here to a theme of the introductory essay which distinguished the emotional or *sensibility* dimension of social order and the negotiated abstraction we call *social structure*. When the symbols and meanings in a society come to be defined as inadequate to the job of expressing the nature of the social bonds which exist in that society, segments of that society search for alternative symbols and meanings which may once again express for them a sense of continuity in time and space in terms of their own biographical and historical situations.

Within this framework, a whole panoply of modern phenomena take on additional significance. Through an examination of rock music, for example, we may probe the nature of the relationships between a sensibility shared by a social group and the larger social structure in which they find themselves. Charles Reich (1970) summarizes the development of the new rock music which burst forth from San Francisco and London in the late sixties.* His observations reproduce the sociological features of the change, from which we may infer a change in sensibilities. Reich asserts that (a) the once separate music traditions of blues, rock, jazz and eastern music were brought together; (b) a full range of electronic and electric instruments was utilized; (c) the music stood in the context of other media; it became part of a multimedia experience; (d) each band developed a personality—erstwhile outsiders, communitarians, marginal observers of the social scene; (e) through drugs and shared experience of playing instruments, audience-performer rapport was heightened; (f) new energy, largely generated from non-cognitive sources flowed into music; (g) the music attained a relatively great complexity (this in comparison to the simple rock formulae of the fifties and given the basic instruments which constituted rock music: the guitar, piano and drums); (h) many groups composed their own music. The Who, an English group, composed an entire rock opera, "Tommy." The music expressed for its listeners and performers a representation and understanding of the world. In summary, according to Reich, a very complex, loud music, played in the context of other media by youthful performers with distinctive personalities, both individually and collectively, symbolized youthful experience, and because many of the young also played rock instruments and took drugs, they were able to identify with these performers and their music.

Sociologically, there are several ways to explain these changes prior to a discussion of the underlying themes they illustrate. First, the music came to pass because population growth and a corresponding growth of radio stations permitted some stations to develop a youth audience, and to play youthful music. This change was paralleled by a change in the social structure of the music business itself, the new equipment and the large potential market in a

---

* See also Melly, 1970; Goldman, 1971; Eisen, ed., 1969; Nuttall, 1968.

time of great affluence allowed a number of smaller, original entrepreneurs to enter the rock music market (see Tom Wolfe's article on Phil Spector, a teen-age record entrepreneur, in *The Kandy-Kolored Tangerine Flake Streamline Baby* (1966)). With the growth in numbers and affluence of the young (see the Douglas essay below), small record companies could produce records directed at the teen-age market and survive in competition against the larger and more conservative companies. Underground FM stations also provided a large and avid following for acid rock music. Thus, the growth of numbers of wealthy young people between 15-25, influenced by the media, and looking for symbolic representations of their own experience and performers who would provide that, generated the revolution in popular music. Changes in social structure, the size of the teen-age market, the number of radio stations, the growing affluence of the young, and the profound affect of media on fads, were the immediate factors or conditions underlying the changes in rock music.

This set of factors or conditions only suggests the structural factors in the industry itself, it does not account for the *content* of the music, the emotional messages found between the lines, in the rhythms, the sounds and the style of singing and playing. In several recent articles by Bell (1965), Berger (1971) and Davis (1967), some of the themes of modern music and culture are explicated. We can take music as a case in point—as a representative form of mass culture where the growth in numbers of people, the kind and amount of interaction, leads to a leveling and massification and values and tastes. Pop culture and rock music are more than just another form of mass culture, for their themes are indicative of issues stressing many of us— autonomy, competence, friendship, intimacy, trust, identity, security. Looking closely at the themes of Reich's analyses, we can see several of the themes of Bell's essay on the sensibilities of the sixties which follows.

First, the "cult of childhood" is in evidence in music; there is a developing market for tunes called cynically "bubble-gum rock," which cater to the teeny-boppers (8-12 year olds), and the most popular recent groups are composed of adolescent brothers with high, reedy, childlike voices. (As Berger observed, it is unlikely that many of the songs could be performed at all by an adult voice.) Recent songs, such as the Who's "My Generation" and another 1970 hit, "I'm 18 and I like it" contain a rejection of adulthood, and a fear of aging. Secondly, in the cult respect mentioned above and in dress and demeanor of rock groups themselves, there is an apparent reversal of values, a veneration of the bizarre, the outlandish, the absurd, a reversal of the middle class canons of taste. Although unmentioned by Reich, there is an underlying theme of violence, cruelty and the sexually perverse in several recent groups and their music: the cannibalistic song, "Timothy," "Burn Down the Mission" by Elton John; Crosby, Stills, Nash and Young's "Ohio" and the on stage destruction of The Who and Alyce Cooper. The noise level of modern rock music has promoted some investigators to test the hearing levels of rock musicians and their audiences. (To his disappointment perhaps, he has not yet established conclusively that there is hearing damage.) In the words of Dylan's songs, and dramatically in the songs and performances of the Rolling Stones, the middle-class concern with rationality, deferred gratification and restraint are ridiculed, and intellectualism in general sustains harsh, cynical attack.

Thirdly, the music tends to diminish distance between self and other, between art and life, between politics and experience (Cf. (c), (d), (e), (f), (h), (i) ). Fourthly, the music is the possession of adolescents, who set style and tone and, furthermore, "own" the creative dimensions of the art form insofar as they write, compose, play and sing the music written by their peers and themselves. Bell's remark that present artistic styles are adolescent may have always held for popular culture, but the degree to which the popular culture, created and performed by the young, is *the* dominant culture in American society is astounding. Fifthly, the music and its performance replicates the experience and feelings of adolescent life. The free-flowing interchange of personnel to form super groups (composed of performers from other groups who come together for occasional recording sessions under a new name) such as Jefferson Starship; Blind Faith; and Bonnie, Delaney and Friends is something unprecedented (except informally in jazz). They parallel adolescent clique and dating patterns, and the diffuse nature of adolescent self and identity. In this example, many of the characteristics of the young in America are illustrated. However, the significant aim of this excursion into rock music is to show how a set of conditions patterns the emergent mood of a segment of a population, and how these moods, in turn, may feed back into the patterns, creating new patterns and new human relationships. We have seen and will see that changes in feeling and mood may not "fit" the extant social structure, with revealing consequences in the institutions of education, politics and family.

The Bell essay, as we noted, contains a number of important insights and commentary, and does work within the context of the relationships between the symbols which express the experience of given social relationships and the social structure as a set of relationships. Bell notes, as does Roszak in *The Making of the Counter Culture* (1969), and such violent enemies of the youth movement as Lewis Feuer (1968), that there has been a general tendency in the society to withdraw from "adult" models of behavior in politics, art, sex and education, and to look to the style of the young. This theme is repeated in the essays in this collection.

The Douglas segment here reprinted also deals with the relationship of the objective facts, in this case the numbers of students in higher education, and the proportion of people under the age of 25 in American society, and the subjective definitions of those facts. Douglas argues that although the relationships between higher education and actual earning power over the lifetime of the graduate is quite problematic and subject to interpretation, the subjective reality, the "definition of the situation," is that without a higher degree, one will suffer not only the danger of the draft, but will be a victim, relegated to the lower ranks of society. In Douglas' presentation, there is a careful interweaving of the meanings of the higher education and the potential this represents for large numbers of discontented students, with the actual numbers of students who increasingly populate our colleges and universities.

In these two selections, then, we have not only an attempt to set the stage by information describing American society, we also have an attempt to deal with a major question in sociology, the development of a model of society which interdigitates both the actor's views and feelings as they define a situation, and the outside observer's critical concepts and frame of reference.

# 1. Sensibility in the 60's

## DANIEL BELL

Each decade—we think now of decades or generations as the units of social time—has its hallmarks. That of the 1960's was a political and cultural radicalism. The politics is, for the moment, spent, but cultural radicalism follows a more complicated course. I propose to examine here the cultural radicalism of the 60's through the prism of its sensibility, in order to cast light on changes in the society itself.

In defining the sensibility of the 60's, one can see it in two ways: as a reaction to the sensibility of the 50's; and as a reversion to, and yet also an extension of, an earlier sensibility which reached its apogee in the modernism of the years before World War I.

The sensibility of the 50's was largely a literary one. In the writings of such representative critics of the period as Lionel Trilling, Yvor Winters, and John Crowe Ransom, the emphasis was on complexity, irony, ambiguity, and paradox. These are properties peculiar to the mind. They foster a critical attitude, a detachment and distance which guard one against any overwhelming involvement, absorption, immolation in a creed or an experience. At worst a form of quietism, at best a mode of self-consciousness, this attitude is essentially moderate in tone. The sensibility of the 60's rejected that mood in savage, even mindless fashion. In its fury with the times, the new sensibility was loud, imprecatory, prone to obscenity, and given to posing every issue, political or otherwise, in disjunctive correlatives.

The more enduring mood, however, derives from the earlier impulses. The modernist innovations that flared so effulgently between 1895 and 1914 wrought two extraordinary changes in the culture. First there was a set of

From *Commentary*, **51** (June, 1971), pp. 63–73.

*formal* revolutions in the arts—the breakup of poetic syntax, the stream-of-consciousness in fiction, the multiplicity of the picture plane on the canvas, the rise of atonality in music, the loss of sequence in temporal representation and of foreground and background in spatial pictorialization. And second there was a new presentation of the self which Roger Shattuck (in *The Banquet Years*) has characterized in terms of four traits—the cult of childhood; the delight in the absurd; the reversal of values so as to celebrate the baser rather than the higher impulses; and a concern with hallucination.

That earlier sensibility—at least judging from these four traits—was still very much with us in the 60's, albeit in a shriller and harsher form. The stress on the pain of childhood was replaced, in the "confessional" poetry of Robert Lowell, Anne Sexton, and Sylvia Plath, by the revelation of the most private experiences—even psychotic seizures—of the poet, though the sense of innocence remained intact in the work of poets like Allen Ginsberg, with its visionary emphasis derived from Whitman; Blake, and the Indian Vedas. The sense of absurdity was extended so that—as in the plays of Ionesco—objects began to take on a life of their own. The reversal of values became virtually complete, though all joy and prankishness were drained out of the celebration of the base. Hallucination, of course, was enthroned in the drug and psychedelic experience.

Yet to all this the sensibility of the 60's also added something distinctly its own; a concern with violence and cruelty; a preoccupation with the sexually perverse; a desire to make noise; an anti-cognitive and anti-intellectual mood; an effort once and for all to erase the boundary between "art" and "life"; and a fusion of art and politics. To take each of these traits briefly, in turn:

The violence and cruelty that one saw splashed on film was not meant to effect catharsis, but sought instead to shock, to maul, to sicken. Films, Happenings, paintings vied with each other in presenting gory detail. One was told that such violence and cruelty simply reflected the world around us, but the 1940's, a gorier and far more brutal decade, did not produce the lingering on sanguinary detail one found in films of the 60's like *Bonnie and Clyde* and *M\*A\*S\*H.*

The sexually perverse is as old as Sodom and Gomorrah, at least in recorded time, but rarely has it ever been flaunted as openly and directly as in the 60's, In such films as Andy Warhol's *The Chelsea Girls*, in the Swedish *I Am Curious (Yellow)*, in such plays as *Futz* and *Ché*, one found an obsessive preoccupation with homosexuality, transvestism, buggery, and most pervasive of all, publicly displayed oral-genital intercourse. What this obsession seemed to represent was a flight from heterosexual life, perhaps in response to the release of aggressive female sexuality which was becoming evident at the end of the decade.

The 50's, one could almost say of its sensibility, had been a period of silence. The plays of Samuel Beckett tried to achieve a sense of silence, and the music of John Cage even attempted an aesthetic of silence. But the 60's was preeminently a period of noise. Beginning with the "new sound" of the Beatles in 1964, rock reached such soaring crescendos that it was impossible to hear oneself think: and that may indeed have been its intention.

The anti-cognitive, anti-intellectual mood was summed up in the attack on "content" and interpretation, in the emphasis on form and style, in the turn to "cooler" media like film and dance—a sensibility, in Susan Sontag's words, "based on indiscriminateness, without ideas [and] beyond negation."

Erasing the boundary between art and life was a further aspect of the breakup of genre, the conversion of a painting into a Happening, the taking of art out of the museum into the environment, the turning of all experience into art, whether it had form or not. By celebrating life, this process tended to destroy art.

Art and politics were probably more intensely fused in the 60's than at any time in modern history. During the 1930's, art had served politics, but in a heavyhanded ideological way. In the 60's the emphasis was not on ideological content, but on temper and mood. Guerrilla theater and demonstration art had little content except anger. One would have to go back to the anarchism of the 1890's, when art was also flushed with politics, to find a comparable tone, but what was most evident in the 1960's was the scale and intensity of feeling that was not only anti-government, but almost entirely anti-institution and ultimately antinomian as well.

And yet what is striking about the 60's is that with all the turbulence, there was not one noteworthy revolution in aesthetic form. The preoccupation with machines and technology only served to recall the Bauhaus and Moholy-Nagy; the theater echoed the practices of Alfred Jarry and the theories of Antonin Artaud; the japes in art repeated Dada or drew rhetorically from surrealism. Only in the novel, perhaps, in the linguistic brilliance of Nabokov, the spatial dislocations of Burroughs, and in some elements of the *nouveau roman* in France, did any interesting innovations appear. It was a decade, despite all the talk of form and style, empty of originality in both. But in sensibility, there was an exacerbation of tone and temper, the fruits of an anger, political in origin, which spilled over into art as well. What remains of importance for cultural history was the mood, which turned against art, and the effort by large masses to adopt and act out the life style which hitherto had been the property of a small and talented elite.

## II
## The Dissolution of "Art"

The arbiters of culture in the 1950's prided themselves on holding out against the indiscriminate, the meretricious, and the trashy which were pouring from the mass media, and the pretentious and the arty which were the stamp of what was then universally known as "middlebrowism." They sought to do this by insisting on a classic conception of culture and by setting forth a trans-historical and transcendental criterion for the judgment of art.

Perhaps the most incisive formulation of this point of view was Hannah Arendt's. "Works of art," she wrote, "are made for the sole purpose of appearance. The proper criterion by which to judge appearance is beauty . . . in order to become aware of appearances we must first be *free to establish a certain distance* between ourselves and the object. . . ."

We have here a Greek view of art in which culture is essentially contemplative. Art is not life, but in a sense something contrary to life, since life is transient and changing while art is permanent. To this Miss Arendt adds the Hegelian concept of *objectification*. A work of art is the projection by the creative person of an idea or an emotion into an object outside himself: ". . . What is at stake here," Miss Arendt wrote, "is much more than the psychological state of the artist; it is the objective status of the cultural world which insofar as it contains tangible things—books and paintings, statues, buildings, and music—comprehends, and gives testimony to, the entire recorded past of countries, nations, and ultimately of mankind. As such the only nonsocial and authentic criterion for judging these specifically cultural things is their relative permanence and even eventual immortality. Only what will last through the centuries can ultimately claim to be a cultural object."

The paradox is that this view—which in the 1960's came to seem so archaic —was undercut not by the lowbrows or middlebrows but by the highbrows— the very prelectors of modern culture themselves. For in seeking to define what was distinctive about the new sensibility, they denied precisely the terms set forth by Miss Arendt. The locus of art and culture, they argued, had moved from the independent work to the personality of the artist, from the permanent object to the transient process. It was Harold Rosenberg, explicating the work of Jackson Pollock, Willem de Kooning, Franz Kline, and other "action painters," as he called them, who first stated the concept forcefully:

"At a certain moment," Rosenberg wrote, "the canvas began to appear to one American painter after another as an arena in which to act—rather than as a space in which to reproduce, re-design, analyze, or 'express' an object, actual or imagined. *What was to go on the canvas was not a picture but an event.* . . . In this gesturing with materials the aesthetic, too, has been

30

subordinated. Form, color, composition, drawing . . . can be dispensed with. What matters always is the revelation contained in the act."

If painting is an action, there is no difference between the preliminary sketch and the finished object. The second cannot be "better" or more complete than the first. There are no preliminaries or hierarchies in art, and each act is an event by itself. In effect, the work *qua* work is dissolved in the act, and so is the critic. "The new painting," Mr. Rosenberg concluded, "has broken down every distinction between art and life. It follows that anything is relevant to it. Anything that has to do with action—psychology, philosophy, history, mythology, hero-worship. Anything but art criticism. The painter gets away from art through his act of painting; the critic can't get away from it. The critic who goes on judging in terms of schools, styles, form—as if the painter was still concerned with producing a certain kind of object (the work of art) instead of living on the canvas—is bound to seem a stranger."

Mr. Rosenberg proved a formidably accurate prophet. The entire movement of art in the 60's sought to dissolve the work of art as a "cultural object," and erase the distinction between subject and object and between art and life. Nowhere was this more apparent than in sculpture, or in the fusion of sculpture and painting, and the dissolution of both into spaces, environments, motions, media-mixes, Happenings, and the creation of "man-machine" interaction systems.

Sculpture classically dealt preeminently with objects. It concerned itself with mass as solid form, and was anchored in three-dimensional space. It was placed on a base or plinth that removed it spatially from the mundane ground or wall. In the 60's all this went. The base was removed so that the sculpture fused with its surroundings. Mass dissolved into space and space turned into motion.

Thus the "minimal sculpture" (of Donald Judd, Robert Morris, Dan Flavin) abandoned imagery altogether. It sought to be nothing other than what it set forth; boxes, shapes, relations which were neither organic nor figurative nor emblematic nor anthropomorphic. They were literally *Dinge an sich*. Similarly in the case of a show organized by the Whitney Museum in the summer of 1968, which was labeled "Anti-Illusion: Procedures and Materials." The materials were hay, grease, dirt, dog food, etc. The catalogue notes by James Monte opened with the observation: "The radical nature of many works in this exhibition depends less on the fact that new materials are being used by the artists than on the fact that the acts of conceiving and placing the pieces take precedence over the object quality of the works." The sculptures "each exist in either a deobjectified or scattered or dislocated state and in some instances the three conditions simultaneously."

Painting has followed a similar trajectory. From its origins in the distant past, painting always based itself on two elements: a symmetrical, geometric field and a flat surface. The first cave painter who put a line around the image he drew on the wall separated the picture from the environment; painting then became a symbol, rather than a magical manipulation, of reality.

Over the last hundred years, there have been many revolutions in painting. Pictorial space was broken up in many different ways: after Post-Impressionism, the shutters were closed on the interior distance, as Maurice Denis has put it, and painters became concerned primarily with surface, with color, with catching a sense of simultaneity, as in Cubism, by placing several planes on one plane, or, as in the paintings of Hofmann and de Kooning, with pigment itself.

In the last decades, we have witnessed the final break with field and surface, the traditional arena of painting. Pasted matter, as in collage, breaks up the surface; shaped canvases break up the geometrical field. Assemblages come off the wall. Environments surround the individual. In these two milieus, as Allan Kaprow, a leader of the new movement, points out, the illusion of space in the painting becomes the literal distance between all the solids in the work.

Environmental art erases the boundary between the space and the person. Happenings erase the distance between the situation, or event, and the spectator. In Happenings, not just color and space but also heat, smell, taste, and motion become aspects of the work. As Allan Kaprow puts it: "Fundamentally, Environments and Happenings are similar. They are passive and active sides of a single coin whose principle is *extension*."

A Happening is a pastiche that combines an environment as art-setting with a theatrical performance. It was originally a painters' theater in which one saw the manipulation of objects and materials that made up the field of painting taken down from the wall, and put into the open. It brings the spectator into the process of "creation" itself.

In a Happening, as Jan Kott has observed, "all the signs are literal: a pyramid of chairs is only a pile of chairs placed one on top of the other; a stream of water which drenches the audience is merely a stream of water which drenches the viewers. In reality, there is not even a partition between the viewer and actors. . . ."

In this, the mimetic and symbolic functions of theater, to use Kott's language, are eliminated. The expressive content becomes dissolved in the literal, and meanings as metaphor or emblems disappear. Even the idea of the evocative loses meaning because the event does not represent or picture something—it *is*. The emphasis on the literal is part of the attack on metaphysical expression. In Zen, for example, a philosophy which during the 60's attracted many painters and poets, one does not use words like *hard* or *soft*, for these are attributes or qualities of a substance; and qualities and substance are metaphysical terms. One has to be exactly literal, and if comparisons are made they must refer to specific tactile experiences denoted by stone, wood, water, etc.

Such immersion in experience is a disruption of aesthetic distance, for one has lost control over the experience if one cannot step back and conduct one's own "dialogue" with the work of art. This eclipse of distance, as I have characterized it,* represents the overturning of the rational cosmology—the orderly sequence of time, of beginning and middle and end, as well as the "internal" organization of divided space, of foreground and background, of figure and ground—which has shaped Western conceptions of aesthetic experience since Alberti in the 15th century. It is not only the dissolution of the cultural object, the work of art, into a process. It is the dissolution of the self into experience.

## III
## The Democratization of Genius

If there was a democratization of culture in which a radical egalitarianism of feeling superseded the older hierarchy of mind, there was also, by the end of the 60's, a democratization of "genius." The idea of the artist as genius, as a being apart who (in the description of Edward Shils) "need not regard the laws of society and its authorities" and who "aimed only to be guided by the inner necessities of the expansion of the self—to embrace new experiences," goes back to the early 19th century. The artist, it was thought, looked at the world from a special point of view. Whistler proclaimed that artists were a class apart whose standards and aspirations stood outside the comprehension of the vulgar. If there was "a conflict between a genius and his public," Hegel declared in a sentence which (as Irving Howe has noted) thousands of critics, writers, and publicists have echoed through the years, "it must be the public that is to blame . . . the only obligation the artist can have is to follow truth and his genius."

In France, where the "man of letters," as Tocqueville observed, had long taken the lead in "shaping the national temperament and the outlook on life," this tradition took particularly deep hold. Not only were artists different, by virtue of their genius, from other mortals, they were also intended to be, as Victor Hugo put it, the "sacred leaders" of the nation. Indeed, with the decline of religion, the writer was more and more invested with the prerogatives of the priest, for he was seen as a man endowed with supernatural vision. In a stultifying world, the writer alone was the unadaptable man, the wanderer—like Rimbaud—in perpetual flight from the mundane. Joyce in Trieste, Pound in London, Hemingway in Paris, Lawrence in Taos, Allen Ginsberg in India, are the very prototypes of this artist-hero type in the 20th

* *Encounter,* May 1965.

century. The pilgrimage to places far from the bourgeois home had become a necessary step in attaining independence of vision.

Underlying all of this is the belief that art tells a truth which is higher than that perceived via the ordinary cognitive mode, that the "language" of art, in the words of Herbert Marcuse, "must communicate a truth, an objectivity which is not accessible to ordinary language and ordinary experience."

But what if, as Lionel Trilling has wryly observed (in a view which even "rather surprises" himself), ". . . art does not always tell the truth or the best kind of truth and does not always point out the right way"? What if art "can even generate falsehood and habituate us to it, and . . . on frequent occasions . . . might well be subject, in the interests of autonomy, to the scrutiny of the rational intellect"? This question is perhaps too large to be gone into here. But the exaltation of the artistic vision above all others also raises another, more pressing question: If the language of art is not accessible to ordinary language and ordinary experience, how can it be accessible to ordinary people?

One solution of the 60's was to make each man his own artist-hero. In May 1968, the students at the École des Beaux Arts in Paris called for a development of consciousness which would guide the "creative activity immanent in every individual" so that the "work of art" and "the artist" become "mere moments in this activity." And a 1969 catalogue of revolutionary art at the Moderna Muséet in Stockholm carried this injunction further by declaring that "Revolution is Poetry. There is poetry in all those acts which break the system of organization." But such activist pronouncements—and the 60's were not lacking in them—do not solve the problems of modernism, they only evade it.

At the heart of the problem is the relationship of culture to tradition. When one speaks of a classical culture, or a Catholic culture, for example, one thinks of a long-linked set of beliefs, traditions, and rituals which over the course of history have achieved a distinctive style. The style results not only from an internally cohesive set of commonsense perceptions or formal conventions, but also from some notion of an ordered universe and of man's place in it. By its very nature, modernity breaks with the past, *as* past, and erases it in favor of the present or the future. Men are enjoined to make themselves anew rather than to extend the great chain of being. Aristocracy, Tocqueville once said, links all members of the community from king to peasant, while democracy breaks the chain, severing each of its links. As a result, democracy "makes every man forget his ancestors." Such an idea was of course attractive to an archetypal American artist like Walt Whitman, for whom culture was the enemy, evoking a literature "smelling of prince's favors . . . and built entirely [upon] the idea of caste."

Where culture is related to the past, accessibility to culture is shaped by tradition and expressed in ritual. Personal experiences and feelings are seen as idiosyncrasies, irrelevant to the great chain of continuity. But when culture is concerned with the individual personality of the artist, rather than with institutions and laws, then singularity of experience becomes the chief test of what is desirable, and novelty of sensation becomes the main engine of change. Where culture is bound up with tradition, the individual strives to become cultivated. Where culture is concerned with the self, the striving is for "fulfillment" defined, as often as not, as the experiencing of sensations derived from exploring hitherto restricted areas of experience.

Modernist culture is a culture of the self par excellence. Its center is the "I" and its boundaries are defined by identity. The cult of singularity begins, as so much in modernity does, with Rousseau, who declares in the opening lines of his *Confessions*: "I am commencing an undertaking, hitherto without precedent. . . . Myself alone! I know the feelings of my heart." And indeed, this pronouncement *is* completely without precedent in literature in its assertion of absolute singularity ("I am not made like any of those in existence") and its dedication to absolute frankness ("I have neither omitted anything bad nor interpolated anything good").

Yet it would be a mistake to confuse the "I" which begins every sentence of the first page of this book with simple narcissism (though that too is there); or to view the studied effort to shock the reader with dismaying detail (". . . in agonies of death she broke wind loudly") as nothing more than a form of exhibitionism. What Rousseau was attempting in the *Confessions* was to exemplify, as ruthlessly as seemed necessary, his dictum that truth is grasped through instinct or feeling, rather than through rational judgment or abstract reasoning. "I feel, therefore I exist," Thus Rousseau's Vicar revises the axiom of Descartes and at one stroke overturns the classical definition of authenticity as well as the definition of artistic creation which flows from it.

How can one know whether an experience is "authentic"—i.e., whether it is true and therefore valid for all men? The classical tradition had always identified authenticity with authority, with mastery of craft, with knowledge of form, and with the search for perfection, whether aesthetic or moral. Such perfection could be achieved, in Santayana's words, only through "purification," though a purging away of all accidental elements—the sentimental, the pathetic, the comic, the grotesque—in the quest for that essence which signifies completeness of form. Even where art is identified with experience, as in the theories of John Dewey, the emphasis remains on completeness as a criterion of aesthetic satisfaction. For Dewey, art was a process of shaping which involved an interaction between the "directive intent" of the artist and the refractory nature of experience. The work of art was complete when the artist had achieved "internal integration and fulfillment." Art, in other words, remained a matter of pattern and structure, and the relationships among its separate elements had to be perceivable for a work of art to have meaning.

But the new sensibility that emerged in the 1960's scorned such definitions completely. Authenticity in a work of art was defined almost exclusively in terms of the quality of immediacy, both the immediacy of the artist's intention and the immediacy of his effect upon the viewer. In the theater, for example, spontaneity was all; the text was virtually eliminated and the reigning form became improvisation—exalting the "natural" over the contrived, sincerity over judgment, spontaneity over reflection. When Judith Malina, the director of the Living Theatre, said, "I don't want to be Antigone [onstage], I am and want to be Judith Malina," she aimed to do away with illusion in the theater, as the painters have eliminated it in art.

But to forgo the "representation" of another, in this instance, is not merely to forgo a text, it is to deny the commonality of human experience and to insist on a false uniqueness of personality. Antigone is a symbol—traditionally acted out on a stage spatially separated from the audience—which restates certain perennially recurrent human problems: the demands of civil obedience, the faithfulness of vows, the nature of justice. To eliminate Antigone, or deny her corporeality, is to repudiate memory and to discard the past.

Similarly, writing in the 60's was judged by its genuineness of feeling, by its success in projecting "the unvarnished imaginative impulse," and by its assertion that thought should not mediate spontaneity. Allen Ginsberg has said that he writes "to let my imagination go [to] scribble magic lines from my real mind." Two of his best-known poems, we were told over and over, were written without forethought or revision: the long first part of *Howl* was typed off in one afternoon; *Sunflower Sutra* was completed in twenty minutes, "me at my desk scribbling, Kerouac at cottage door waiting for me to finish." And in the same improvisatory manner, Jack Kerouac came to the point of typing his novels nonstop onto enormous rolls of paper—six feet per day— with never a revision.

Most of these reports from the artist's workbench were approving, for the critics of the new sensibility were hardly less personal in tone than the artists. Faced with a play, a book, or a film, their purpose seemed less to evaluate it in traditional aesthetic terms than to express themselves about it: the work served mainly as an occasion for a personal statement. Thus did each work of art, whether painting, novel, or film, become a pretext for "another" work of "art"—the critic's declaration of his *feelings* about the original work. "Action" art thus brought "action" response, and every man became his own artist. But in the process, all notion of objective judgment went by the board.

The democratization of genius is made possible by the fact that while one can quarrel with judgments, one cannot quarrel with feelings. The emotions generated by a work either appeal to you or they don't, and no man's feelings have more authority than another man's. With the expansion of higher education, and the growth of a semi-skilled intelligentsia, moreover, a significant change has taken place in the scale of all this. Large numbers of people who might previously have been oblivious to the matter now insist on the right to participate in the artistic enterprise—not in order to cultivate their minds or sensibilities, but to "fulfill" their personalities. Both in the character of art itself and in the nature of the response to it, the concern with self takes precedence over any objective standards.

This development has not been unforeseen. Thirty years ago Karl Mannheim warned that:

". . . the open character of democratic mass society, together with its growth in size and the tendency toward general public participation, not only produces far too many elites but also deprives these elites of the exclusiveness which they need for the sublimation of impulse. If this minimum of exclusiveness is lost, then the deliberate formulation of taste, of a guiding principle of style, becomes impossible. The new impulses, intuitions and fresh approaches to the world, if they have no time to mature in small groups, will be apprehended by the masses as mere stimuli. . . ."

Other theorists of mass society like Ortega y Gasset, Karl Jaspers, Paul Tillich, Emil Lederer, and Hannah Arendt, whose writings were so influential in the 1950's, were also concerned with the social consequences of the loss of authority, the breakup of institutions, and the erosion of tradition; but their emphasis was political rather than cultural. They saw mass society as highly unstable and a prelude to the onset of totalitarianism. But while their theory about the relation of the "masses" to society seems in retrospect overly simple in its judgments about social structure and crude in its analysis of the nature of politics, it did prove startlingly relevant to one segment of society—the contemporary world of culture. What these theorists called "massification"—to use one of their clumsier terms—is now taking place in the world of the arts. Style has become synonymous with fashion, and "new" styles in art displace one another in constant and bewildering succession. The cultural institutions do not work in opposition to the present, thereby providing the necessary tension for testing the claims of the new, but surrender without struggle to the passing tides.

High art, as Hilton Kramer has observed, "has always been elitist, even if the elite was only an elite of sensibility, rather than of social position. High art requires exceptional talent, exceptional vision, exceptional training and dedication—it requires exceptional individuals. . . ." Such a requirement is of course repugnant to any kind of populist ideology—including the populist ideology which holds sway in present-day American culture.* Hence the haste with which so many critics have rushed to align themselves on the side of mass culture.

For the serious critic the situtaion poses a real dilemma. "The profession of criticism," as Hilton Kramer points out, "made its historical debut at the very moment when high art needed to be defended against a large, ignorant public for the first time." But that situation has long since changed. High art itself is in disarray, if not "decadent" (though that term has never been adequately defined); the "public" is now so culturally voracious that the avant-garde, far from needing defenders among the critics, is in the public domain. The serious critic, then, must either turn against high art itself, thereby pleasing its political enemies, or, in John Gross's phrase, "resign himself to being the doorman at the discothèque." This is the trajectory of the democratization of cultural genius.

# IV
## The Loss of Self

The situation is most grave, perhaps, in the area of literature. The novel came into being some two hundred years ago, created by the sense of a world in upheaval. It was a means of reporting on the world of fact through the imagination, and the touchstone of the novel was involvement with experience—in all its variety and immediacy—refracted through the emotions and disciplined by the intellect. A novelist is, so to speak, a sample of one whose personal experiences are a kind of *ur*-experience. When he goes back into his own unconscious to scrape the burns of his psyche, he is in touch—if he is a good novelist—with the collective unconscious as well.

For the first hundred years or so of the novel's existence, the task of the novelist was to elucidate society. But that task was eventually to prove impossible. As Diana Trilling has written, in seeking to define the contemporary burden of the novelist: "For the advanced writer of our time, the self is his supreme, even sole referent. Society has no texture or business worth bothering about; it exists because it weighs upon us and because it conditions us so absolutely. . . . [The] present-day novelist undertakes only to help us define the self in relation to the world that surrounds us and threatens to overwhelm it."

---

* "Ours is the first cultural epoch," Lionel Trilling has written, "in which many men aspire to high achievement in the arts and, in their frustration, form a dispossessed class which cuts across the conventional class lines, making a proletariat of the spirit." "On the Modern Element in Modern Literature," in *The Idea of the Modern*, edited by Irving Howe.

This is a brilliantly accurate statement about the first of the century; by the time we reached the 60's, however, the novelist had lost even the self as referent, as the boundaries between the self and the world grew increasingly blurred. Mary McCarthy has said that a new kind of novel, "based on statelessness," was beginning to be written at this time, and she cites as evidence the writings of Vladimir Nabokov and William Burroughs. I think this is to some extent true. In any event, writing in the mid-1960's became increasingly autistic, and the voice of the novelist grew more and more disembodied.

In reading the novelists who have touched the nerve of the age, one finds that the major preoccupation of the 60's was *madness*. When the social life has been left behind, and the self, as a bounded subject, has been dissolved, the only theme left is the theme of dissociation, and every important writer of the 60's was in one way or another involved with this theme. The novels are hallucinatory in mode; many of their protagonists are schizoid; insanity, rather than normalcy, has become the touchstone of reality. Despite all the social turmoil of the decade, not one novel by these writers was political; none (with the exception of Bellow's *Mr. Sammler's Planet*) dealt with radicalism, youth, or social movements—yet all were anagogical in one way or another. What all this adds up to in the sensibility of these writers is an apocalyptic tremor—like the swallows before a storm—that seems to warn of some impending holocaust.†

The "simplest" writers are the Black Humorists—Joseph Heller, J. P. Donleavy, Bruce Friedman, Thomas Pynchon, and, for the "pop" audience, Terry Southern. They deal with absurd and nihilistic situations, the plots are nutty and mischievous, the style cool, farcical, zany, and slapstick. In all of the situations the individual is a kind of shuttlecock, batted back and forth by the inanities of huge and impersonal institutions. In *Catch-22*—one of the most popular novels of the 60's—the protagonist cannot escape from the Air Force because by invoking a rule to show that he is mad, he proves he is really sane. It is the classical theme of folly.

In the science fiction and futurism of Anthony Burgess, Kurt Vonnegut, and William Burroughs the absurdities are heightened as the characters undergo actual changes in their physical form. The emphasis is on the gratuitousness of events and on the blurring of good and evil. In John Barth's *Giles Goat Boy*, the world is fought over by two giant computers. In Thomas Pynchon's *The Crying of Lot 49*, the "plot" centers on a worldwide conspiracy

† This reading, I know, completely ignores many prominent novelists of the decade—such as Updike, Salinger, Cheever, J. F. Powers, Styron, Roth, Malamud, and Baldwin. I can only say that these men have busied themselves with the more traditional concerns of the novelist—which is to report the doings of man in a social framework, though Malamud, to be sure, has often gone off into the exploration of fantasy. Given my own sociological reading of the apocalyptic temper of the times, I feel that the novelists I have chosen are the ones making the more characteristic statements.

—a theme that also occurs in Burroughs—and we await the end of America in an onrush of doomsday saturnalia.

Schizoid themes are made explicit in Ken Kesey's *One Flew Over the Cuckoo's Nest*, Barth's *The End of the Road*, and Mailer's *An American Dream*. In Kesey's book, parts of it written under the influence of peyote and LSD, a character fakes insanity to escape a jail term but ends up being lobotomized, while a schizoid Indian giant who has been a patient in the same hospital breaks out and "goes sane." In Mailer's *An American Dream* —with its obviously symbolic title—the protagonist Stephen Rojack acts out a variety of omnipotence fantasies—including confrontation by the CIA and other mysterious forces—and ends up by celebrating the power of thought waves to reach out to the beyond.

In the other major novelists of the period—Nabokov, Bellow, Burroughs, and Genet—the themes of fantasy predominate. Nabokov's *Pale Fire* is a kind of fantastic detective story (as well as a melodramatic, labyrinthine conceit about power, love, and learning) consisting of an elaborate commentary on a long poem by a protagonist who may be a spy or the deposed king of an imaginary country resembling Russia—the confusion of identity is crucial. *Ada* (or *Ardor*, or many other versions) is an equally complex fantasy about love, which deliberately plays with anachronism to obliterate all distinctions between past and future time.

Saul Bellow—the only writer who in the end is anti-apocalyptic—raises the question: "Was it the time . . . to blow this great, blue, white, green planet, or to be blown from it?" *Mr. Sammler's Planet* revolves, in large part, around the plan of an Indian physicist to colonize the moon as an escape from the over-crowding of the earth. Interwoven with Dr. Lal's plan is a purported memoir of the life of one of the pioneering futurists, H. G. Wells. And Mr. Sammler himself—the novel's beautifully rendered protagonist—is stateless, as though to emphasize the dissolution of all past structures.

Nabokov and Bellow are by temperament observers of the world, but with Burroughs and Genet the apocalypse is upon us. The world is literally and symbolically dismembered. In Burroughs, the excremental vision becomes tactile. Though *Naked Lunch* is ostensibly about the author's battle with drug addiction, the theme of feculence runs like an open sewer through the book: there is a great preoccupation with anality, with bodily discharges of all kinds, with a horror of the female genitalia, and a lingering upon such images as the reflexive ejaculation of a hanged man during an execution. People are turned into crabs, or huge centipedes, or carnivores. Burroughs has said that the "novelistic form is probably outmoded," and writers will have to develop more precise techniques "producing the same effect on the reader as lurid action photos." His novels—*Naked Lunch*, and the trilogy including *The Soft Machine*, *Nova Express*, and *The Ticket That Exploded*—are "cut-up" books:

"You can cut into *Naked Lunch* at any intersection." It is a "continuous show-ing," for *Naked Lunch* has no use for history. The other novels are written in strips and pasted up arbitrarily. Reality has no reality, for there are no more dimensions and no more boundaries.

Similar preoccupations run through the work of Jean Genet, but his writ-ing is above all a celebration of the underclass. As Susan Sontag has written, "Crime, sexual and social degradation, above all murder, are understood by Genet as occasions for glory." Genet sees the world of thieves, rapists, and murderers as the only honest world, for here the profoundest and most for-bidden human impulses are expressed in direct, primitive terms. For Genet, fantasies of cannibalism and bodily incorporation represent the deepest truth about human desires.*

# V
## The Dionysian Pack

Nowhere was the apocalyptic mood acted out more tirelessly than in that movement which called itself the "Dionysiac theater," and which regarded the acting troupe as a kind of Dionysiac pack. Its main emphasis was on spon-taneity, on orgiastic release, on sensory communication, on Eastern mysticism and ritual; its intention, unlike that of the older radical theater, was not to change the ideas of the audience so much as to reconstruct the psyches of both audience and actors through joint participation in ceremonies of liberation. The movement fostered a school of theater which was anti-discipline and anti-craft, on the ground that any shaping of performers or text, any form of artifice or calculation, was "non-creative and anti-life."

In the traditional theater of the well-wrought play, there are no loose ends, no moral ambiguities, no unused bits of plot; there is always an underlying logic that guides the action to its conclusion, for the playwright wants to make a point. But the "new theater" distrusts what is olderly and condemns it as arbitrary and selective. Necessarily such a theater is not one of playwrights, for a written play is to some extent circumscribed and bounded, while the new theater wants to break open the action, to erase the distinction between spectator and stage, between audience and actor. Distrusting thought, it seeks to recapture in the theater a sense of primitive ritual.

The prototype of the new sensibility in the drama was the Living Theatre,

---

\* It may seem strange to include Genet in an "American" group, and to label him a writer of the 1960's. Yet though his major writing was done in the 1940's and 1950's, the books which won Genet an American following—*Our Lady of the Flowers, The Thief's Journal,* and *Funeral Rites*—did not appear in translation until the 1960's. Burroughs, too, was writing in the 1950's, but both men emerged fully in the American consciousness only in the 1960's.

organized by Julian Beck and Judith Malina. After traveling in Europe for several years, the troupe evolved a new style of random action and preached a form of revolutionary anarchism. In their new credo, "the theater must be set free" and "taken out into the street." In words reminiscent of Marinetti's Futuristic Manifesto, Beck launched an attack on the theater of the past:

"All forms of the theater of lies will go. . . . We don't need Shakespeare's objective wisdom, his sense of tragedy reserved only for the experience of the high-born. His ignorance of collective joy makes him useless to our time. It is important not to be seduced by the poetry. That is why Artaud says, 'Burn the Texts.'

"In fact the whole theater of the intellect will go. The theater of our century, and centuries past, is a theater whose presentation and appeal is intellectual. One leaves the theater of our time and goes and thinks. But our thinking, conditioned by our already conditioned minds, is so corrupt that it is not to be trusted. . . ."

Accordingly, in *Paradise Now*, the star piece of the Living Theatre, audiences were invited to cross the footlights and join the actors onstage, while other performers wandered all through the house smoking marijuana and engaging members of the audience in conversation. Now and then one or another actor would return to the stage, strip down to a loincloth, and encourage the audience to follow his lead. The intention (seldom achieved) was to organize some sort of mass saturnalia. Finally everyone was exhorted to leave the theater, convert the police to anarchism, storm the jails, free the prisoners, stop the war, and take over the cities in the name of "the people."

Traditionally, violence has been repugnant to the intellectual as a confession of failure. In discourse, individuals resorted to force only when they had lost the power of persuasion by means of reason. So, too, in art the resort to force—in the sense of a literal reenactment of violence on the canvas, on the stage, or on the written page—signified that the artist, lacking the artistic power to suggest the emotion, was reduced to invoking the shock of it directly. But in the 1960's violence was justified not only as therapy, but as a necessary accompaniment to social change. Watching the children of the French upper bourgeoisie mouth the phrases of violence and chant from Mao's Little Red Book in Jean-Luc Godard's *La Chinoise*, one realized that a corrupt romanticism was covering some dreadful drive to murder. Similarly in Godard's *Weekend*, where a real slaughter of real animals takes place, one realized that the roots of a sinister blood-lust were being touchd, not for catharsis but for kicks.

What the rhetoric of revolution permits—both in the new sensibility and the new politics—is the eradication of the line between playacting and reality, so that life (and such "revolutionary" actions as demonstrations) is played out as theater, while the craving for violence, first in the theater and then in the street demonstrations, becomes a necessary psychological drug, a form of addiction.

# VI
## In Place of Reason

By the end of the 60's the new sensibility had been given a name (the counter-culture) and an ideology to go with it. The main tendency of that ideology —though it appeared in the guise of an attack on the "technocratic society"— was an attack on reason itself.*

In place of reason, we were told to give ourselves over to one form or other of pre-rational spontaneity—whether under the heading of Charles Reich's "Consciousness III," the "shamanistic vision" of Theodore Roszak, or the like. "Nothing less is required," said Mr. Roszak, one of the movement's most articulate spokesmen, "than the subversion of the scientific world view with its entrenched commitment to an egocentric and cerebral mode of consciousness. In its place, there must be a new culture in which the non-intellective capacities of personality—those capacities that take fire from visionary splendor and the experience of human communion—become the arbiters of the true, the good, and the beautiful."

Revolutionary change, we heard over and over, must embrace psyche as well as society. But when we sought clues as to what this might mean in real terms—what form this new, presumably post-revolutionary, culture might take—we were given only further exhortations to cast off the deadening weight of cognition, and further celebrations of "the shaman's rhapsodic babbling."

Do these exhortations add up to anything more than a longing for the lost gratifications of an idealized childhood? This has been the recurrent yearning of all utopian movements. What is new, however, about the present Arcadian fantasy—other than its being dressed up in the language of psychology and anthropology—is that while in the past such longings were largely rhetorical (regard only the "eupsychia" of Fourier), in the 1960's one found the fantasies and sexual demands of childhood acted out during adolescence on a mass scale unprecedented in cultural history. For what else was the demand

---

* It would be a mistake and distortion to see this attack as coterminous with all radicalism. In fact, there is an older radical tradition which detests irrationalism, and a number of its adherents—Philip Rahv, Robert Brustein, Lionel Abel, Irving Howe—have in different essays attacked aspects of the new sensibility. The difficulty with many of their arguments is that intellectually and aesthetically they are all allied with modernism and accept its premises. Yet all the new sensibility has done is to carry the premises of modernism through to their logical conclusions.

for negotiation and indiscriminateness than a denial of those necessary distinctions—between sexes and among ideas—which are the mark of adulthood? What else was the youth culture of the Aquarian Age, the rock-drug dance of springtime, than the democratization of Dionysus?

## 2. The Growing Importance of Youth and of College Students in American Society

### JACK D. DOUGLAS

The young have become evermore important in our society. This is true in terms of "objective fact," such as their number and their contributions to society. But it is far more true as a "subjective fact"—a "social reality." Regardless of their numbers or their contributions to society, the young are increasingly important to our society because the members of our society *believe* they are more important, *feel* they are more important, and act in accord with this belief and feeling.

This is more true of college youth than of any other group of the young. It is the college youth who have been paid evermore attention, who have been wooed for years by political parties and groups, who have been endlessly eulogized as the "leaders of tomorrow," and who have been minutely scrutinized by the mass media for portents of the future. Formerly, generations of adults were almost exclusively concerned with the "evils" of lower class youth and paid great attention to gang wars and motorcycle gangs, making such splinter groups as the Hell's Angels world famous. But today these erstwhile celebrities have become has-beens as the mass media have devoted their coverage almost exclusively to the "hell-raising" of campus splinter groups.

There are many important "subjective" reasons for the growing importance of the young and especially of the young who attend college. But most of these do build to some extent on the "objective" factors, the facts about the growing importance of youth—especially the college educated youth—in our society. At the least, these socially recognized facts form the background against which these more "subjective" factors are judged by the influential

From *Youth in Turmoil*. Washington: USGPO, 1970, pp. 1–7, 10–15.

members of our society. If there is no "objective" substance to the belief and feeling that the young are of growing importance, then we can be sure that the vast attention paid to them will be transitory, as the interest in the Hell's Angels seems to have been (they *do* still exist, though many people would probably be surprised to learn this). And, if we expect public and official concern to be transitory, then there is far less reason for any of us to be concerned with social policy concerning college youth.

Our first concern, then, must be with the facts about the importance of youth in our society, especially of the college youth. The facts about youth are all too few, so it is all the more important that we be as aware as possible of the relevant facts that are available.

## The Growing Number and Proportion of Youth in American Society

It is common knowledge today that the median age of the American population has been decreasing for a number of years, so that more than half of our population is still safely under the traumatic age of 30. In fact, today the majority of the American population is (approximately) twenty-five years or less. Heralded by the leisure industries as a tidal wave of consumers, and bemoaned by school administrators as an avalanche of pupils, in recent years the young have grown rapidly in absolute number and, far less strikingly, in their percentage of the total population. And census projections make it clear that the number and percentage of the young will continue to increase for at least the next decade.

As can be seen in Series A of Table I, census projections show an expected increase in the number of 18-to-24-year-olds of approximately three million from 1966 to 1970, of three million more by 1975, and of two million more by 1980. The percentage of the total population increases will be from 10.8 in 1966 to 11.8 in 1970, to 12.1 in 1975, and then a drop back to 11.8 by 1980. In the same time periods the age group from 25 to 34 years will show even more marked increases of three million by 1970, six million by 1975, and five million by 1980, representing percentage growths from 11.5 in 1966 to 12.1 in 1970, to 13.8 in 1975, and 14.8 in 1980.

While these will certainly be important changes, the truly striking increases in the number and percentage of the young are not shown in these figures because they had largely occurred just prior to 1966. The reason for this is simple and is probably the most important single fact about the distribution of the American population today: *in the period from approximately 1960 to 1968 the War Babies came of age.*

In the depression years of the 1930's the birth rate in the United States was exceptionally low, so low that the percent of the total population constituted by the 18-to-24-year-old group declined by 1.19, as this 1930's cohort reached the 18-to-24-year group from 1950 to 1960. But the period during and immediately after the war saw the dramatic increase in the birth rate that was commonly called the Baby Boom. The results of this succession from the

## TABLE I

Estimated and Projected Distribution of the Population by Age:
1966 to 1990[1]

Numbers in thousands. Figures relate to July 1 and include Armed Forces abroad. Boldface figures depend, in whole or part, on projections of births; all percentages are affected by the projections of births.

| Age | 1966 | Series A | | | | |
| --- | --- | --- | --- | --- | --- | --- |
| | | 1970 | 1975 | 1980 | 1985 | 1990 |
| All ages ............ | [1]196,842 | 208,615 | 227,929 | 250,489 | 274,748 | 300,131 |
| Under 5 years ........ | 19,851 | **21,317** | **27,210** | **31,040** | **33,288** | **35,015** |
| 5 to 13 years ......... | 36,525 | 37,224 | 37,884 | **45,215** | **53,497** | **58,690** |
| 14 to 17 years ......... | 14,300 | 15,808 | 16,896 | 16,005 | **19,006** | **23,080** |
| 18 to 24 years ......... | 21,326 | 24,589 | 27,535 | 29,612 | **28,956** | **32,459** |
| 25 to 34 years ......... | 22,567 | 25,315 | 31,423 | 36,998 | 40,699 | 42,449 |
| 35 to 44 years ......... | 24,225 | 22,961 | 22,458 | 25,376 | 31,384 | 36,863 |
| 45 to 54 years ......... | 22,331 | 23,326 | 23,532 | 22,147 | 21,705 | 24,542 |
| 55 to 64 years ......... | 17,261 | 18,490 | 19,831 | 21,032 | 21,236 | 20,027 |
| 65 to 74 years ........ | 11,568 | 12,097 | 13,191 | 14,457 | 15,570 | 16,602 |
| 75 years and over ...... | 6,889 | 7,488 | 7,968 | 8,606 | 9,407 | 10,404 |
| Percent ............ | 100.0 | 100.0 | 100.0 | 100.0 | 100.0 | 100.0 |
| Under 5 years ........ | 10.1 | 10.2 | 11.9 | 12.4 | 12.1 | 11.7 |
| 5 to 13 years ......... | 18.6 | 17.8 | 16.6 | 18.1 | 19.5 | 19.6 |
| 14 to 17 years ........ | 7.3 | 7.6 | 7.4 | 6.4 | 6.9 | 7.7 |
| 18 to 24 years ......... | 10.8 | 11.8 | 12.1 | 11.8 | 10.5 | 10.8 |
| 25 to 34 years ......... | 11.5 | 12.1 | 13.8 | 14.8 | 14.8 | 14.1 |
| 35 to 44 years ......... | 12.3 | 11.0 | 9.9 | 10.1 | 11.4 | 12.3 |
| 45 to 54 years ........ | 11.3 | 11.2 | 10.3 | 8.8 | 7.9 | 8.2 |
| 55 to 64 years ......... | 8.8 | 8.9 | 8.7 | 8.4 | 7.7 | 6.7 |
| 65 to 74 years ......... | 5.9 | 5.8 | 5.8 | 5.8 | 5.7 | 5.5 |
| 75 years and over ...... | 3.5 | 3.6 | 3.5 | 3.4 | 3.4 | 3.5 |

[1] Bureau of the Census, *Publication Estimates*, Series P-25, No. 381, Washington, D.C.: United States Department of Commerce; United States Government Printing Office, December 18, 1967, p. 6.

Depression Babies (The Baby Bust) to the War Babies (The Baby Boom) can be clearly seen in the census figures of Table II.

*From 1960 to 1968 the 18-to-24-year age group increased by 43 percent.*

Since it is this group from approximately 18 years to 24 years that constitutes the core of what is increasingly coming to be known as "youth" or "the young" (which we shall discuss in more detail in Chapter 2), *The coming of age of the War Babies*, in less than a decade, especially when coupled with the greatly decreased number and percentage of adults in the most productive

## TABLE II

Age of the Population in 1968, 1960, and 1950 With Average Annual Rate of Change[2]

Numbers in thousands. Total population including Armed Forces overseas.

| | | | | Percent distribution | | |
|---|---|---|---|---|---|---|
| | Population | | | | | |
| Age | July 1, 1968 | April 1, 1960 | April 1, 1950 | July 1,1968 | April 1, 1960 | April 1, 1950 |
| All ages ........... | 201,166 | 180,007 | 151,718 | 100.0 | 100.0 | 100.0 |
| Under 5 years ....... | 18,521 | 20,321 | 16,243 | 9.2 | 11.3 | 10.7 |
| 5 to 13 years ......... | 37,239 | 32,726 | 22,255 | 18.5 | 18.2 | 14.7 |
| 14 to 17 years ........ | 15,053 | 11,162 | 8,473 | 7.5 | 6.2 | 5.6 |
| 18 to 24 years ........ | 22,842 | 15,975 | 16,150 | 11.4 | 8.9 | 10.6 |
| 25 to 34 years ........ | 23,966 | 23,007 | 23,999 | 11.9 | 12.8 | 15.8 |
| 35 to 44 years ........ | 23,649 | 24,181 | 21,572 | 11.8 | 13.4 | 14.2 |
| 45 to 54 years ........ | 22,889 | 20,503 | 17,403 | 11.4 | 11.4 | 11.5 |
| 55 to 64 years ........ | 17,880 | 15,573 | 13,328 | 8.9 | 8.7 | 8.8 |
| 65 years and over ..... | 19,129 | 16,560 | 12,295 | 9.5 | 9.2 | 8.1 |

| | Change | | | | Average Annual Percent Change | |
|---|---|---|---|---|---|---|
| | 1960 to 1968 | | 1950 to 1960 | | | |
| Age | Number | Per-cent | Number | Per-cent | 1960-1968 | 1950-1960 |
| All ages .......... | +21,158 | +11.8 | +28,200 | +18.6 | +1.3 | +1.7 |
| Under 5 years ....... | −1,800 | −8.9 | +4,073 | +25.1 | −1.1 | +2.2 |
| 5 to 13 years ......... | +4,513 | +13.8 | +10,471 | +47.1 | +1.6 | +3.9 |
| 14 to 17 years ........ | +3,891 | +34.9 | +2,689 | +31.7 | +3.6 | +2.8 |
| 18 to 24 years ........ | +6,867 | +43.0 | −176 | −1.1 | +4.3 | −0.1 |
| 25 to 34 years ........ | +959 | +4.2 | −992 | −4.1 | +0.5 | −0.4 |
| 35 to 44 years ........ | −533 | −2.2 | +2,609 | +12.1 | −0.3 | +1.1 |
| 45 to 54 years ........ | +2,386 | +11.6 | +3,099 | +17.8 | +1.3 | +1.6 |
| 55 to 64 years ........ | +2,306 | +14.8 | +2,246 | +16.8 | +1.7 | +1.6 |
| 65 years and over .... | +2,569 | +15.5 | +4,265 | +34.7 | +1.7 | +3.0 |

[2] Bureau of the Census, *Population Estimates*, Series P-25, No. 46, Washington, D.C.: United States Department of Commerce; United States Government Printing Office, February 17, 1969, p. 5.

age group from approximately 35 to 45 years, has been a profound demo-graphic change which has in turn had profound social effects.

From the end of the Second World War through the 1950's there was a great deal of discussion in the mass media of the importance of the Baby Boom during and immediately after the Second World War to American society. Journalists, government officials and, apparently, everyone else believed that this Baby Boom phenomenon would have profound effects on American society. There were strong demands for social planning to meet the important changes that would result from the Baby Boom. There were many predictions of the great effects this crop of War Babies would have on education, consumption, investment, real estate, and almost every other aspect of American society. There was a great deal of discussion of the great over-crowding in schools that would occur when this unprecedentedly large group of students hit the schools (and the emphasis was generally placed on such striking terms as "hit"). There was widespread speculation about what would happen when this group inundated the colleges and the labor market. There were some expressions of impending doom, though these were generally balanced by the optimistic economic forecasts of businessmen looking at the consumer potential of this wave of young people.

For some unexplained reason, in the 1960's almost all of the speculation, portentous prediction, and optimistic planning died away almost completely. Just as the pupil invasion was hitting the schools the hardest, especially the State colleges and universities, and just as the demand for public investment in schools and social services was reaching its peak, thereby placing an ever growing demand on the tax base of society, the Baby Boom phenomenon almost disappeared from the public arena. Though some of the grimmest predictions, such as chaos in the schools and widespread unemployment, were effectively prevented by a rapid increase in investment in schools and by the continuing economic prosperity of the Nation, some of the grim predic-tions had indeed come true. Double and triple sessions in elementary and secondary schools were common, State colleges and universities were, in fact, inundated with new pupils, the demands for all public services for this massive group of (relatively) economically unproductive citizens was very intense, so that taxes on the productive segment of society had to increase very rapidly, and in turn led to a "taxpayers' revolt"; but the public had apparently for-gotten that many of these grim details had been effectively forecast by those who knew the demographic details of the Baby Boom.

In terms of their numbers and their proportion of the total population, there could be little doubt that young people, especially those in the 18-24 age group, from 1960 up to the present have grown at an extremely rapid rate, and have, in this sense, become evermore important in our society. These young people have been of growing importance in our society also in that they have placed ever greater demands on public services and, thereby, public tax investment. All this may appear to be of negative importance, rather than of importance because of the contributions of the young to society. It is, nevertheless, a matter of fundamental importance. (It should also be kept in mind that this negative aspect, their cost, is a shortrun phenomenon that will be reversed in the next decade as this group becomes the most productive group of society.)

## The Growing Importance of College Students in American Society

It would be a mistake, however, to conclude that the many strains placed on social services by the young in the past decade have been simply the result of the War Babies coming of age. There have been other, perhaps even more important factors, especially in the causation of the strain on schools and colleges.

There has been almost steady increase in the percentage of young people enrolled in American schools over the last half century and more. In the early part of this century there was an accelerating rate of attendance of elementary schools and secondary schools. Today the great majority of the young under 18 years of age are enrolled in schools and only sudden increases in the number of students due to the Baby Boom and some upgrading of standards caused any strains on the elementary and secondary schools.

At the same time there was a steady but slow increase in the percentage of people attending college in the early part of the century. In the post-war period, however, this percentage grew rapidly and at a slowly accelerating, if erratic, rate. As can be seen in Table III, there was a 2 percent increase from 1946 to 1951, a 9.5 percent increase from 1951 to 1956 (probably due partly to the men returning from Korea), a 4 percent increase from 1956 to 1961, and an 8 percent increase from 1961 to 1966. But it must also be noted that this percentage increase from 22 percent to 46 percent did not simply lead to a doubling in the absolute number of college students. Because the War Babies came of age in the late 1950's and early 1960's, there were more than four million more 18–21 year olds by 1967. *The absolute number of college students had tripled in twenty years.*

The rapidly growing percentage of the population in the 18-21-year-age group enrolled in college and universities has been the result of a number of basic changes taking place in American society which have increasingly made formal education and research the foundation of much of the rest of our society. Since these changes are continuing and, very possibly, accelerating, we can expect education and research to continue to grow in importance and to involve an ever greater number of young people.

The number of the young going to college has grown rapidly, primarily

## TABLE III

Enrollment in Institutions of Higher Education Compared With
Population Aged 18–21: United States, Fall 1946 to Fall 1967[3]

| Year | Population 18–21 years of age[1] | Enrollment | Number enrolled per 100 persons 18–21 years of age | Year | Population 18–21 years of age[a] | Enrollment | Number enrolled per 100 persons 18–21 years of age |
|---|---|---|---|---|---|---|---|
| 1 | 2 | 3 | 4 | 1 | 2 | 3 | 4 |
| 1946 | 9,403,000 | 2,078,095 | 22.1 | 1957 | 8,844,000 | 3,036,938 | 34.3 |
| 1947 | 9,276,000 | 2,338,226 | 25.2 | 1958 | 8,959,000 | 3,226,038 | 36.0 |
| 1948 | 9,144,000 | 2,403,396 | 26.3 | 1959 | 9,182,000 | 3,364,861 | 36.6 |
| 1949 | 8,990,000 | 2,444,900 | 27.2 | 1960 | 9,550,000 | 3,582,726 | 37.5 |
| 1950 | 8,945,000 | 2,281,298 | 25.5 | 1961 | 10,252,000 | 3,860,643 | 37.7 |
| 1951 | 8,742,000 | 2,101,962 | 24.0 | 1962 | 10,761,000 | 4,174,936 | 38.8 |
| 1952 | 8,542,000 | 2,134,242 | 25.0 | 1963 | 11,154,000 | 4,494,626 | 40.3 |
| 1953 | 8,441,000 | 2,231,054 | 26.4 | 1964 | 11,319,000 | 4,950,173 | 43.7 |
| 1954 | 8,437,000 | 2,446,693 | 29.0 | 1965 | 12,127,000 | 5,526,325 | 45.6 |
| 1955 | 8,508,000 | 2,653,034 | 31.2 | 1966 | 12,888,000 | [b]5,885,000 | 45.7 |
| 1956 | 8,701,000 | 2,918,212 | 33.5 | 1967 | 13,632,000 | [b]6,348,000 | 46.6 |

[a] These Bureau of the Census estimates are as of July 1 preceding the opening of the
academic year. They include Armed Forces overseas.

[b] Estimated.

because a college education has become evermore important in our society. A
college education has most obviously become more important from the
economic vantage point of a young person considering whether he should go
to college and then to work or opt for immediate employment after leaving
high school. From the commonsense standpoint of most members of our
society, a college education has been closely associated with financial success:
commonsensically, going to college means far more money. There have, in
fact, been a great number of statistical studies done to show how much
greater the lifetime incomes of college graduates are, and these kinds of

[3] Simon, Kenneth A., and Vance Grant, *Digest of Educational Statistics*, Washington,
D.C.; U.S. Department of Health, Education, and Welfare, Office of Education, U.S.
Government Printing Office, 1968, p. 8.

Note: Beginning in 1960, data are for 50 states and the District of Columbia data for
earlier years are for 48 States and the District of Columbia. Beginning in 1953, enrollment figures include resident and extension degree-credit students; data for earlier years
exclude extension students.

figures have become the spearheads of many advertising campaigns. The results of a typical study of this sort are presented in Table IV.

## TABLE IV

Estimated Total Income of Males From the Year of Specified
Number of Years of School Completed Through
Age 64 by Region and Race, 1954[4]

| Years of School Completed | Non-South White Males | Non-South Non-White Males | South White Males | South Non-White Males |
|---|---|---|---|---|
| 8 | $224,000[a] | $172,000[a] | $197,000[a] | $115,000[a] |
| 12 | 300,000[b] | 195,000[b] | 274,000[b] | 138,000[b] |
| 16 | 371,000[c] | 215,000[c] | 346,000[c] | 157,000[c] |

[a] Assumes that eight years of school are completed in the year that the person is 14 years of age.

[b] Assumes that 12 years of school are completed in the year that the person is 18 years of age.

[c] Assumes that 16 years of school are completed in the year that the person is 22 years of age.

[4] Lassiter, Roy L. *The Association of Income and Educational Achievement*, Florida: University of Florida Press, 1966, p. 7.

The conclusions of these studies are always rosy—for the college graduate or the prospective graduate. The figures always show him winning by $50,000 to $100,000 over the high school graduate and far outdistancing the hapless dropout. The college degree would appear to be a guaranteed meal tciket.

The actual relations between income and education are clearly very complex. There may well be no general positive relationship between actual income and degree of formal education. If there is, the difference is not terribly great for most individuals, but the general relationship may not be nearly so important as specific relationships. What does seem to be very clear is that there is a direct positive relationship between technical education and income and that this relationship has been growing rapidly in recent years. It is, in fact, only in rather technical fields that there is any direct relationship between what an individual learns in formal education and the nature of the job that he performs through his career. Wolfle, for example, found that in the natural sciences, 42 percent of the graduates entered corresponding occupations, whereas, in psychology the percentage was only 20 percent, in the social sciences only 13 percent, in the humanities and arts only 24 percent, and so on.[8] Over the years even these relations may greatly decrease as many of the more successful individuals in technical fields enter managerial occupa-

[8] Wolfle, quoted in Harris, *op. cit.*, p. 50.

tions where their technical skill is not so directly related to the job. Individuals who graduate in the general education courses, such as English, philosophy, and so on, probably do not receive any great economic advantage from their formal education unless they go on to business school, law school, medical school, or some other form of professional training of a technical nature.

However, after having considered how uncertain the objective facts about relationships between economics and formal education are, it is of crucial importance to note that this may not be nearly so important in determining what has happened to education as the "social reality" of the relationship between college and success. Whether it is or is not true, most members of our society have believed for at least a century that graduation from college will lead to far more money, far more financial success. Perhaps this belief was largely the result of the fact that in the 18th and 19th centuries college was largely attended only by the already affluent. In fact, certainly most people who graduated from college were financially very well off, or were destined to become so by assuming lucrative jobs in their fathers' businesses. However it came about, this belief in the great financial value of a college education became a firmly entrenched "social reality" by the 20th century and has served to create a strong motivation for individuals to attend college. It became a basic force behind the immigrant's dream of sending his children to college.

Even more importantly, it seems highly likely that college in more recent days has come to be seen by young people as a gateway to something of at least equal importance to financial success. College has come increasingly to be seen as the gateway to social respectability, prestige, and interesting kinds of work. Certainly any young man who reads the newspapers, or listens to his reasonably knowledgeable parents discuss such matters, would recognize that the average carpenter, plumber or electrician earns two or three times more money than does a typical elementary or high school teacher. Indeed, there are probably some cities in which the trash collectors with very low educational levels earn significantly more money than do the teachers. While any high school graduate advised of these facts might be saddened by them, and might certainly prefer that they were not so (unless he is already dedicated to one of the higher paying jobs), there is little reason to believe that most individuals are profoundly affected by such facts. It seems apparent that most of the young people would prefer a far less well-paying job if they find the work of interest and, especially, if they find it prestigious and important in itself.

The college degree has increasingly become a gateway—a "license"—not merely to generalized prestige, but to very specific kinds of jobs, such as teaching, which are not greatly demanding, but which individuals expect to be far more interesting than occupations that would be open to them without the college degree. It might very well be that this social belief is also false, as indeed, many of those who have taught, especially in the elementary and secondary levels, would urge is true; but this, too, is not very important. Today it is a growing "social reality" to the young that the kinds of jobs that college leads to are more interesting and prestigious than other jobs. For this reason, then, a college education has become far more important in our society, especially to the highly motivated, hard-working young people, even if there is not a positive economic relationship of significant degree.

But colleges and universities have become vastly more important in our society than such practical and "subjective" considerations might lead one to expect. As we shall see at greater length below, our society has increasingly become a technological society, a society in which the basic source of wealth and the basic mental and emotional preoccupation is increasingly the result and goal of technological knowledge and production. As this has happened, the so-called knowledge industry has increasingly become the focal point of our society, the social fulcrum point about which the rest of society turns. As the primary centers of technical research and education, the colleges and universities have been at the center of the center: they have been at the center of the knowledge industry. Because of this, the colleges and universities have vastly increased their social influence in the last few decades. In his work on *Notes on the Post Industrial State*, Daniel Bell has excellently summed up this increasingly central position of the universities in our society:

"The university, which is the place where theoretical knowledge is sought, tested and codified in a disinterested way, becomes the primary institution of the new society. Perhaps it is not too much to say that if the business firm was the key institution of the past one hundred years because of its role in organizing production for the mass creation of products, the university will become the central institution of the next hundred years because of its role as the new source of innovation and knowledge."

In addition, everyone is aware of how much the Federal Government, and, increasingly, local governments are dependent upon the universities for advice for the basic policies by which the government is run. Everyone is aware that industry has turned increasingly to the colleges and universities for such advice. In fact, the colleges and universities have probably become seen as far more the center of the knowledge industry and of the society than they actually are; yet, again, the power of the universities is important as a "social reality"—beyond the objective facts of such power. Indeed, so great has been this belief in the influence of the colleges and universities, that there has been a very specific form of anti-intellectualism, that of *anti-academism*, growing throughout the society in recent decades as individuals come increasingly to resent the power of the universities, their faculties, and students. (This resentment is now breaking forth in great force in the current social debate over the problems of the colleges and the universities.)

As the colleges and universities have been seen increasingly as of vital importance in society, as perhaps the cornerstone of the society's economic development, artistic glory, intellectual achievement, and national defense, they have come to be seen increasingly as the source of social influence. The colleges and universities, therefore, have come increasingly to be seen as the wellsprings of national leadership. As the advertisements and the graduation oratory put it, the colleges and universities have become the "trainers" of "tomorrow's leaders." Since most people in our society are very much interested in social influence and power for its own sake, and since prestige, economic success, and all kinds of other things can plausibly be believed to go along with such influence and power, it is no wonder that there has grown a "panic to get one's children into college." The panic has grown as well among the young who do not wish to be left out in the society's development or left out of interesting and valued paths of life—and this panic has led to much resentment on the part of those subjected to it, the students. High school has come increasingly to be seen by those with much motivation as a stepping-stone to college, and, as the enrollment and graduation numbers have spiraled in the colleges, the panic to get into the graduate schools has grown. College students, at least once they face getting a job as seniors or graduates, have come increasingly to feel that the B.A. or B.S. is not very significant, that in order to get that added economic edge, that added edge of influence, that added edge of prestige, one must have an M.A. and, of course, the panic among those with M.A.'s has grown, so the desire for Ph.D.'s has grown rapidly. The result has been a rapid spiraling upward in degree aspirations and in the number of degrees granted. As we have seen, the number of college graduates has grown very rapidly in the last 20 years, and the number of advanced degrees has grown even more rapidly. There are already approximately 5 percent of the population between the ages of 25-34 enrolled in some form of formal education and this percentage is still growing rapidly. It is now relatively common for individuals to remain "students" until the age of 30, and vast numbers over the age of 30 are still tied to universities through thesis committees.

## Numbers, Power, and Action

The numbers of the young, especially of college youth, and the growing power of the universities have been of fundamental importance in several ways in the development of the political activist groups, the student protest movements. They have, of course, been important in producing the focusing of the mass media on college youth: now that they are more important and have more present and future power from both their numbers and their central position in our society, the adult world is vitally concerned with what they do, and certainly with their apparent attacks on the adult world. In the growth of their sheeer numbers, their proportion of our society, their subjective importance to the adults, and their financial power as consumers, the young have come to have an ever greater effect on the nature of everyday life in our society: they are everywhere and everywhere they go they carry their own subcultural styles of dress, speech, behavior, and values. In terms of numbers alone, those under thirty have come to be the basic element of the public context of our everyday lives: movies, television, books, stores, cars, and almost anything else meant for the mass audience or mass consumption must take youth as *the* basic element in the mass market—youth sets the tune, quite literally in the case of popular music. Popular music *is* youthful music.

But there are some far less obvious ways in which the numbers and proportions of youth give them power and thus help to produce youthful activists. Very importantly, the rapid growth in their absolute numbers, especially, once again, in higher education, produces some qualitative differences in political power and action. In the first place, it is probably quite true that there has been no great change in the number of committed radical youth in colleges, though it is also true that there have been recent changes in this area. We shall examine some more of the details of this question later, such as the recent changes and the changing proportion of college youth who are highly liberal, but Seymour Martin Lipset has adequately summarized the general findings on this point of the small proportion of outright radicals:

"It remains true, as Herbert Marcuse pointed out recently, that the majority of the students in all countries are politically quiescent and moderate in their views. According to national surveys of student opinion taken by the Harris Poll in 1965 and the Gallup Poll in 1968, approximately one-fifth of the students have participated in civil rights or political activities (17 percent in 1964–1965, the year of the Berkeley revolt, and 20 percent in 1967–1968, the year of the McCarthy and Kennedy campaigns). The radical activist groups generally have tiny memberships. Students for a Democratic Society (SDS) claims a total membership of about 30,000 out of a national student body of 7 million of which about 6,000 pay national dues. A Harris Poll of American students taken in the spring of 1968 estimates that there are about 100,000 radical activists or somewhere between 1 and 2 percent of the college population. A Gallup survey also conducted in the spring of 1968 reports that 7 percent of male students indicate that they will refuse to go, if drafted. Given that the activists are such a small minority, the question must be raised as who are they (sic), and what are the factors that contribute to activist strength.[9]"

But even if there had been no increase at all in the percentages of radical youth, which is certainly not the case, the vast increase in the absolute numbers would be sufficient to produce a vastly larger absolute number that would have more absolute power and be more socially noticeable, since attention is determined more by such absolute magnitudes than proportionate magnitudes. Martin Meyerson, making use of roughly the same figures as Lipset, has made this point very well by making a few simple calculations and arguing from them:

"With five and a half million students, a third of whom are women, American colleges and universities have a larger population than Denmark, Ireland, or any one of a majority of the independent nations in the United Nations. At such a scale, higher education increasingly contains the divergences and convergences of the larger American culture. With these vast numbers, paradoxically, even a small minority may be large. If 98 percent of the students are "silent," and the other 2 percent dissenting, the latter category would have over 100,000 students, a large figure for any kind of protest. (No single national group devoted to student protest is that large; for example, the Students for a Democratic Society claimed a national membership of over 3,000 in mid-1965.) However, even a relatively small number can, if concentrated at a few influential institutions, have a potent national impact.[10]"

But I believe there is far more to it than such objective considerations of power. The absolute numbers and the proportions do give the young more power, a power which we shall see is being mobilized by the development of a generalized youth subculture and a student subculture, but they also produce a far greater subjective *sense of power* than the objective facts taken together would justify. The profound egocentrism of youth, that Thomas Wolfe feeling that they are immortal, that they are the finest, the most beautiful, the strongest who have ever lived, and that what they do is the most important thing ever done—all of this gives youth a sense of power, a feeling of the great things they will surely do as soon as they can. And their proverbial impatience makes them want to rush in and get it done right now: "Never mind the cautions! Forget all the miserable failures of history! *We* know how! *We* can do it!" This straining against all constraints to take over, to do

[9] Lipset, Seymour Martin, "The Activists: a Profile," p. 46–57 in *Confrontation*, Daniel Bell and Irving Kristol, eds., New York: Basic Books, Inc., 1968, p. 51.

[10] Meyerson, Martin, "The Ethos of the American College Student: Beyond the Protests," pp. 266–291, in *The Contemporary University: U.S.A.*, Robert S. Morison, ed., Boston: Houghton Mifflin Company, 1966, p. 267.

it one's own way, is all an ancient part of youth. But in a time of such rapid absolute and proportional growth in the number and apparent power of youth, of those who will surely agree with one because they are like him, the sense of power found among youth is very heady indeed. It is a time when the young over-reach their power, but in so doing they produce social change, though rarely what they seek. Herbert Moller may be wrong in arguing that all the basic changes in Western society have come during periods of rapid demographic growth (increases in the percentages of youth), but he is surely getting at an important point.[11]

---

[11] Moller, Herbert, "Youth as a Force in the Modern World," pp. 237–260, in *Comparative Studies in Society and History*, Geneva, Switzerland: The Hague, 1968.

# SECTION II

# Politics

A number of recent observers of youth have concluded that a great deal of their frenetic activity is directed toward boundary creation and maintenance. In the process of discrediting age, rationality, traditional politics and the established forms in art, music and literature, the young have raised protest itself into a style (Melly, 1970). However, undercutting previously maintained limits on sensibilities, on thought, or on reasoning may leave the person floating, having a vague sense of *disconnectedness* with symbols of the social order (Lifton, below; 1967, Keniston, 1966). It is this disconnectedness and feeling of loss of control over body and fate that seems to underlie the appeal of the drugged experience. At the same time, disconnectedness creates pressures to attain a new feeling of intimacy, of closeness, of togetherness. In art, literature, and rock music one can discover evidence of this attempt to reduce boundaries, to create a new wholeness. One finds additional evidence in the writings of Burroughs, with his lack of attention to space and time and his technique of "cut up," an attempt to mix linear and nonlinear modes of thinking, and to accentuate them by near-random juxtaposition in nonlinear expressionistic art; in *dada*, which rejects the forms of art and, indeed, rejects art itself; in atonal music; and in Eastern music. In each of these forms the conventional sense of order and of distance between artist, art, life, and observer is reduced explicitly, often violently.

These trends represent more than a change in the social organization of art; they are a profound challenge to the larger institutional structure that rests on order, rationality, linear thinking, tonal and rational music, and an art that represents "reality." (Socialist realism is the classic case of the political nature of all art—the Soviet state attempts to prescribe the form and content of art so that it might better glorify the state.) Many writers identify

59

the source of this sense of revolt: the technological superstructure dominating the everyday lives of citizens. According to such insightful commentators as Roszak, Reich, Zijderveld, Matson, Lifton, and others, the "enemy" is the abstract, rationalized society with its supertechnological engine. As Flacks points out later in this book, the enemy in this conceptualization can never be the old, for they are also victims of the new depersonalization and dehumanization. In this way, the new Left, composed of such intellectual spokesmen as Richard Flacks, Paul Goodman, and Herbert Marcuse, with its emphasis on dangers inherent in the technology creating "one-dimensional men," differs from the old Left's emphasis on the exploitive nature of the class system. The class system creates victims at the bottom, systematically grinding down the bourgeoisie into a proletariat, bifurcating society into owners and workers. The new Left sees the enemy everywhere—in the organizational structure of society itself, in its rationalized, bureaucratically governed, and depersonalized system. In Roszak's terms (1969, pp. 5–7), society has adopted a new technocracy that assumes that all human needs are technical, that all major problems can be solved by specialists using modern technology, and that given enough technical knowledge and its application specialists can know and define all needs.

There is a new romanticism in this antitechnology position, as Laqueur points out brilliantly in his essay, and which Nisbet notes as a central theme of his essay. (In *The Greening of America*, Reich offers a sacred text rationalizing and justifying this romanticism of consciousness). Flacks argues that the future of the left movement rests on the failure of the potential that the system has for coopting, absorbing, and buying off discontent with material goods. (In a sense, we are returning to the *ad hoc* explanation for the absence of socialism in the United States that was offered at the turn of the century. The affluence of the United States, the absence of a feudal past and the row were said to provide in America "safety valves" for discontent that short-circuited the revolutionary potential of the labor movement and the socialist parties in the United States. It is in somewhat the same vein that present writers are attempting to predict the growth or decline of the student-radical political movement in America.) Flacks presents evidence that this movement, discussed in the following papers, will grow, spreading to a variety of discontent groups in the society—the old, Catholic laymen, the young, some of the alienated intellectuals, marginally skilled labor people, and the blacks (although this is the most problematic of all). In Lipset's summary (below) of the conditions that stimulate student activist groups, one discovers conditions that are characteristic of modern societies in general. Flacks' analysis is a useful contrast, for it is sensitive to the difficulties of a revolutionary movement—the very things that stimulate activism seem to limit its scope to the young, to campuses, and to limited settings and times.

On this point, however, there is a great disaffiliation of the older Left types and the new Left, as well as a disaffiliation of the cultural and artistic radicals from the political radicals. In the works of Melly (1970), Nuttall (1968), Neville (1971), and Rubin (1970) we see attempts to integrate these strands. The task is to weave together the radical political implications of questioning social structure by explicating in art and music, literature and drama, its moment-to-moment reconstitution, its tenuous nature, and the underlying basis of the social order in such fundamental notions as reciprocity, trust, love, fear, hope, and despair.[7]

Although Reich's argument is weak, it is this wedding of the political and cultural radicalism that he foresees in the *Greening of America* (1970). It is in the extent to which cultural dimensions are seen as political weapons that the old and the new Left differ. In the selections below, we see in historical perspective, and in the university environment, an assessment of the meanings of student activism of the late 1960s and early 1970s.

[7] See Gouldner's *The Coming Crisis of Western Sociology* (1970), for a brief discussion of the political implications of phenomenological sociology (ethnomethodology). In response to a recent critique, Gouldner admitted that he underestimated the political implications of ethnomethodology (Social Problems Theory Session, SSSP, 1971).

# HISTORICAL AND COMPARATIVE BACKGROUND

## 3. Reflections on Youth Movements

BY WALTER LAQUEUR

I can well imagine that on Saturday nights across this country, at hundreds of faculty parties where a year and a half ago the main subject of discussion was the war in Vietnam, thousands of professors and their wives now passionately debate the pros and cons of the student movement, the tactics of the SDS, and the significance of the generational conflict. I myself have attended several such gatherings, and have been struck not so much by the intensity with which the actions of the students are either approved of or condemned by their elders, as by the baffled consensus among those elders that the movement is both unprecedented and totally inexplicable in terms of what the university has historically represented. When I am asked, as I invariably am, for the European view on these matters, I rarely manage more than a few words, to the effect that the American situation is unique and that anyway history never repeats itself—which, needless to say, is of no great help to anyone. And yet, I believe there is something to be learned from the European experience, even if the lesson is an ambiguous one. Not the least thing to be learned is that the Western university has by no means always represented that tranquil meeting-ground, so fondly misremembered now by American professors, of those who would gladly learn with those who would gladly teach.

Quite the contrary. Organized youth revolt has for a long time been an integral part of European history. That, on the one hand. On the other, the idea of the university as a quiet place, devoted to the pursuit of learning and unaffected by the turbulence of the outside world, is of comparatively recent

From *Commentary*, 47 (June, 1969), pp. 33–41.

date. The medieval university certainly was no such place. As Nathan Schachner has pointed out, it was a place characterized more by bloody affrays, pitched battles, mayhem, rape, and homicide: "Indeed by the frequency of riots one may trace the rise of the University to power and privilege." In his monumental study, Universities of Europe in the Middle Ages, Hastings Rashdall relates the violence of the medieval university to the violence of medieval times in general, when the slitting of a throat was not regarded even by the Church as the worst of mortal sins. Thus, a Master of Arts at the University of Prague who had cut the throat of a Friar Bishop was merely expelled, while in the case of other offenders punishment consisted in the confiscation of scholastic effects and garments. The police were openly ridiculed by students, and the universities did nothing to exact discipline from their own scholars. In dealing with the subject of students' morals, Rashdall is constrained to write in Latin. According to Charles Thurot's history of Paris University in the Middle Ages, masters frolicked with their pupils and even took part in their disorders. The university was a great concourse of men and boys freed from all parental restrictions; morality, as Schachner notes, was a private affair, as were the comings and goings of the students. Nor was the trouble localized; the same complaints were to be heard from Oxford to Vienna and Salamanca.

As for the professor, his position in the medieval university was not what it became in later days. He was, first of all, paid by the students. A professor at Bologna needed his students' permission if he wanted to leave town even for a single day; he had to pay a fine if he arrived late in class or if he ended his lecture before the chiming of the church bells; should his lectures not meet with favor, there was a good chance that he would be interrupted, hissed, or even stoned. Supported by King and Church, medieval students enjoyed almost unlimited freedom. It was an unwritten rule, for instance, that they were always in the right in their clashes with townspeople. Of course, from time to time the citizenry would get even by killing a few students; the Oxford town-and-gown riots of 1354 were one such response, if a major one, to student provocation—provocation that took the form, in the words of a contemporary chronicler, of "atrociously wounding and slaying many, carrying off women, ravishing virgins, committing robberies and many other enormities hateful to God." To be sure, the real troublemakers were a minority, some of them not even students but rough vagabonds enjoying the immunities of the scholar, drifting from master to master and from university to university. For every scholar involved in felonious offenses there were dozens whose story is unknown. "They studied conscientiously, attended lectures and disputations, worked hard, ate frugally, drank their modest stoup of wine, and had no time for the delights of tavern and brothel. The

63

annals of the virtuous, like the annals of a happy people, are short and barren" (Schachner). Nevertheless, it is a fact that only in later ages did the university begin to impose stricter discipline on its students.

If student violence in the Middle Ages can be ascribed mainly to the high spirits of youth, by the 18th century a new figure had appeared on the scene: the student as freedom fighter. *Die Raeuber* ("The Robbers"), the play that made Schiller famous, tells the story of a group of students who, disgusted by society and its inequities, take to the mountains to lead partisan warfare against the oppressors. (In the 1920's when Piscator staged the play in Berlin, he had Spiegelberg, one of the leaders of the gang and incidentally a Jew, appear in the mask of Trotsky.) *Sturm und Drang*, the first real literary movement of youth revolt, combined opposition to social conventions with a style of life that is familiar enough today: wild language, long hair, and strange attire. Within a few decades after its inception, the romantics had made this movement fashionable, if not respectable, all over Europe. Suddenly there was Young England and Young Germany, Young Italy, Young Hungary, and Young Russia—all up in arms against the tyranny of convention, tradition, and outworn beliefs. One of the very few places untouched by the cult of youth at that time was America, itself a young country, unencumbered by the dead weight of tradition: *America*, Goethe apostrophized, *du hast es besser. . . .*

Some youth groups in the modern period have done much good, while others have caused a great deal of harm. It has been the custom in writing about them to divide them into the progressive and the reactionary, the wholesome and the decadent, so that, for example, the revolutionary Russian student movement of the 19th century, the Italian Risorgimento, and the Chinese May 1919 movement fall in one camp, and the fascist youth movements fall in the other. But this scheme is at best an oversimplification, since almost all movements of youthful revolt have contained in themselves both elements at once. The historical role a movement finally played depended in each case on political conditions in the society at large, the gravity of the problems the movement faced, the degree of its cultural development, and the quality of the guidance it received from its mentors.

The dual character of youth movements is illustrated wih particular clarity by the example of the early German student circles, the *Burschenschaften*. In his recent book, Lewis Feuer characterizes the members of these circles as "historicists, terrorists, totalitarians and anti-Semites"—all of which is perfectly true.* But they were also genuine patriots who dreamed of German unity and set out to combat the tyranny and oppression of the Holy Alliance. Most of them, in addition, were democrats of sorts and their movement was regarded by the liberals of the day as one of great promise. Their story is

---

* *The Conflict of Generations.* Basic Books, 543 pp. $12.50.

briefly told. The leader of the group was Karl Follen, a lecturer at Jena, of whom a contemporary wrote that "no one could be compared with him for purity and chastity of manners and morals. He seemed to concentrate all his energies upon one great aim—the revolution." In 1818, a certain Karl Sand, an idealistic and highly unstable student of theology who had come under Follen's influence, assassinated a minor playwright by the name of August Kotzebue who was suspected of being a Russian agent. Sand genuinely expected that this action, undertaken in the service of a holy cause, would trigger a revolution. But the choice of victim was haphazard, and the consequences regrettable: the government seized the opportunity to suppress the *Burschenschaft* as well as the whole democratic movement. Follen escaped to America, where he became professor of German literature and preacher at Harvard (he later drowned at sea in a shipwreck). It took almost thirty years for the movement he had led to recover from the blow dealt it by the authorities.

The idealism, spirit of sacrifice, devotion to one's people, and revolutionary fervor that marked the *Burschenschaft* have been an inherent part of all youth movements over the last hundred years. It is a mistake to assume that the fascist youth movements were an exception to this rule, that their members were mainly sadistic, blindly destructive young thugs. To be sure, they preached a doctrine of violence, but as Mussolini said, "there is a violence that liberates, and there is a violence that enslaves; there is moral violence and stupid, immoral violence" (compare Marcuse: "In terms of historical function, there is a difference between revolutionary and reactionary violence, between violence practiced by the oppressed and by the oppressors"). The ideological foreruners of Italian fascism, men like Corradini and Federzoni, were second to none in their condemnation of capitalism and imperialism and in their defense of the rights of the "proletarian nations." Early fascist programs demanded a republic, the abolition of all titles, a unified education, the control and taxation of all private income, and the confiscation of unproductive capital. They also placed great stress on youth. Giovanni Gentile, the philosopher of fascism, considered the sole aim of the new movement to be the "spiritual liberationof the young Italians." The very anthem of the fascist regime was an appeal to the young generation: *Giovinezza, Giovinezza, primavera di bellezza.*

Similarly in Germany, where the student movement after the First World War was strongly nationalist; the Nazi student association emerged as the leading force in the German universities (and in Austria) in 1930, well before Hitler had become the leader of the strongest German party. With 4,000 registered members out of a total of 132,000 students, the Nazis easily took control of the chief organization of German students several years before the party's seizure of national power. The declared aim of the Nazi student association was to destroy liberalism and international capitalism; point two on its program was to "purge the university of the influence of private capital"; point nine called on students to join the ranks of the workers. The slogan of "student power" made its first appearance at the *Goettingen Studententag* in 1920. Later on it was linked to the demand that the university be made political, a real "people's university," and that all the academic cobwebs and so-called "objective sciences" be cleaned out. Even before Hitler came to power, leading German professors attacked the "idea of false tolerance" of the humanist university. Invoking Fichte, Hegel, and Schleiermacher, they held that liberal democracy was the main enemy of the true scientific spirit, and demanded that henceforth only one political philosophy be taught. The Nazis, needless to say, were still more radical: academic life, they said, had largely become an end in itself; located outside the sphere of real life, the university educated two types of students—the only-expert and the only-philosopher. These two types produced a great many books and much clever and refined table-talk, but neither they nor the universities which sustained them were in a position to give clear answers to the burning questions of the day.

Criticisms like these were common at the time all over Europe. An observer of the French scene wrote in 1931 that the main characteristic of the young generation was its total rejection of the existing order: "almost no one defends the present state of affairs." One of the most interesting French youth groups was *L'Ordre Nouveau*, whose manifesto, written by Dandieu and Robert Aron, had the title, *La Révolution Nécessaire. Ordre Nouveau* stood for the liberation of man from capitalist tyranny and materialistic slavery; Bolshevism, fascism, and National Socialism, it declared, had assumed the leadership of the young generation and for that reason would prevail everywhere. The young in France were deeply affected—to quote yet another contemporary witness—by a "tremendous wave of revolutionary enthusiasm, of holy frenzy and disgust." When several prominent young socialists seceded from the SFIO in opposition to the rule of the old gang and established a movement of their own, this too was welcomed as one more manifestation of the rebellion of the young generation. All these people were deeply troubled by the existing state of affairs and no doubt well meaning in their intentions; together with Jean Luchaire, the leader of *Ordre Nouveau*, many of them ended up as Nazi collaborators during World War II.

The tactics adopted by these youth groups vis-à-vis the universities were the tactics of agitation. Even before the First World War, members of the *Action Française* had made it a custom to disrupt systematically the lectures of professors at the Sorbonne who had provoked their ire for political reasons. Nazi students perfected the system, forcing universities to dismiss Jewish professors, and even one Christian pacifist, well before 1933. But the question must be asked again: was this rowdyism, or an action undertaken in the genuine conviction that one's country was in grave danger and that the professors were enemies of the people who had to be removed? Among the fascist youth movements in the late 20's, one of the most sinister was the Rumanian terrorist band, the *Archangel Michael*, which later became the Iron Guard. Yet even the members of this group were not devoid of sincerity and idealism; Eugen Weber recently wrote of their leader: "From a mendacious people he demanded honesty, in a lazy country he demanded work, in an easy-going society he demanded self discipline and persistence, from an exuberant and windy folk he demanded brevity and self-control." Whoever describes a youth movement as idealistic only states the obvious. Youth movements have never been out for personal gain; what motivates them is different from what motivates an association for the protection of the interests of small shopkeepers. The fascist experience has shown that the immense potential which inheres in every youth movement can be exploited in the most disastrous way; but the potential itself must be seen as neutral.

Almost everything that is great has been done by youth, wrote Benjamin Disraeli, himself at one time a fighter in the ranks of generational revolt. Professor Feuer would counter: many disasters in modern European politics have been caused by students and youth movements. The exploits of the *Burschenschaften*, he argues, set back the cause of German freedom thirty years. Russian student terrorism in the 1880's put an end to progress toward constitutionalism in that country. But for the terror and stress of the First World War (inaugurated by a bomb thrown by yet another student hero, Gavrilo Princip), Russia would have evolved in a liberal capitalist direction, and European civilization would not have been maimed by fascism and a second World War. According to Professor Feuer, the qualities needed to bring about peaceful social and political change are not those usually found in youth movements, and he accuses students of almost always acting irrationally in pursuing their objectives. Unfortunately, however, peaceful change is not always possible in history, nor are patience and prudence invariably the best counsel. Take the Munich students who revolted against Hitler in 1943 and the student rebels who were recently sentenced in the Soviet Union; had they acted entirely rationally, they might well have convinced themselves that as a consequence of long-term political and social processes, the dictatorship would disappear anyway or at least be mitigated in its ferocity. Why therefore endanger their lives? To their eternal credit, such rational considerations did not enter the students' minds. The impetuosity, the impatience, and sometimes the madness of youth movements has been a liberating force in the struggle against tyranny and dictatorship. Tyranny cannot be overthrown unless at least some people are willing to sacrifice their lives, and those willing to do so usually do not come from the ranks of the senior citizens. It is only when youth movements have launched a total attack against democratic regimes and societies—in Germany, France, and Italy in the 20's and in other countries later on—that they have come to play by necessity a reactionary and destructive role.

Most of the basic beliefs and even the outward fashions of the present world youth movements can be traced back to the period in Europe just before and after the First World War. The German *Neue Schar* of 1919 were the original hippies: long-haired, sandaled, unwashed, they castigated urban civilization, read Hermann Hesse and Indian philosophy, practiced free love, and distributed in their meetings thousands of asters and chrysanthemums. They danced, sang to the music of the guitar, and attended lectures on the "Revolution of the Soul." The modern happening was born in 1910 in Trieste, Parma, Milan, and other Italian cities where the Futurists arranged public meetings to recite their poems, read their manifestoes, and exhibit their ultra-modern paintings. No one over thirty, they demanded, should in future be active in politics. The public participated actively at these gatherings, shouting, joking, and showering the performers with rotten eggs. In other places, things were not so harmless. "Motiveless terror" formed part of the program of a group of young Russian anarchists, the *Bezmotivniki*, in their general struggle against society. The *Bezmotivniki* threatened to burn down whole cities, and their news sheets featured diagrams for the production of home-made bombs. Drug-taking as a social phenomenon, touted as a way of gaining new experience and a heightened sensibility, can be traced back to 19th-century France and Britain. The idea of a specific youth culture was first developed in 1913–14 by the German educator Gustav Wyneken and a young man named Walter Benjamin who later attained literary fame. In 1915, Friedrich Bauermeister, an otherwise unknown member of the youth movement, developed the idea of the "class struggle of youth." Bauermeister regarded the working class and the socialist movement (including Marx and Engels) as "eudaimonistic"; the socialists, he admitted, stood for a just order and higher living standards, but he feared that once their goals were achieved they would part ways with the youth movement. Bauermeister questioned whether even the social revolution could create a better type of man, or release human beings from their "bourgeois and proletarian distortions."

The ideas of this circle were developed in a little magazine called *Der Anfang* in 1913–14. Youth, the argument ran (in anticipation of Professor Kenneth Keniston), was *milieulos*, not yet integrated into society. Unencumbered by the ties of family or professional careers, young people were freer than other elements of society. As for their lack of experience, for which they were constantly criticized by their elders, this, far from being a drawback, was in fact a great advantage. Walter Benjamin called experience the "mask of the adult." For what did the adult wish above all to prove? That he, too, had once been young, had disbelieved his parents, and had harbored revolutionary thoughts. Life, however, had taught the adult that his parents had been right after all, and now he in turn smiled with condescending superiority and said to the younger generation: this will be your fate too.

For the historian of ideas the back issues of the periodicals of the youth movement, turned yellow with age, make fascinating reading. The great favorites of 1918–1919 were Hermann Hesse, Spengler's *Decline of the West*, Zen Buddhism and Siddharta, Tagore's gospel of spiritual unity (*Love not Power*), and Lenin. It is indeed uncanny how despite all the historical differences, the German movement preempted so many of the issues agitating the American movement of today as well as its literary fashions.

Some youth movements in the last hundred years have been unpolitical in character. Most, however, have had definite political aims. Of this latter group, some have belonged to the extreme Left, others have gravitated to the extreme Right, some have sought absolute freedom in anarchy, others have found fulfillment in subordinating themselves to a leader. To find a common denominator seems therefore very nearly hopeless. But the contradictions are often more apparent than real, not only because many of those who originally opted for the extreme Left later moved to the Right, or vice versa, or because the extremes sometimes found common ground as in the National Bolshevik movement which gained some prominence in various countries in the 1920's. Whether a certain movement became political or unpolitical, whether it opted for the Left or the Right, depended on the historical context: it hardly needs to be explained in detail why youth movements were preponderantly right-wing after the First World War, while more recently most have tended toward the left. But beyond the particular political orientation there are underlying motives which have remained remarkably consistent throughout.

Youth movements have always been extreme, emotional, enthusiastic; they have never been moderate or rational (again, no major excursion into the psychology of youth is needed to explain this). Underlying their beliefs has always been a common anti-capitalist, anti-bourgeois denominator, a conviction that the established order is corrupt to the bones and beyond redemption by parliamentary means of reform. The ideologies of democracy and liberalism have always been seen as an irretrievable part of the whole rotten system; all politicians, of course, are crooks. Equally common to all youth groups is a profound pessimism about the future of present-day culture and an assumption that traditional enlightened concepts like tolerance are out of date. The older generation has landed the world in a mess, and a radical new beginning, a revolution, is needed. Youth movements have never been willing to accept the lessons of the past; each generation is always regarded as the first (and the last) in history. And the young have always found admiring adults to confirm them in their beliefs.

This leads us to the wider issue of *Kulturpessimismus*. The idea that the world is in decline—an idea that is about as old as the world itself—had an impact on modern youth movements through the mediating influence of neo-romanticism. The themes of decadence and impending doom can be traced like a bright thread through the 19th century from Alfred de Musset (*"Je suis venu trop tard dans un monde trop vieux"*), to Carlyle, Ruskin, and Arnold with their strictures against the universal preoccupation with material gain. So widespread a fashion did *Kulturpessimismus* enjoy that one can scarcely find a single self-respecting 19th-century author who did not complain about the disjunction between mankind and the world, between idea and reality, or about the spiritual bankruptcy and moral consumption of his age. In Germany, as *mal du siècle* turned into *fin de siècle*, a whole phalanx of Cassandras raised their voices, denouncing mass culture, crass materialism, and the lack of a sense of purpose in modern life. *Kulturpessimismus* induced in some a sense of resignation and gave rise to decadent moods in literature and the arts; at the same time, however, it acted as a powerful stimulus to movements of regeneration. Whereas dissatisfaction led some to ennui and perversions (*La jeune France*, an all-out revolt against social conventions, was decadent and wholly unpolitical in character), elsewhere and in other periods boredom gave birth to activism. Thus, on the eve of the First World War, a whole generation of young Europeans, having pronounced themselves culturally suffocated, welcomed the outbreak of hostilities as heralding a great purge, a liberation that would somehow put things right. The close connection between *Kulturpessimismus* and boredom deserves more study than it has received so far, as does the connection between boredom and prosperity. Max Eyth, the German popular writer, astutely diagnosed the illness of his age in autobiography he wrote during the Wilhelminian era: *"Es is uns seit einer Reihe von Jahren zu gut gegangen"* (We had it too good for a number of years).

One of the main problems facing the decadents was that of combining their hatred of modern civilization with their love of the refinements that civilization had made possible. (This is still very much of a problem, although some of today's revolutionaries seem to have solved it on the personal if not on the ideological level.) The decadents also faced the dilemma of squaring their *langueur*—Verlaine: *Je suis l'Empire à la fin de la décadence*—with their fascination with violence and revolutionary action. The indiscriminate assassinations and bombings carried out by the French anarchists found many admirers among both the decadents and the right-wing futurists. "What matter the victims, provided the gesture is beautiful," Laurent Tailhade wrote. D'Annunzio's career as a writer progressed from descriptions of courtesans in modish clothes, luminous landscapes, and villas by the sea, to the most lavish praise of the freshness and joy of war. Having begun by calling on youth to "abolish all moral restrictions," he ended as the prophet of moral regeneration and the poet laureate of fascism. The list could be lengthened: Maurice Barrès made his way from the decadent movement to the *Action Française*; Johannes R. Becher, who in the early 20's was known in Germany as the mad expressionist poet who had killed his girl friend, was to become in later life minister of culture in Walter Ulbricht's East Germany.

If the youth movements of the early 20th century arose, then, in a milieu in which the sense of decadence was widespread, they represented at the same time an attempt to overcome it. Their leaders were moralists, foever complaining about the evils of corporate guilt. Like all moralists, they exaggerated those evils, speaking out of the anti-historical perspective which is a hallmark of the moralist. For the study of history teaches that other periods have, broadly speaking, not been much better than one's own. This is why the moralist and the revolutionary regard history as a reactionary discipline, the story of big failures and small successes. The study of history is a breeding-ground of skepticism; the less the moralist knows of it, the more effectively will he pursue his mission with an untroubled conscience. Thomas Mann, pleading in a famous speech to German students in the 1920's for "aristocratic skepticism in a world of frenetic fools," was sadly out of touch with the mood of an audience longing for firm belief and certain truths.

If in what I have said up till now my remarks have indicated a certain ambivalence of feeling toward youth movements in general, it is because I have been trying to distinguish between the various ideas which they have espoused—ideas which are certainly deserving of criticism—and, what I take to be of even greater significance, the depth of emotional experience which they have provided their members. * (I say this as one who shared that experience at one stage in life.) The politics and culture of youth movements have always been a reflection of the Zeitgeist, a hodgepodge, often, of mutually exclusive ideas. A proto-Nazi wrote about the unending and fruitless discussions of German youth movements in 1920: "Look at those *Freideutsche* leaders and their intellectual leap-frogging from Dostoevsky to Chuang-tse, Count Keyserling, Spengler, Buddha, Jesus, Landauer, Lenin, and whichever literary Jew happens to be fashionable to the moment. Of their own substance they have little or nothing." There was, let's face it, more than a grain of truth in this criticism; a list of the main formative intellectual influences on the American movement would look even more incongruous. But what was essential about the German youth movement, at least in its first phase, was not its "intellectual leap-frogging" and confused politics but something else

---

* Although I originally intended this as a statement about youth movements of the past, I now read in Martin Duberman's review of Christopher Lasch's new book, *The Agony of the American Left:* "I think what is most impressive about the radical young people is that their politics or their social theories, but the cultural revolution they have inaugurated—the change in life style."

entirely. The movement represented an *un*political form of opposition to a civilization that had little to offer the young generation, a protest against the lack of vitality, warmth, emotion, and ideals in German society. (Hoelderlin: "I can conceive of no people more dismembered. . . . You see workmen but no human beings, thinkers but no human beings, priests but no human beings, masters and servants, youth and staid people, but no human beings. . . .") It wanted to develop qualities of sincerity, decency, open-mindedness, to free its members from petty egoism and careerism, to oppose artificial conventions, snobbery, and affectation. Its basic character was formless and intangible, its authentic and deepest experience difficult to describe and perhaps impossible to analyze: the experience of marching together, of participating in common struggles, of forming lasting friendships. There was, of course, much romantic exaltation as well, but although it is easier to ridicule the extravagances of this state of mind than to do it justice, the temptation should be resisted: experiences of such depth are very serious matters indeed.

The non-political phase of the German youth movement ended roughly speaking with the First World War. Summarizing that early phase, I wrote several years ago that "if lack of interest in politics could provide an alibi from history, the youth movement would then leave the court without a stain on its character."† In retrospect, this judgment seems a trifle misplaced; the truth is that the movement was simply not equipped to deal with politics. Being romantic and opposed to "arid intellectualism," its thought was confused and its outlook illiberal. Oriented toward a mythic past and an equally mythic future, it was darkly suspicious of the values of the Enlightenment— an attitude that did not have much to commend it in a country where the Enlightenment had not met with conspicuous success anyway—and it was easily swayed in different directions by philosophical charlatans and political demagogues preaching all kinds of eccentric doctrines.

All this appeared very clearly in the second, political phase of the German youth movement after the First World War. By 1930, the youth movement was displaying an incontinent eagerness to rid Germany of democracy. Almost all its members shared the assumption that anything at all would be better than the detested old regime. Lacking experience and imagination, they clearly misjudged the major political forces of their time. One of their leaders wrote much later: "We had no real principles. We thought everything possible. The ideas of natural law, of the inalienable rights of man, were strange to us. As far as our ideas were concerned we were in mid-air, without a real basis for our artificial constructions." It was, in brief, not an intellectual movement, and any attempt to evaluate it on the cultural and political level alone will not do it justice; it moved on a different plane. The movement arose in response to a certain malaise; it attempted, without success, to solve

† *Young Germany: A History of the German Youth Movement.*

72

the conflicts facing it; and it was, in retrospect, a splendid failure. With all its imperfections, it did succeed in inspiring loyalties and a deep sense of commitment among its members.

I am not sure whether today's youth movements can achieve even this much. "People who screw together, glue together," claims the Berkeley SDS, but if that were true, the Roman Empire would still be in existence. Some time ago, I happened to meet with members of a radical pacifist communal settlement in upstate New York. This settlement had had its origins in the early German youth movement; its members were believing Christians who took their cue from the New Testment: "Ye cannot serve God and Mammon," and "the love of money is the root of all evil." Setting out to realize the ideal of social justice in their own lives, they established two settlements in Germany, moved to England in 1934, then to Paraguay, and finally to New York State. Still convinced that their way of life is the best of all possible ways, the surviving members have recently been trying to find supporters and active followers. On their tours of college campuses they are invariably met with tremendous enthusiasm and a great show of willingness to join. Then, a few days after each appearance, they send a bus around to take prospective candidates for a tour of the settlement. No one shows up. One could argue that it is unfair to compare the depth of commitment and the ardor of present-day revolutionaries with that shown by those who challenged less permissive societies in bygone days. Where the 19th-century revolutionary risked the gallows or a lifetime in Siberia, the rebel of the 60's risks a warning from a disciplinary committee. In these adverse circumstances a breed of devoted revolutionaries is unlikely to arise. That may be finally all to the good, but I for one confess to a certain nosalgia for the breed.

It has been said of youth movements: blessed is the land that has no need of them. For a long time, America was such a land. In the 19th and early 20th centuries, it alone among the major Western countries did not experience a widespread movement of generational conflict. The reasons for this are not particularly obscure. For one thing, the burden of the past was not felt as heavily in America as it was in Europe. Less distance separated parents and children, teachers and students; adventurous young men went West, the country was forever expanding; society as a whole was far less rigid. Then in the 20th century, when these factors had ceased to be quite so important, America was spared a movement of youth revolt by a series of economic and foreign political crises. For it is a rule of youth movements that, like *Kulturpessimismus*, they prosper only against a background of rising affluence. Another rule appears to be that they cannot strike deep roots in a country whose general mood is basically optimistic.

America in the 60's is a prosperous society, but it is no longer optimistic: the American dream has been lost on the way to affluence. It was thus in a sense inevitable that when the worldwide wave of youth revolt broke earlier in this decade, American youth should assume a leading role. (I am not speaking here of the black student revolt, because this is not a generational conflict but part of a wider movement for full political and social emancipation, and the success or failure of this movement will depend ultimately on the blacks themselves.) But the American situation is a complicated one, not only because it is accompanied by such factors as a general breakdown of authority, a crisis in the universities, and a widepread sense of cultural malaise, but also because of the response it has elicited in the society at large. Youth movements have come and gone, but never before has one been taken so seriously. Never in the past has an older generation been so disconcerted by the onslaught of the young. Previous generations of adult, more certain of their traditions and values, less ridden by feelings of guilt, have shown little patience with their rebellious sons and daughters. The middle-aged, middle-class parents of today clearly do not feel themselves to be in any such position of certainty. The milieu in which the youth of America have grown up bears striking resemblance to the European 1890's as described by Max Nordau:

"There is a sound of rending in every tradition and it is as though the morrow would not link itself with today. Things as they are totter and plunge, and they are suffered to reel and fall because man is weary, and there is no faith that it is worth an effort to uphold them. Views that have hitherto governed minds are dead or driven hence, meanwhile interregnum in all its terrors prevails and there is confusion among the powers that be . . . what shall inspire us? So rings the question from the thousand voices of the people, and where a market-vendor sets up his booth and claims to give an answer, where a fool or a knave begins suddenly to prophesy in verse or prose, in sound or color, or professes to practice his art otherwise than his predecessors and competitors, there gathers a great concourse around him to seek in what he has wrought, as in Oracles of the Pythia, some meaning to be divined and interpreted. . . . It is only a very small minority who honestly find plaesure in the new tendencies, and announce them with genuine conviction as that which is sound, a sure guide for the future, a pledge of pleasure and of moral benefit. But this minority has the gift of covering the whole visible surface of society, as a little oil extends over a large area of the surface of the sea. It consists chiefly of rich educated people, or of fanatics. The former give the *ton* to all the snobs, the fools, and the blockheads; the latter make an impression upon the weak and dependent, and it intimidates the nervous. . . ."

Nordaus' *Degeneration* is an exaggerated, polemical tract, but much of what he wrote about the malady of his age was pertinent; he realized correctly that ideas, books, and works of art exercise a powerful, suggestive influence far beyond the small circle of the avant-garde: "It is from these productions that an age derives its ideals of morality and beauty. If they are absurd and anti-social they exert a disturbing and corrupting influence on the views of a whole generation." The moral and aesthetic ideals of today's avant-garde theater and cinema have certainly had their effect—as have the works of Jean Genet and Frantz Fanon. The deliberate gibberish of recent movies and novels finds its reflection in the involuntary gibberish of certain strands of youth politics; the message of John Cage's "Silent Sonata 4.33" (in which a performer sits in front of a piano for precisely that amount of time, poised to play but never playing) has its parallel in certain aspects of the wider cultural revolution; the theater of the absurd is not unconnected with the politics of the absurd. Indeed, the crisis of rationality has had a powerful impact: affirmation replaces analysis and argumentation; *fin de siècle* revolutionaries arrange happenings and call it a revolution, or discuss *salon* Maoism before enthusiastic audiences and call it radical commitment. Afraid to appear unfashionable or out of step with the avant-garde, those who ought to know better seem willing to take every idiocy seriously, trying to "understand" if not to accept.

*Corruptio optimi pessima.* The American youth movement, with its immense idealistic potenial, has gone badly, perhaps irrevocably, off the rails. For this, a great responsibility falls on the shoulders of the gurus who have provided the ideological justification for the movement in its present phase—those intellectuals, their own bright dream having faded, who now strain to recapture their ideological virginity. There is perhaps some tragedy to be glimpsed in this endeavor of the old to keep pace with the young, but at the moment one cannot permit himself the luxury of a tragic sense. The doctors of the American youth movement are in fact part of its disease. They have helped to generate a great deal of passion, but aside from the most banal populism they have failed to produce a single new idea. Most of them stress their attachment to Marx. But one need only read *The Eighteenth Brumaire* to find Marx's opinion on the value of bohemianism in the revolutionary struggle; and his polemics against Bakunin leave little doubt as to his feelings with regard to the idea, first propagated one hundred years ago, of a coalition between *lumpenproletariat* and *lumpenintelligentsia*. Students should not be criticized for ignoring lessons of the past and the dangers of chiliastic movements. They always do; the historical memory of a generaion does not usually extend back very far, and the lessons of historical experience cannot be bequeathed by will or testament. But their mentors do remember, and their betrayal of memory cannot be forgiven.

The American youth revolt was sparked off by Vietnam, by race conflict, and later on by the crisis of the university. At any point along the line rational alternatives could have been formulated and presented. Instead, the movement preferred a total, unthinking rejection, and so became politically irrelevant. Yet a revolution is in fact overdue in the universities. There is nothing more appalling than the sight of enormous aggregations of students religiously writing down pearls of wisdom that can be found more succinctly and profoundly put in dozens of books. There is nothing more pathetic than to behold the proliferation of social-cience non-subejcts in which the body of solid knowledge proffered stands usually in inverse ratio to the scientific pretensions upheld. Whole sections of the universities could be closed down for a year or two, and the result, far from being the disaster to civilization which some appear to anticipate, would probably be beneficial. Unfortunately, this is about the last thing that is likely to happen, for it is precisely the non-subjects, the fads, and the bogus sciences to which the "radicals" in their quest for social relevance are attracted as if by magnetic force. As for the consequences of all this, one thing can be predicted with certainty: those to be most directly affected by the new dispensation in the universities will emerge from the experience more confused and disappointed than ever, and more desperately in need of certain truths, firm beliefs.

An American youth movement was bound to occur sooner or later; youth revolt is a natural phenomenon, part of the human condition. But the particular direction the American movement would take was not at all foreordained, and it is therefore doubly sad that in its extreme form it has taken a destructive course, self-defeating in terms of its own aims. It seems fairly certain at this point that the American movement will result in a giant hangover, for the more utopian a movement's aims, the greater the disappointment which must inevitably ensue. The cultural and political idiocies perpetrated with impunity in this permissive age have clearly gone beyond the borders of what is acceptable for any society, however liberally it may be structured. No one knows whether the right-wing backlash, so long predicted, will in fact make its dreadful appearance; perhaps we shall be spared this reaction. It is more likely that there will be a backlash from within the extremist movement itself, as ideas and ideologies undergo change and come into conflict with underlying attitudes. Insofar as those attitudes are intolerant and irrational, they will not quickly mellow, and for that reason America is likely to experience a great deal more trouble with its *enragés*.

The American youth movement of the 60's, infected by the decadence of the age, missed the opportunity to become a powerful agent of regeneration and genuine social and political change. But decadence, contrary to popular belief, is not necessarily a fatal disease. It is a phase through which many generations pass at various stages of their development. The boredom that gives rise to decadence contains the seeds of its own destruction, for who, after a time, would not become bored with boredom? In 1890, the prevailing mood in France was expressed in the *terin fin de siècle*; the most popular sport was national self-degradation; and everyone was convinced that the decay of the country had reached its ultimate stage. Charles Gide, the economist, compared France with a sugarloaf drowning in the sea. Fifteen years later the crisis was suddenly over. Almost overnight, pessimism was transformed into optimism, defeatism into aggressive nationalism, a preoccupation with eroticism into a new enthusiasm for athletics. No one knew exactly why this happened: French society and politics remained essentially the same, the demographic problem was still in full force, moral and religious uncertainties were as rampant as before. I do not mean to suggest that recovery is always so certain; indeed, the form the cure takes is sometimes almost as bad as the disease. But generations seldom commit collective suicide. As they rush toward the abyss, a guardian angel seems to watch over them, gently deflecting them at the very last moment. Nevertheless, even the patience of angels must not be tried too severely.

# 4. American Student Activism in Comparative Perspective[1]

## SEYMOUR MARTIN LIPSET

How can we interpret the rather fantastic explosion of student protest and sit-ins from Warsaw and Prague to West Berlin, Rome, London, Madrid, Rio de Janeiro, Madison, San Francisco, Tokyo, Jakarta, Calcutta, Cairo, and many other places? Various writers dealing with individual countries and university situations have suggested explanations specific to the particular time and place. Germans have explained their student movement as a response to either the decline in institutionalized opposition resulting from the formation of the coalition of the two big parties or the coming of age of a student generation whose members are the grandchildren of the Nazi generation and able to attack the German past directly without talking about the behavior of their own parents. Italians and Germans both point to the inability of a highly traditionalistic, almost feudal, university structure to adapt to the needs of a rapidly expanding system. The London School of Economics, the center of British student protest, blew up against the appointment of a director who was charged (falsely) with sponsoring segregated institutions in Rhodesia. The Berkeley revolt occurred in reaction to adminis-

From *American Psychologist*, 25 (July, 1970), pp. 675–687.

[1] This report is one in a series of proceedings of Seminars on Manpower Policy and Program sponsored by the Manpower Administration. It presents a condensed transcript of the seminar held in Washington, D.C., May 1, 1968. Expressions of opinion by the speaker and those participating from the audience are not to be construed as official opinions of the United States Government or the Department of Labor. Copies of this publication or additional information may be obtained from the United States Department of Labor's Manpower Administration, Washington, D.C. 20210.

trative measures which seemingly restricted the political rights of civil rights activists.

Many people have attempted to give various kinds of sociological explanations for student activism. But given the widespread character of student activism in the United States and other countries, and the special circumstances of the university system in these countries, the character of the initiating or catalytic events can have been no more than aggravating factors—sparks setting off fires that were ready to go off.

Some of the glib and easy explanations given when the current wave of student activism first started have been undermined by more recent events. For example, I was convinced that the administration at Berkeley was primarily responsible for initiating the affair by changing the rules governing student activities. I argued that complete tolerance for student politics, and limitation of university regulations solely to rules governing campus traffic, would have avoided organized protest directed at the university itself. At the time, 1964–65, I pointed to San Francisco State as an example of a school which allowed its students almost total political freedom and which, as a result, was relatively quiet as far as aggressive student politics were concerned. But during 1967–68 there were more violent confrontationist politics at San Francisco State than at any other school in the country, with the possible exception of Columbia—and yet the policy of the school with regard to student rights had not been changed.

Many people have suggested that student tension reflects the lack of student participation in the affairs of the university and that some realization of student power in the university structure would reduce the potential for strong confrontation tactics. They suggest that if students feel they can communicate effectively to university authorities, they will limit the expression of their demands to legitimate conventional channels. While there can be little doubt that this proposition has some validity, one must also point to the fact that the one university in Germany, the Free University of Berlin, in which students have been represented on the faculty Senate and other organs is the Berkeley of West Germany. It is the school in which the greatest and most aggressive student movement was organized and from which other German student movements have stemmed. Similarly, co-government in many Latin American countries has not made for a docile or institutionally responsible student movement. In fact, many analysts of the Latin American university have argued that the political representatives of the students tend to be institutionally irresponsible, bring politics into faculty appointments, and often resist efforts to upgrade the institution.

The thesis that student protest is caused by large size and bureaucratization, impersonality, and lack of contact with professors is also valid to some degree; yet it, too, is insufficient. Studies of attitudes of American students do show that students in large State universities are more dissatisfied with the quality of education and life than those at small private schools, but this is not the whole story. A survey of the attitudes of students at the major first-rate, large State universities, such as Berkeley, Madison, or Ann Arbor—which have been among the leading centers of activism—generally indicate positive sentiments toward the quality of the education they receive, and these schools receive many transfers from first-rate, small private schools. Berkeley studies, at the time of the Free Speech Movement (FSM), showed no relationship between attitudes toward the school as an educational institution and involvement in the movement.

On the other hand, a number of small, elite, private institutions, such as Reed, Brandeis, Antioch, Oberlin, Swarthmore, Haverford, and Chicago, have been strongholds of political activism, at times even of resistance to the school administration itself. Chicago, the smallest of the major universities, had a 2-week sit-in in the president's office before the Berkeley revolt. Brandeis last year had a strike or boycott against the university directed to the complaint that classes were too large. The largest were 75 or so. Reed, which has 900 students, has had systematic protests against various administrative policies, including a sit-in protesting the fact that a gym was being built when the students felt that the college should not be spending money on gyms.

In citing these cases, I do not want to suggest that the various interpretations seeking to relate student unrest to actual structural grievances, bad political rules, inadequate channels of communication, bureaucracy and impersonality, lack of involvement in the decision-making process, or inadequate instruction are wrong. In fact, I will try to demonstrate later that they are valid. But it is important to recognize that these internal sources of grievance cannot come close to accounting for the presence of large numbers of political activists in our universities and certainly do not explain the current revival of student protests.

## Politics as the Cause of Activism

Essentially, the sources of political activism among students—that is, the factors which differentiate those who are active on the left from those who are not—must be found in politics or in the factors associated with different types of politics. The explanations for more political activism at one time rather than another must also be found on a political level, in the sources of variations in political response.

If one looks at the history of student involvement in politics, or politics in general, it's clear that students as a group are more responsive to political trends, to changes in mood, and to opportunities for action than almost any other group in the population, except possibly intellectuals. As a result, students have played a major role in stimulating unrest and fostering change in many countries. The special role of students has been particularly noted in the French Revolution of 1848: in the Russian revolutionary movement, which was largely a student one until 1905; in the various Chinese movements during the 20th century; and in many other revolutionary actions.

Although it may be argued that student activism is the result, rather than the cause, of social malaise, it is important to recognize that, once activated, student groups have played a major role in mobilizing public opinion behind the causes and ideologies they espouse. Social unrest causes student unrest; but once students and intellectuals start expressing their disquiet, they have been in many ways the vanguard of the evolution. They are the most articulate segments of society; they are, therefore, able to communicate their opinions to other groups. Thus the first members of many revolutionary parties were recruited from student movements in many countries. In Czarist Russia, student groups organized the workers and peasants against the regime. In recent years student movements supported by intellectuals initiated the process that led to a break in the totalitarian regimes in Communist Poland and Czechoslovakia. In Russia today, the student and intellectual groups constitute the principal source of opposition. In the United States, the campus-based antiwar movement has been responsible for the eventual growth of large-scale opposition to the Vietnam war. The McCarthy campaign, which seemingly resulted in Lyndon Johnson's withdrawal as a candidate for reelection, would have been impossible without student participation and organization. One can look at the newspapers and see current examples of the same process in Germany and France.

In periods in which belief in the accepted verities of a society begins to break down, in which events undermine the stability and even the legitimacy of a society's socioeconomic arrangements, in which drastic social change occurs, or in which the political elite become sharply divided about the direction of policy, there should be a sharp increase in student activism. In societies in which rapid change, instability, or weak legitimacy of political institutions is prevalent, there appears to be almost constant turmoil among students.

In various underdeveloped countries and new states which are chronically unstable, whose political institutions lack legitimacy, or which have been developing rapidly, there is a wide gap between the social outlook of the educated younger part of the population and that of the more traditional, less educated older section.

The wide divergence between the social expectations set by intellectuals and universities and the reality of underdeveloped societies motivates students and intellectuals to accept radical ideologies that define the status quo as unacceptable and seek drastic institutional changes to foster modernization—

which means adopting the values of the "advanced" societies. Thus, the intellectuals and students of Eastern Europe in the 19th century rejected the institutions of their own societies as backward compared to those of France and Britain.

Support for radical student activism, like that for other forms of extra-parliamentary politics, should occur less frequently and be less prevalent in the developed stable democracies of Northern Europe and the English-speaking countries. Although present, the tensions between the universalistic values inherent in a modern industrial society and the egalitarian concepts and free competition of ideas fostered by the university should be relatively weak and the gap fairly small. One would, therefore, expect what has been true until recently, that there should be a lower level of student activism in the developed democracies.

## Current Student Unrest Started with the Race Issue

The current wave of student unrest in the United States arose as a response to the one issue, race relations, on which the United States has retained a remnant of premodern traditional caste values that are basically at odds with the norms of a democratic industrial society. Concern for civil rights, for the status of the Negro, is the supremely moral issue of American society, precisely because it is the one area where the egalitarian values of the society, which are taught to the young, which are preached in the schools, and which are approved by almost everyone in theory, are most violated in practice. The continued oppression of the Negro challenges the legitimacy of American institutions in a way that no other issue can.

Students, who tend to accept the basic values of the society in a more absolute fashion than do older generations accustomed to the reality of compromise, became involved in the civil rights struggle beginning in the late 1950s. The story is well known, and it need not be repeated here other than to point out that, in this particular situation, the conservative or traditional elements introduced the tactics of civil disobedience. Southern whites refused to accept the law as laid down by the Supreme Court, and this taught the advocates of civil rights, both black and white students, that the regular peaceful methods of democracy would not work. The confrontationist tactics of civil disobedience, which first emerged in the South, were then spread by the student movement to other issues, particularly in recent years to the protest against the Vietnam war.

The question may be raised as to why students became particularly sensitive to the race issue in the 1960s, when relatively few of them had been actively concerned previously. Obviously, this question does not have one set answer. I would suggest, however, that a generation gap emerged among

82

politically conscious Negro and white youth on the race issue. This gradually took form following the Supreme Court's 1954 decision, which stimulated the struggle for equal rights. It was followed by various actions by the courts, administrative agencies, and legislative bodies; each of these attested to the value of political action, but none resulted in any major visible change in the status of the bulk of the Negro population. They remained poor, segregated, and uneducated, securing only the leavings of the job market. To each group of civil rights-oriented youth who came to political consciousness, the gap between what ought to be and what actually existed increased rather than decreased, while the reverse was true to older generations. Youth took for granted the existing structure, including the changes that had occurred but a year or two ago, and reacted with outrage against the continued sources of Negro deprivation. Racially sensitive members of the older generations, on the other hand, often pointed with pleasure to the progress that had been made within the past few years. Thus, an inevitable age-related split occurred within the liberal and Negro political communities. To each new political generation, the older generations seemed like smug members of the liberal establishment; to those older members who had experienced political and juridical enactments supporting Negro rights, which went far beyond their greatest dreams, the American political process appeared to demonstrate its capacity to adjust to pressures for reform.

The division between the generations on the race issue has been particularly acute within the Negro community. To younger Negroes, the gains made since the 1950s appear empty in face of the existing pattern of Negro social and economic inferiority. And on the major campuses of the Nation, the growing minority of Negro students have found themselves in a totally white-dominated world, facing few—if any—black faculty and a largely white student body, whose liberal and radical wing turned increasingly after 1964 from involvement in civil rights protest to activity directed against the Vietnam war. The concern with black power, and with Negro control over civil rights organizations, won growing support among black college students. And most recently, these students have played a major role in confronting university administrations with demands for more Negro students and faculty and for changes in the curriculum. Black students have been among the major forces initiating sit-ins during the 1967–68 school year at schools as diverse and separated as San Francisco State, Columbia University, Boston University, Northwestern University, and many predominately Negro institutions as well.

The issue of the acceptable pace of reform, which devided the liberal white as well as the black community on an age basis, was also affected by events abroad, particularly in Cuba. The triumph of the Castro Revolution, dominated by young men, produced an example of successful rapid change, just off the shores of the United States, and helped to generate the idea that revolution was possible and desirable as a way to eliminate social evils. Again, generational experiences divided the liberal-left community. The older generation had learned from experience that revolutions usually lead to totalitarianism, to new forms of exploitation, or to cynical betrayals of popular will, as in Czechoslovakia in 1948 or Hungary in 1956.

## Activism Has Focused on Vietnam

Opposition to the Vietnam war has, of course become the dominant political issue affecting student activism in the United States and other developed countries. The generational difference, particularly between older liberals dominating public policy and liberal youth, has perhaps been greater in this case than in others. For political generations that had experienced the rise of nazism: the transformation of communism into Stalinist terror; the Stalin-Hitler pact of 1939, which made the start of World War II possible; the reemergence of Stalinist terrorism and anti-Semitism within the Soviet Union after the war; and the ways in which the Soviet Union placed and kept Communist parties in power in Eastern Europe; the cold war made sense. Communism was experienced as an expansionist totalitarian empire with undertones of racism. The United States, and the rest of the free world, had an obligation to resist its expansion. Thus, to the older generations, Vietnam was but the most recent episode in a two-decade-long struggle against Communist imperialist expansion. To support resistance to communism in Vietnam needed no special justification; it was a continuation of existing policies, the bases of which were clearly understood.

For this reason the United States Government did not feel the need to issue propaganda concerning the inequities of the North Vietnamese regime or the terror tactics of the Viet Cong. In part, this policy was dictated by a desire to restrain the pressures of the "hawks" who sought to escalate the war and by the hope of keeping the United States' role as limited as possible. But the failure to undertake any significant propaganda campaign in support of the war was also clearly a result of the feeling among those who ran the Government that there was no need to justify a war against a Communist effort to take over another country, that almost all Americans regarded communism as a totally evil social system, and hence could be expected to back the Government.

For some years, then, it would appear that the Johnson administration mistakenly thought that its principal domestic political problem with respect to the war came from the right, rather than the left. Again, as in the case of the race issue, a gap increasingly emerged between the older liberals and the younger ones, the students inclined to the left, who had no personal experience of Stalin, the Czech coup of 1948, the Hungarian revolution, or the Berlin Wall.

To the generations who came of age in the 1960s, anticommunism had become a relatively unimportant issue. European communism no longer could be identified with Stalinist oppression, with the slaughter of innocents, or with monolithic absolutist power. Though still dominated by authoritarian one-party regimes, the states of Eastern Europe clearly faced internal rifts, and students and intellectuals were able to oppose their governments publicly, even if at the risk of loss of employment or imprisonment. Polycentrism, resistance to Soviet policy, now characterized the relationships among Communist states.

The Vietnam issue became defined, for the younger generation, in terms that placed American action at odds with certain basic American beliefs. The very failure of the gigantic, powerful United States to defeat quickly its small, poor Vietnamese opposition was evidence of the oppressive character of the war—a war in which a foreign power sought to impose its will by force over another people. Such a war, inherently, violated for American liberals the value that the United States has always proclaimed as its own in international affairs, the self-determination of peoples. The same values that led Americans to be suspicious of and opposed to the British, French, and Dutch empires and that were called into play to justify World Wars I and II have now been turned against the United States and its allies.

The revival of student activism in the West has had obvious effects on Eastern Europe as well. As in the underdeveloped countries, in the Communist world there is a gap between norms which are a regular part of university and intellectual life, namely academic and intellectual freedom, and the structure of the society. Intellectual and scientific life requires freedom. The obligation to support party truth is antithetical to this, so there is a predisposition among those involved in the world of the intellect, whether inside or outside of the university, to resist authority on this issue. As with the race issue in the United States, improvements—that is, a relaxation of controls—often serve to stimulate increased criticism of the system among those who take the values of freedom seriously. For new generations of Eastern European or Spanish university students, the fact that there is more freedom now than in Stalin's day, or than 3 years ago, is an ineffective argument. They know only that the present system is not free and that the present rulers are repressive, even if they happen to be men who pressed for more freedom a few years earlier. Thus, once the issue of freedom arises in authoritarian states, we may expect stuents and intellectuals to fight to drop the existing restrictions, a struggle which can lead either to greater liberalization or to a return to absolutist controls. Events in Czechoslovakia and Poland, unfortunately, have shown the validity of the latter part of this generalization.

A general discussion of the political sources of student unrest, of course, does not explain why students as students have played such an important role in stimulating protest, reform, and revolution. The factors to which attention has been called in the growing literature on the subject may be differentiated between those that motivate students to action and those that facilitate their participation.

## What Motivates Student Activism?

Among the motivating factors are the frustrating elements of the student role. Students are marginal men. They are in transition between being dependent on their families for income, status, and security and taking up their own roles in jobs and families.

Basically, the college years are a tension-creating period. The rapid growth in the number of American students, 7 million today as compared with 1½ million at the end of the 1930s, places young people in a highly competitive situation. This means both that the composition of the college population has been democratized, as a group they come from increasingly less privileged families, and that the value of a college degree for status placement has declined. The pressures to conform to the requirements of the educational establishment begin for many middle-class and aspiring working-class youth in elementary school and intensify in high school, with hard work and ability serving only to qualify the individual to enter even more difficult competition at the next rung in the educational ladder. While some succeed, many students must show up as mediocre or must rank low. There is a variety of evidence which suggests that these tensions affect the emotional stability of many teenagers and college youth. Such tensions may find varying outlets, including rejection of the social system which forces them into a rat race for grades. Although such tensions have always been present in the student role, it should be noted that the increased enrollment in universities around the world over the past 15 years has made the situation more competitive than ever before.

Reference is frequently made to the idealism of youth, another factor motivating student activism. Societies teach youth to adhere in absolute terms to the basic values of the system, such as equality, honesty, democracy, socialism, and the like. There is a popular saying which exists in many forms in many countries: "He who is not a radical at 20 does not have a heart; he who still is one at 40 does not have a head." This statement is properly interpreted as a conservative one; it clearly assumes that radicalism is an unintelligent response to politics. But the first part of the maxim may be even more important than the second, for it denotes a social expectation that young people sould be radicals and that the older generation believes that youthful radicalism is praiseworthy behavior. It is the young conservative, the young "fogie" and not the young radical, who is out of step with social expectations.

The emphasis on youthful reformism is greater in the United States than in many other countries, for American culture places a premium on being youthful and on the opinions of youth. It tends in general to glorify youth and to deprecate age. Americans dislike admitting their increased age. Hence to look youthful, to behave youthfully, to adopt the dress, the sports, the dances, or the political and social views that are identified with youth and to gain acceptance from youth by such behavior are ways of holding back age.

Thus, many American adults are reluctant, even when they consciously disagree, to call students or youth sharply to task. Instead, they may encourage youth and students to take new, independent positions rather than emphasize the worth of experience. This ties in with the American self-image of the United States as a progressive country which accepts reform and change. The truism that youth will inherit the future is linked with the idea that youth are bearers of the progressive ideas which will dominate the future.

The real world, of course, deviates considerably from the ideal, and part of the process of maturation is to learn to compromise, to operate in a world of conflicting role and value demands. But youth view such compromises as violations of basic morality. Students retain absolute beliefs longer than others do. As Max Weber has suggested, they tend to develop an ethic of "absolute ends" rather than of "responsibility"; they tend to be committed to ideals rather than to institutions. As a result, those events which point up the gap between ideals and reality stimulate them to action.

The pressures causing youth to act idealistically and politically in different societies are linked to the existence of youth as a separate social category to some extent independent of the various divisions which separate adults. In developing societies youth generally find themselves in an intergenerational communications gap. They are exposed, on one hand, to the familiar values of the elders of the society who attempt to keep them within the traditional framework. On the other hand, students are attracted by the new values most likely fostered within the university and intellectual community, and the emerging institutions of modern society, although these may appear unfamiliar and threatening. Age groups organized around political ideologies often emerge in developing societies, where they both fulfill the function of socialization into the new thought frameworks and offer status security, suggesting avenues of collective penetration into the strange adult society. They give students a sense of group identity which enables them to cope with the problem of differing with their elders.

Modern societies, in turn, are characterized by a prolongation of adolescence, usually devoted to educational development. The very nature of the university calls for a withdrawal from the mainstream of society into an ivory tower, free from the constraints of politics and religion. Although physiologically mature, and often above the age legally defined as adult, students are expected to refrain from full involvement in the adult world—a world which places great stress on individual achievement. Such a situation can be highly frustrating. The student requires, in addition to the opportunity to acquire an education, the chance both to experiment with adult roles and to exhibit his ability to achieve a position on his own. Erik Erikson has pointed out that, by creating distinct age-bound groups, students and others who remain in a sociological adolescent role may satisfy some of their needs to act as adults, in a political or social heterosexual sense, and to acquire personal status.

## Universities Foster Dependency

Dependency is, of course, built into the very essence of the university system. Students are dependent on their standing with the faculty for their future placement. The faculty, with the power of certification through its control over grades, can influence what students read and how they spend much of their time. The American university, with its stress on frequent examinations and faculty judgments, emphasizes this dependent relationship even more than do universities in most other countries. Hence, the student who leaves home to attend a university finds that he remains in a tightly controlled situation, much like the high school, while he is urged to become independent.

The constraints imposed on students living in university dormitories have proved to be particularly burdensome. By acting in loco parentis, universities in America take on the role of a constraining agent over the social life of individuals who have increasingly claimed the right to be independent. Inevitably, in a world in which 18-year-olds are eligible for the draft, the effort of the university to maintain these controls has been doomed to failure. With the decline in the average age at which Americans reach physical sexual maturity and the accompanying changes in the accepted norms concerning heterosexual relations, the university has placed itself in the impossible position of seeking to enforce a status of social dependency, which even middle-class parents have found difficult to maintain.

In essence, it may be argued that student life in general and student activism in particular are, among other things, expressions of youth culture. There is an array of age-group symbols, such as unique patterns of personal appearance, peculiar modes of communication, dances, special styles of life, relatively low standards of living with major expenditures on music or travel, or use of drugs, which sets students apart from others in society, and from adults in particular. Political extremism, the formation of student political groups which are unaffiliated or at odds with adult political parties, would seem to be another expression of youth culture.

Involvement in university life makes politics a particularly critical source of self-expression. Evidence drawn from surveys of student attitudes indicates that colleges have a liberalizing effect on young people, particularly in areas linked to universalistic principles such as racial equality, freedom of speech, internationalism, peace, and the like. Students are given ample opportunity to discuss and study political matters.

The university itself, in spite of its emphasis on being nonpartisan and "value free," is becoming increasingly involved in politics as professors take over roles as party activists, intellectual commentators on political events, advisors, consultants, and researchers on relevant policy matters. Most faculty political involvement, although generally to the left of the spectrum in the United States, occurs within the establishment. While many students are in centers of great political significance, they have little or no share in the political status of the university. Hence, if students are to express a sense of separate identity, politics as part of the student culture phenomenon must be outside of and in opposition to that of most of the adults in the society.

A variety of circumstances have changed the relationship of the university to the student. The increase in the importance of the university as a center of influence and power and as the major accrediting institution of the society has reduced the influence of students within it. Faculty are under greater pressure to do research, publish, and take part in extramural activities, and they increasingly give a larger proportion give a larger proportion of their teaching time to graduate students. This reflects the increased profesionalization of the faculty and the extent to which teaching as such has declined as the main identification of the professor. And many of the small elite schools have also adapted to this phenomenon, in order to secure and retain first-class faculty, that is, faculty who have a national reputation as scholars.

University administration involves fund raising, lobbying, handling of research contracts, and concern for recruiting and retaining prestigious faculty. There can be little doubt that undergraduate students are of much less concern to the faculty and administration than in earlier periods of American education. Yet the administrators and faculty have sought to maintain their traditional authority and prerogatives while yielding their personal "responsibility" for the personal and intellectual lives of their students.

It may be argued that today's students are subject to greater strains and fewer rewards than those of previous generations, with the exception of the depression generations. The fantastic increase in numbers of students, as we have seen, means that higher education has become an increasingly competitive and coercive institution. A "gentleman's C" no longer qualifies graduates for good jobs or for graduate school, and accreditation means hard work and conformity to course requirements. Although the demand for "student power" in the decision-making process of the university tends on the whole to be raised by the left-wing activist groups, the wide receptivity accorded this demand may reflect the increased awareness that the university demands much yet gives little in the form of personal relations between the students and the faculty and administration. Thus, as in the case of workers and employees in bureaucratized industry, a sort of student syndicalism seems to be emerging and seeking to regain for students the influence they have lost as a result of changes in the organization of universities. Conversely, the often unconceptualized sense of grievance with their situation, not always consciously directed against the university, may make many students, particularly those with a politically critical background, more receptive to political action directed against trends in the larger society. The two sources of activism thus reinforce each other: the one uses campus discontent as a set of issues around which to build a movement, while in the other campus discontent may express itself in political issues.

Thus far, I have dealt only with general aspects of the situations which may motivate some students to support activist politics. Now I will consider the many factors which facilitate such activity, making it easier to recruit students for such action.

## Students Are Easy to Recruit

Young people are more available for new political movements than adults. As new citizens, as people entering the political arena, they are less committed to existing ideologies—they have few or no explicit political commitments, they have no previous personal positions to defend, they are less identified with people and institutions which are responsible for the status quo, and they know less recent history than adults. The members of each generation have absorbed the experiences of their lifetimes into their political perspectives, and they interpret new events in the context of opinions formed about previous ones. As we have seen, communism has meant something evil for the generations that experienced the use of terror tactics against a popular uprising, as in Hungary, or the willingness to risk the danger of atomic war by an armed attack, as in Korea. These events are ancient history to the generation that has helped form the new left. For this younger generation, the key formative events have been the Vietnam war, in foreign policy terms, and heightened awareness of the oppressed position of the American Negro domestically. Thus, older generations are inhibited from reacting in simple, moralistic terms to new events and issues; younger ones see new events as moral issues and are unaffected by emotional and intellectual ties to the conflicts and lessons of the recent past.

Students are also more available because of lesser commitments to their "occupational" role, as compared to adults. Max Weber, many years ago, pointed out that political activity is to a considerable degree dependent on the extent to which it does not conflict with job requirements. In his terms, those who can take time off from work without suffering economic consequences are much more likely to be active than those who have to punch a time clock or remain the entire time at their work.

Students and professors have perhaps the most dispensable jobs of all. Students may drop out of school, may put off their studies for short or long periods, or may often delay taking examinations without paying a great price. Although the American system with its frequent examinations puts more pressure on students to spend time on their studies than do other systems—a factor which may account for the limited participation in the past and for the relatively small numbers active even now as compared with students elsewhere—students remain an extremely dispensable group. The numbers who dropped their books to take part in the McCarthy campaign are a recent illustration of this point. The extent of dispensability will, of course, vary with the discipline being studied. Those majoring in the hard sciences, and various professional schools, are more restricted than are humanities and social science students. The latter generally are in a position to catch up with their studies, even if they put them off completely for a time.

Linked to the concept of student dispensability is the factor of "irresponsibility." As compared to other groups students simply have fewer responsibilities in the form of commitments to families and jobs. Thus, the existence of punitive sanctions against extremist activism will not affect students as much as it will affect those with greater responsibilities to others or to a career.

As noted earlier, students are considered adolescents or juveniles sociologically and are often treated as such legally. Punishments meted out to students for infractions of society's moral codes are relatively lenient, in part because they are thought of as irresponsible youth who are "sowing their wild oats." The notion mentioned earlier that leftist students generally outgrow their politics as they mature contributes to this attitude. Students sometimes relate to sections of the elite which generally favor leniency. For example, in many societies, a number of students involved in politically or otherwise motivated infractions are literally children of the elite, a fact that often serves to lessen the desire to punish them. In addition, universities are generally run by liberal individuals who are disinclined to invoke severe sanctions against those they view as being in their care—namely, the students. Hence, students are under less pressure to conform than are other groups.

Still within the category of factors which facilitate student political involvement, there are aspects of the university situation which make it relatively easy to mobilize students who are disposed to act politically. The campus is the ideal place to find large numbers of people in a common situation. Many schools have over 30,000 students concentrated in a small area. Cothinkers can reach each other more easily on a campus than in other large communities, and new ideas which arise as a response to a given issue may move easily among the students and quickly find their maximum base of support. Often a large demonstration or meeting is composed of only a small percentage of a massive student body. Thus in 1965–67, although opinion polls indicated that the great majority of American students supported the Vietnam war and that antiwar sentiment within the student group was no greater than in the population as a whole, campus opposition to the war was able to have a great impact on the body politic because it could be mobilized. The antiwar student minority could and did man impressive antiwar demonstrations.

## The Majority of Students Are Not Activist

So far, I have discussed various factors which are conducive to students playing a major role in politics, a role which is more likely to be activist, or even extremist, in style than that of adult groups. In spite of the impact of these factors, it remains true that the large majority of students in all countries for which opinion data exist are politically inactive and moderate in their views.

The radical activist groups generally have small memberships. Out of a total student population of 7 million, the American new left Students for a Democratic Society (SDS) claims a total national dues-paying membership of about 7,000 with another 25,000 as active participants in local activities. The German Sozializtischen Deutschen Studentbund, also SDS, claims 2,500 members and is credited by observers with 10,000 supporters. Opinion surveys of American student population indicate that a large majority are within the mainstream of American politics and are not sympathetic with racial doctrines and tactics.

Yet, the relatively small activist elements, both liberals and leftists, have played a major role in influencing American politics in the 1960s. They have formed the mainstay behind the two movements which have had considerable impact in affecting national trends: the civil rights and the antiwar struggles. It is no exaggeration to conclude that activist students brought down the Johnson administration. The pressure for university reform in the United States and other countries, which has affected campus life in major ways, is also a product of student activism. Given the fact that the activists are a relatively small minority, questions must now be raised as to who they are and what the factors are that contribute to activist strength.

The major conclusion to be drawn from a large number of studies in the

United States, and other countries as well, is that students—while they may be more idealistic and more committed—generally hold views similar to those of their parents. Thus research agrees that leftist students are usually the children of leftist or liberal parents. The activists, particularly, are more radical or activist than their parents, but both are located on the left side of the spectrum. Conversely, studies of those active in conservative student groupings, like the Young Americans for Freedom (YAF), indicate that they are largely from rightist backgrounds.

In line with these findings, the available data indicate that the student left in the United States is disproportionately Jewish. Adult Jews, of course, are overwhelmingly liberal or radical. A comparison of delegates to the national conventions of SDS and YAF shows that the majority of SDS delegates are of liberal Jewish background, while the large majority of YAF delegates come from Protestant conservative families. Studies of activists at the Universities of Chicago, Wisconsin, and California all report that Jewish participation in leftist activism has far outweighed the proportion of Jews in the student bodies of these schools. Studies of hippie populations in different cities indicate similar findings.

Intellectuals, academics, writers, and musicians, among others, in the United States are usually found on the left. They may be either liberal Democrats or supporters of left-wing minor parties. And studies of student populations suggest that students who are intellectually oriented, who identify as "intellectuals," or who aspire to intellectual pursuits after graduation are also much more prone to be on the left and favorable to activism than students inclined to business and professional occupations.

Among faculty and students, there are clear-cut correlations between disciplines and political orientations. On the whole, those involved in the humanities and social sciences, or in the more purely theoretical fields of science, are more likely to be on the left than those in the more practical, applied, or experimental fields. Such a distinction, however, would appear to be more a result of the factors affecting entrance into the different disciplines than of the effects of the content of the fields. Thus, studies of entering freshmen—those who have not yet taken a single lecture—report the same relationships between intended college major and political attitudes as are found among seniors, graduate students, and faculty. One panel study of students (repeating interviews with the same people 2 years apart) reports that political orientation proved to be a major determinant of shifts in undergraduate major. A large proportion of the minority of conservatives who chose liberal majors as freshmen changed to subjects studied by conservatives, while many liberals who had selected conservative majors tended to shift to fields which were presumably more congenial with their political outlook.

The interrelationship between political outlook and intellectuality affects matters of style and occupational choice. Undergraduates who identify as liberals or leftists are likely to state their occupational preferences as intellectual ones (professors, for example, or writers) and exhibit intellectual tastes in their reading, music, and the like. Therefore, the political liberalism of university faculty, particularly those in the colleges of liberal arts, would seem to be part of the general structure which places the modern intellectual on the left.

## University Issues and Student Orientation

The distinct political character of some schools may be linked to selective recruitment and the resulting political orientation of their students. In this country, universities with large numbers of Jewish students or black students tend to be centers of leftist activism. High-level liberal arts colleges with an intellectual aura attract students oriented to becoming intellectuals. This accounts for the pattern of student protest at schools like Reed, Swarthmore, Antioch, and others. The best State universities, judged in terms of the scholarly prominence of faculty, such as California, Michigan, and Wisconsin, are schools which have also become the most important centers of confrontationist politics since they attract a disproportionate number of intellectually oriented students.

The political traditions and images of certain universities may play an important role in determining the orientations of their students and faculty. The main center of confrontationist politics in Britain, the London School of Economics, has a reputation dating back to its founding of being a radical institution. Waseda, the main center of activist politics in Japan, has also had a continuing history of student demonstrations. In the United States, Madison and Berkeley have maintained records as centers of radicalism. The University of Wisconsin image goes back to before World War I, and the strength of Progressive and Socialist politics in that State contributed to its political character. Berkeley is another interesting case in point. Since the turn of the century the San Francisco Bay area has had a history of being among the most liberal-left communities in the Nation, and more recent data point up the continuity of this image. In his *Memoirs*, George Kennan reports puzzlement that during his 1946 West Coast academic lectures the audiences—and those at Berkeley in particular—tended to be much more sympathetic to the Soviet Union than those at other universities. Berkeley was the only large university in the country to sustain a major protest against restrictive anti-Communist personnel policies in the form of the loyalty oath controversy of 1949–50. A 1954 national opinion survey of the attitudes of social scientists, conducted to evaluate the effect of McCarthyism on universities, indicated that the Berkeley faculty was more liberal than that of any other school sampled. In 1963–64, the year before the celebrated Berkeley student revolt, San Francisco Bay area students received national publicity for a successful series of massive sit-in demonstrations designed to secure jobs for Negroes at selected business firms.

Prior to the emergence of the Free Speech Movement (FSM), the Berkeley campus probably had more different and more numerous left-wing and activist groups than any other school in the country, and the vigor and effectiveness of the FSM of 1964 must, in some part, be credited to the existence of a well-organized and politically experienced group of these activist students. A study of the 600 students who held a police car captive in the first major confrontation of the FSM in October 1964 reported that over half of them had taken part in at least one previous demonstration, while 15% indicated they had taken part in seven or more. A number of opinion studies of Berkeley students conducted during the FSM protest indicated that general political orientation was the best predictor of attitudes toward the demonstrations.

In stressing that involvement in leftist student activism is primarily a function of the general political orientation which students bring to the university, rather than a result of the university experience itself, I am not trying to argue that changes in attitude do not occur, or even that conversions do not take place. Universities do have a liberalizing effect so that there is a gradual shift to the left. A significant number of students in the 1960s have been much more radical in their actions and opinions than postwar generations of American students, or than their parents. The larger events which created a basis for a renewed visible radical movement have pressed many students to the left of the orientation in which they were reared. Many students of liberal parents have felt impelled to act out the moral imperatives endemic in the seemingly "academic" liberalism of the older generation. Political events combined with various elements in the situation of students pressed a number of liberal students to become active radicals. The principal predisposing factors which determine who among the students will become activist exist before they enter the university.

The political activities of university students are, of course, not simply a function of family political socialization or other politically relevant preuniversity experiences. Some students obviously change considerably as a result of campus events. If we hold preuniversity orientation constant, it obviously will make a difference which school a student attends, what subject he decides to major in, who his friends are on campus, what his relations are with faculty of varying political persuasions, what particular extracurricular activities he happens to get involved in, and the like. But the relationships between the orientation which students form before entering the university and the choices they make which help maintain their general political stances while in it are only correlations, and many students behave differently from the way these relationships would predict.

The fact that young people, with fewer ties to the past, are undoubtedly more likely to change than older ones may explain the drastic changes in belief or political identity which occur among students. However, there is also a special aspect of university life which increases the chances that some students will be more likely to find satisfactions in intense political experiences.

## Studies of Student Activism

Various studies of political extremism and of the factors associated with the rise of new social movements suggest that mobility—particularly geographic mobility, putting a person in an unfamiliar social context—is conducive to making individuals available for conversion to new religious or political beliefs, particularly those which involve intense commitment. Mobility undercuts the social supports of the old belief system and increases the need to join new groups. Therefore, college communities, particularly those in which students live considerable distances from home, contain many people who sould be recruitable. Students form and join all sorts of groups in order to reduce their initial loneliness, and dynamic activist groups can fulfill these social needs.

Studies of student activism in America indicate that new students, either underclassmen or recent transfers, are more likely to be politically active than those who have been in the social system for longer periods. And, as might be expected, local students or those relatively close to home are likely to be less active than those who are removed from their home communities. In Berkeley, Madison, the London School of Economics, and Berlin, the leading activists have come disproportionately from the ranks of the migrants, and I would hypothesize that those who have experienced real conversions are drawn heavily from this group.

Thus far, I have discussed the influence of factors which seem to have a direct impact on political choice. Many studies of student activism, however, have also sought to account for varying orientations and degrees of involvement in terms of personality traits. Thus, they have looked at such factors as the way different groups of students have been reared by their parents (such as permissive or authoritarian atmospheres), as well as investigating parental relationships, student intelligence, sociality, and the like. Such studies have reported interesting and relatively consistent differences between the minority of student activists and the rest of the student population. At the moment, however, I remain unconvinced of the value of using such variables as explanatory factors, in large part because the existing studies do not hold the sociological and politically relevant factors in the backgrounds of the students constant. For example, the leftist activists tend to be the offspring of permissive families, in terms of child rearing practices, and of families characterized by a strong mother who dominates family life and decisions. Conversely, conservative activists tend to come from families with more authoritarian relationships between parents and children and in which the father plays the dominant role. To a considerable extent these differences correspond to the variations reported in studies of Jewish and Protestant families. Child rearing practices tend to be linked to social, cultural, and political outlooks. To prove that such factors play an independent role in determining the political choices of students, it will first be necessary to compare students with similar ethnic, religious, and political-cultural environments. To my knowledge, this has not yet been done.

The reports that student activists are of higher academic ability or have other personal traits which separate them from the bulk of the student population are also subject to similar methodological doubts. One may not conclude—as some have done—that the intelligent are more likely to be leftists or activists. Leftist and conservative activists should be compared with each other and with those involved in nonpolitical activities. The limited efforts in this direction indicate that some of the characteristics which have earlier been identified as those of leftist activists also characterize involved students in general. For example, both leftist and conservative activists are drawn from the ranks of the academically talented in the United States.

Efforts have also been made to determine if political orientation has a strong effect on whether students direct their extracurricular energies into politics. Studies of student bodies in different countries indicate that those on the left and the small group on the extreme right generally view politics as an appropriate, and even necessary, university activity. Committed morally to the need for major social changes, leftists feel that the university should be an agency for social change, that both they and their professors should devote a considerable portion of their time to political activities. Conversely, the more conservative students are, the more likely they are to disagree with this view and to feel that the university should be an apolitical "house of study." Liberals and leftists, therefore, are much more likely to be politically active than moderates, centrists, and conservatives. A relatively strong conservative stance will not be reflected in membership or activity in a conservative political club since conservative academic ideology fosters campus political passivity. This means that, on any given campus or in any country, the visible forms of student politics will suggest that the student population as a whole is more liberally or radically leftist than it actually is.

## What Is Needed

Most studies on the subject of student activism have been efforts to understand the social sources of contemporary student activism and its effect on contemporary politics. Perhaps more important is the need to evaluate the long-term effects of heightened periods of activism on the outlook of future generations. Since the various elites are necessarily recruited from student populations, the campus mood of a given period may have its most significant impact on national policy two or three decades later. This has led some students of politics to stress the concept of the political generation and to suggest that those who come of age under conditions of war, depression, civil strife, and the like will continue to react in terms of their early beliefs for the rest of their lives. Although, as noted earlier, many assume systematic changes in political outlook with increased age, we as yet have little reliable information on the extent to which youthful activists, whether conservatives or radicals, change.

# A VIEW FROM THE LEFT

## 5. Young Intelligentsia in Revolt

RICHARD FLACKS

Karl Marx expected that capitalist exploitation of industrial workers would lead them to oppose the culture of capitalism—that is, that workers would organize not only on behalf of their own interests but ultimately on behalf of human liberation. What now seems clear is that opposition to capitalist culture arose less in the working class than among tiny groups of artists and intellectuals. Obviously, such people were too few in number and too isolated from the productive process to have any historical significance in Marx's eyes. To the extent that he had any hope for a revolutionary contribution from them, it was that they would follow his example and join the working-class struggle, which of course few did.

What Marx could not anticipate, however, was that the antibourgeois intellectuals of his day were the first representatives of what has become in our time a mass intelligentsia, a group possessing many of the cultural and political characteristics of a class in Marx's sense. By intelligentsia I mean those engaged vocationally in the production, distribution, interpretation, criticism and inculcation of cultural values. Most of the occupations in which the intelligentsia work are located outside the capitalist sector of the economy, either as free professions or in nonprofit educational institutions or other public bureaucracies. If, as in the case of the mass media, they are coordinated by private corporations, the intelligentsia are often officially depicted as serving such values as pleasure, art and truth, rather than commercial values.

It is important to note that these occupations are among the most rapidly growing, numerically, of any in the society. This is due in part to increasing governmental investment in educational, scientific and social service activities, and in part to the increase in leisure time and the consequent demand for entertainment and recreation. But more fundamentally, it is a function of the need in advanced industrial society for people to do the work of planning, prediction, innovation and systematic training, and socialization that the system now requires for its survival and growth. In the past century, then, the intelligentsia has been transformed from a tiny group of marginal status to a fast-growing, increasingly organized mass playing a key role in the functioning of the system.

Several years ago, when some of us at the University of Chicago looked into the social backgrounds of New Left students, we found that our group of activists was distinct from other college students in the degree to which they aspired to be part of the intelligentsia. But we also found, after interviewing their parents, that there was a substantial continuity between basic values and aspirations of the two generations. Both the activists and their parents were hostile to the self-denying, competitive, status-oriented individualism of bourgeois culture, and both sought a way of life that emphasized self-expression, humanism, openness to experience and community. In addition, both the students and their parents were substantially disaffected from the political system—though the students, of course, were more thoroughly alienated than their parents. It seemed clear to us that the students, through their activism, were for the most part attempting to fulfill and extend an ideological and cultural tradition already present in their families, rather than rebelling against the values on which they had been raised.

The fact that there have been, in the United States and Europe, a number of previous examples of political and cultural movements, based in the intelligentsia, with parallel ideological overtones, suggests, as does the generational continuity within activists' families, that the current youth radicalism is an expression of a definite historical process. This process may be described as the effort by many in the ranks of the intelligentsia to articulate and implement values which would serve as alternatives to those prevailing in capitalist culture.

## Intellectuals as a Class

Historically, the revolt against bourgeois culture has taken many, quite divergent, ideological forms, ranging from socialism on the left to romanticism on the right, and it was acted out in a variety of ways, from direct participation in revolutionary movements to withdrawal into bohemian communities. In the first years of this century, however, a characteristically American intellectual radicalism began to emerge, which differed in important respects from the perspectives that prevailed in Europe. Like the Europeans, the new radical American intellectuals expressed their disaffection in a variety of ways: muckraking journalism, literary and social criticism in little magazines, realistic novels, avant-garde poetry and painting, salon conversation, scholarly radicalism, progressive politics, labor-organizing, the socialist movement. But unlike their European counterparts, American intellectuals tended to have a relatively optimistic and rationalist perspective. They believed that social, political and personal reforms were possible, especially if science and reason were brought to bear on pressing problems.

Significantly, the revolt of American writers and intellectuals coincided with the rise of the feminist movement. One consequence of the impact of feminism on the perspective of American intellectuals was a tendency for the boundaries between private and public issues to become blurred or obliterated. Political reform in the larger society was linked to reform of family life and individual character, with the result that many intellectuals emphasized conscious, deliberate and scientific reform of the socializing institutions, the family and the school in order to create new values and character types and thereby to facilitate social change.

## Optimism of the Intelligentsia

The specific hopes of the early twentieth century radical intellectuals were largely abortive. But their assault on Victorianism, the Protestant Ethic and business values had a wide impact. Progressive education, social work, child psychology, psychotherapy—a host of new professions emerged which had their original impulse in the desire to cure the effects of the dominant culture and which embodied implicit or explicit criticism of it. An important result of these new ideas, when combined with the rising status of women, was to create a new kind of middle-class family—less authoritarian, less hierarchical, more child-centered, more democratic, more self-conscious in its treatment of children. In these ways, the criticism of capitalist culture by tiny groups of European and American intellectuals became rooted in American life and incorporated into the value system of large numbers of middle-class Americans who attended the universities or were influenced by university-centered thought.

Now it is not the case, of course, that the rising intelligentsia was predominantly radical politically or unconventional culturally. Rather, what has been characteristic of this class politically is its very substantial optimism about the direction of the society and a whole-hearted acceptance of the legitimacy of the national political system, coupled with a strong hostility to those aspects of politics and culture identifiable as reactionary and regressive. What supported their optimism was their faith in three interrelated instruments of change.

First, they believed that the federal government could be molded into a force for social amelioration, economic progress and equality. This hope was, of course, crystallized during the New Deal and solidified during World War II and the immediate postwar period. Second, they believed that the new vocations, the service, helping and educational professions they had entered, would be significant in curing and preventing social and psychological pathology, extending the possibilities for democracy and upward mobility and raising the intellectual and cultural level of the people. Third, they tended to believe that the values they held were best implemented through self-conscious efforts to create families and a personal life style embodying democratic, humanistic, egalitarian principles, in contradiction to the authoritarian, repressed, Victorian, anti-intellectual and acquisitive style of life they perceived as characteristic of other middle-class people.

These beliefs emerged most strongly in the twenties and thirties, and it was possible to maintain them all during the New Deal period and the forties when it appeared that there was a real chance for the welfare state actually to be realized. Moreover, the horrors of fascism and Stalinism permitted many of the educated to feel that the United States, whatever its flaws, was the major defender of democratic values. Post–World War II prosperity greatly raised living standards and cultural possibilities for this group and also seemed to be creating the conditions for social equality. Thus, the parents of the present generation of student activists, despite their antipathy to traditional capitalist culture, maintained a generally complacent view of American society when they themselves were young and in the years when their children were growing up.

By the late fifties, however, some of this complacency undoubtedly began to break down. The Eisenhower years were a period of political stagnation and anti-Communist hysteria in which it became evident that the drive toward a welfare state and social equality might not be inherent in American political institutions. It also became clear that America's international role was incongruent with humanist, democratic values and beliefs. At a more fundamental level, many of the educated, as they reached middle age, began to have some doubts about the moral worth of their own occupations and about the degree to which they too had participated in the pursuit of status and material comfort. The late 1950s was a period of increasing social criticism much of which revolved around the collapse of meaning in vocation and about the moral callousness of the American middle class.

By 1960, then, the development of the American intelligentsia as a class had come to this. Demographically, it had grown over several decades from small pockets of isolated, independent intellectuals to a substantial stratum of the population, including many in new white-collar vocations. Culturally, it had begun to develop a family structure and value system at odds with the traditional capitalist, Protestant Ethic, middle-class culture. Politically, it had passed through a period of optimistic reformism and seemed to be moving into a period of increasing disillusionment. The newest and largest generation of this stratum was thronging the nation's colleges, at just that point historically when the sustaining ideologies of industrial society—liberalism, socialism, communism—had reached exhaustion. At the same time, the cold war and anticommunism had ceased to be a workable framework for American international policy, and the colored population in the United States and around the world was breaking into active revolt.

## Coming Together

In the decade since 1960, the offspring of the intelligentsia have become politicized and increasingly radicalized, despite the fact that, having been born to relatively high privilege and social advantage, they saw society opening ever wider vistas for personal success and enrichment. Why have they, in large numbers, refused to follow their fathers and mothers—adopting a stance of slightly uneasy acceptance of the prevailing social order while trying to establish a personal life on a somewhat different cultural basis?

In part, the disaffection of these youth is a direct consequence of the values and impulses their parents transmitted to them. The new generation had been raised in an atmosphere that encouraged personal autonomy and individuality. Implicitly and explicitly it had been taught to be skeptical about the intrinsic value of money-making and status and to be skeptical about the claims of established authority. It incorporated new definitions of sex roles. Having seen their parents share authority and functions more or less equally in the family, and having been taught to value aesthetic and intellectual activity, these were boys who did not understand masculinity to mean physical toughness and dominance, and girls who did not understand femininity to mean passivity and domesticity. Moreover, they were young people—young people for whom the established means of social control were bound to be relatively ineffective (and here they were particularly different from the older generation). Growing up with economic security in families of fairly secure status, the normal incentives of the system—status and income—were of relatively minor importance, and indeed many of their parents encouraged them to feel that such incentives ought to be disdained.

In retrospect, it seems inevitable that young people of this kind should come into some conflict with the established order. Because of their central values, they, like the earlier generations of intellectuals, would necessarily be social critics. Because of their material security, they, like earlier generations of high status youth, were likely to be experimental, risk-taking, open to immediate experience, relatively unrepressed. Because of their character structure, they would very likely come into conflict with arbitrary authority in school and other situations of imposed restriction. Because of their values and sex role identifications, they would find themselves out of harmony with the conventional youth culture with its frivolity, anti-intellectualism and stereotypic distinctions between the sexes.

Furthermore, their impulses to autonomy and individuality, their relative freedom from economic anxiety and their own parents' ambivalence toward the occupational structure would make it difficult for them to decide easily on a fixed vocational goal or life style, would make them aspire to construct their lives outside conventional career lines, would make them deeply critical of the compromise, corruption and unfreedom inherent in the occupations of their fathers—the very occupations for which they were being trained.

Much of this had happened before, but the situation of the young intelligentsia of the sixties differed radically from that of their precursors. First, their numbers were enormously greater than ever before. Second, they faced, not a scarcity of jobs, but an abundance of careers—yet the careers for which they were being trained no longer held the promise of social melioration and personal fulfillment that their parents had anticipated. Third, these youth sensed not only the narrowness and irrationality of the prevailing culture but the deeper fact that the dominant values of bourgeois society, appropriate in an age of scarcity and entrepreneurial activity, had become irrelevant to a society which was moving beyond scarcity and competitive capitalism. Thus, by the late fifties, more youth were feeling more intensely than ever before a sense of estrangement from capitalist culture—an estrangement which could not be assuaged by the promise of material security the system offered.

The cultural crisis these youth experienced provided the ground for their coming together. But the transformation of cultural alienation into political protest, and eventually into revolutionary action, was due to more immediate and concrete pressures. It was the emergence of the southern civil rights movement which, more than any other single event, led the young intelligentsia in the early sixties to see the relevance of political opposition and social change to their own problems. The nonviolent movement showed, for one thing, how small groups of committed youth could undertake action that could have major historical impact. It demonstrated how such action could flow directly from humanistic values. But above all, it confronted these white students with the fact that all of their opportunities for personal fulfillment were based on white upper-middle-class privilege and that continued passivity in the face of racism meant that one was in fact part of the oppressive apparatus of society, no matter what one's private attitudes might be.

## Hopes of SDS

Participation in the civil rights struggle seemed, however, to offer a way out of this dilemma, and civil rights protest helped to open the consciousness of many students to other political issues. It made them aware that there was more to their problems than the fact that the culture offered little support for their personal aspirations; it also threatened their existence. But at the same time numbers of students became rapidly sensitive to the fact that the nuclear arms race, the cold war and the militarization of society were not simply facts of life but deliberate, therefore reversible, policies. It was not long before the protest tactics acquired in the civil rights movement began to be applied to the demand for peace.

When one reads today the Port Huron Statement (June 1962) and other documents of the early Students for a Democratic Society (SDS) and the New Left, one is struck by the degree to which the early New Left conceived of itself largely as a political reform movement rather than in clearly revolutionary terms. While it's true, as Todd Gitlin has suggested, that the early new radicals of the sixties were filled with "radical disappointment" with the American way of life, it is also the case that they retained a good deal of optimism about the possibilities for change in the context of American politics. In particular, it was hoped that the labor movement, the religious community, the liberal organizations, the intellectual community, the civil rights movement all could eventually unite around a broad-based program of radical reform.

The role of the student movement was seen by the early SDS leaders as providing the intellectual skills needed for such a new movement and, somewhat later, as important for producing people who would help to catalyze grass root activities in a variety of places. Direct action such as the sit-ins, freedom rides and other forms of protest and civil disobedience was seen, on the one hand, as a vital tactic for the winning of reform and, on the other hand, as a method by which the more established institutions such as the labor movement could be induced to move in the direction of more vigorous action. In this early phase of the student movement, SDS and other New Left leaders were little aware of the possibility that a mass movement of students on the campus could be created and engaged in collective struggles against university authority. Rather the New Left's role on the campus was seen primarily as one of breaking through the atmosphere of apathy, educating students about political issues, so that they could begin to take a role off the campus in whatever struggles were going on.

But the early reformism of the New Left was soon abandoned. The failure of the established agencies of reform to create a political opposition and to mobilize mass support for political alternatives was most decisive in preventing the new movement of the young intelligentsia from becoming absorbed by conventional politics, thereby following in the footsteps of previous movements of American intellectuals. This collapse of the so-called liberal establishment thus marked a new stage in the consciousness of the American intelligentsia—beyond cultural alienation, beyond social reform, beyond protest—toward active resistance and revolution.

The emergence of the student movement in the sixties, then, signifies a more fundamental social change and is not simply a species of "generational conflict." The convergence of certain social structural and cultural trends has produced a new class, the intelligentsia, and, despite the apparent material security of many in this class, its trajectory is toward revolutionary opposition to capitalism. This is because, first, capitalism cannot readily absorb the cultural aspirations of this group—aspirations that fundamentally have to do with the abolition of alienated labor and the achievement of democratic community. Second, the incorporation of this group is made more difficult by the concrete fact of racism and imperialism—facts which turn the vocations of the intelligentsia into cogs in the machinery of repression rather than means for self-fulfillment and general enlightenment. Third, the numerical size of this group and the concentration of much of it in universities make concerted oppositional political action extremely feasible. Finally, the liberal default has hastened the self-consciousness of students and other members of this class, exacerbated their alienation from the political system and made autonomous oppositional politics a more immediate imperative for them. Thus, a stratum, which under certain conditions might have accepted a modernizing role within the system, has instead responded to the events of this past decade by adopting an increasingly revolutionary posture.

In part, this development grows out of the antiauthoritarian impulses in the fundamental character structure of the individual members which provide much of the motivation and emotional fuel for the movement. But, as the history of the movement shows, there was an early readiness to consider whether established political alternatives were in fact viable. That such readiness has virtually disappeared is almost entirely due to the failure of the political system itself—a failure most manifest in the crises of race, poverty and urban life on the one hand and the international posture of the United States on the other.

Over the last decade the American government has consistently failed to enforce new or existing legislation guaranteeing civil rights. It has consistently failed to implement promised reforms leading to social and economic equality. It has demonstrated a stubborn unwillingness and/or incompetence in dealing with the deepening crises of urban life, and it has supported essentially repressive, rather than ameliorative, policies with respect to the black revolt.

Even more crucial in undermining the legitimacy of the system for young people was, of course, the war in Vietnam—the fact that the United States was unable to win the war; the fact that it dragged on endlessly to become the longest war in American history; the fact that the United States in Vietnam was involved in an effort to suppress a popular uprising; the fact that the United States in Vietnam committed an interminable series of atrocities and war crimes, especially involving the destruction of civilian life; the fact that the war was accompanied by a military draft and that alongside the draft a system involving the social tracking of all young males in America had grown up; the fact that the war in Vietnam was not simply an accident of policy but an essential ingredient of what became increasingly identified as a worldwide imperialist policy involving the suppression of popular revolution and the maintenance and extension of American political and corporate power throughout the Third World.

Moreover, alongside the growth of conventional and nuclear military power and the penetration of American institutions, including especially the universities, by military priorities, there grew up a paramilitary establishment which had attempted to control and manipulate organizations and events throughout the world and also at home. This development was perhaps best symbolized for students by the fact that the Central Intelligence Agency had subsidized the National Student Association and had extensive ties with American academics. Finally, the war continued and escalated despite vast expressions of popular discontent.

This, more than anything else, reinforced the New Left's disbelief in the efficacy of conventional political means of affecting policy. By the time of the Democratic Convention in 1968, a very large number of young people were convinced that only extreme action of a disruptive sort could have any substantial effect on major policy and that "working through the system" was a trap, rather than a means to effect change.

Obviously, many young people, fearing the consequences of a full-scale delegitimation of authority, continue to search for a more responsive political alternative within the system. But the stagnation of liberalism in these years along with the astonishing series of assassinations of spokesmen for its revitalization have made such hopes appear increasingly unrealistic. Thus the growth of revolutionary sentiment among the students proceeds apace. As the legitimacy of national authority declines, a process of delegitimation occurs for all in authoritative positions—for instance, university officials—and proposals for melioration and compromise are viewed with deepening suspicion. Political polarization intensifies, and those in the opposition feel, on the one hand, the imperative of confrontation as a means of further clarifying the situation and, on the other hand, that the entire structure of social control is being organized for the purpose of outright repression. And for

American students confrontation is made more urgent by the moral pressure of the black liberation movement, which continuously tests the seriousness of their proclaimed revolutionary commitment.

## New Front Line

The early New Left frequently criticized university life as well as the larger society, but it was also quite ambivalent toward the university as an institution. University authority was seen as paternalistic and as subservient to dominant interests in the society. University education was regarded as a contributor to student indifference towards social questions. At the same time, the Port Huron Statement and other early New Left writing viewed the university as a potential resource for movements for change, university intellectuals as potentially useful to such movements and the university as a relatively free place where political controversy could flourish provided it was catalyzed.

Prior to the fall of 1964, SDS leaders ignored the campus as a base of operation, persuading a considerable number of students to either leave school or to work off the campus in the efforts to organize the urban poor. In large measure, university reform campaigns were felt by the most committed activists to be both irrelevant and, in a certain sense, immoral, when people in the South were putting their bodies on the line. The Berkeley free speech movement of 1964 helped to change this perception of the campus. The police action at Berkeley, the first of numerous large-scale busts of student protestors, suggested that a campus struggle could be the front line. And the political impact of Berkeley in California, and indeed internationally, suggested that there was nothing parochial or irrelevant about an on-campus struggle. Moreover, these events coincided with the turning away of portions of the civil rights movement, especially the Student Nonviolent Coordinating Committee, from efforts to work with white students. Further, Berkeley coincided with the escalation of the war in Vietnam and with the discovery, only dimly realized before, that the universities were major resources in the development of the military potential of the United States.

Beginning in the fall of 1966 attacks on military research installations, on ROTC, on connections between the university and military agencies, on military recruitment and recruitment by defense corporations became the prime activity of SDS and other student groups for a number of months. Every major confrontation mobilized hundreds of students for highly committed direct action and many thousands more for supportive action. Typically the issues raised by the student movement on a campus were supported by as many as two-thirds of the student body, even though large numbers of students were unwilling to participate in disruptive actions as such. And as previously uncommitted students joined these actions, many were radicalized by the experience of participation in a community of struggle, by the intransigence and obtuseness of university administrators and by the violence of police repression of the protests. Institutional resistance was fostering student "class consciousness."

By the late sixties, the movement was no longer the exclusive property of those I've been calling the young intelligentsia. It was having a widening impact on students at nonelite campuses, in junior colleges and high schools, and on nonstudent youth in the streets and in the Armed Forces. To a great extent, the availability of larger numbers of young people for insurgent ideas and actions is rooted in the cultural crisis we alluded to at the outset of this paper. For all youth experience the breakdown of traditional culture, the irrelevance of ideologies based on scarcity. Vast numbers of youth in America today are in search of a less repressed, more human, more spontaneous life style.

The radicalization of youth is enhanced by the peculiar social position of high school and college students, who have achieved some degree of independence from family authority but are not yet subject to the discipline of work institutions. The high school and college situation is, on the one hand, extremely authoritarian but, on the other hand, functions to segregate young people, maintaining them in a peculiar limbo combining dependency with irresponsibility. The impact of the cultural crisis on the school situation is to make really vast numbers of young people ready for new and more liberating ideas, while they have the freedom and energy to spend time in examination and criticism of prevailing values and ideologies.

In addition, the situation of youth is exacerbated by the demands of the imperialist system for manpower and by the increasing bureaucratization of both education and vocation. More concretely, the draft is the reality that undermines the endless promises made to American youth. What the draft means is that one is not really free to pursue self-fulfillment, even though one has been taught that self-fulfillment is the highest goal and purpose of the system. Not only is that promise undermined by the necessity to serve in the army and die in the mud of some distant jungle, a fate reserved for relatively few young men, but the draft serves to facilitate control over the careers of all young men by serving explicitly as a means for tracking youth into occupations believed to be in the interest of the state. The result for school youth is postponement or avoidance of the military but subjugation to an educational system that reproduces many of the worst features of the larger society in terms of authoritarianism, competitiveness, individualism and dehumanization. The growth of a mass youth movement depended on the emergence of a group of young intelligentsia whose own socialization was particularly at odds with the dominant culture, but once such a circle of youth emerged, their expressions, both cultural and political, spread alike wildfire.

Thus, the story of the student movement in the United States over the past decade has been one of continued self-transformation. Once student activism was characteristic of tiny groups of campus rebels, the offspring, as we have suggested, of the educated middle class, who faced severe value and vocational crisis, could find no moral way to assimilate into American society and so searched for a new basis for living in cultural avant-gardism and moralistic dedication to social reform. In the past decade, obviously, the movement has spread well beyond this original group. It has transformed itself from a nonideological movement for vague principles of social justice into a new radical movement in quest of a new social vision and a new framework for social criticism, and finally into a movement spearheaded by revolutionaries tending, more and more, to look to classical revolutionary doctrine as a guiding principle and to embody, more and more, classical models of revolutionary action as their own.

It is a movement that rejects and is at the same time entangled by its roots in what I have called the intelligentsia. Yet it has expressed most clearly the fundamental aspirations of the rising generation of that class for a new social order in which men can achieve autonomy and full participation in determining the conditions of their lives, in which hierarchy and domination are replaced by community and love, in which war, militarism and imperialism are obsolete and in which class and racial distinctions are abolished. It is a movement of surprising strength. It has touched the minds of millions and changed the lives of thousands of young people, both here and abroad. It has severely shaken the stability of the American empire and challenged the basic assumptions of its culture. But its most sensitive adherents have become increasingly despairing, as the movement has reached the limit of its possibilities. This despair is rooted first in the unresponsiveness of the political system to pressure for reform; second, in the narrow class base of the movement; third, in the seemingly overwhelming capacity of the authorities to manage social control. Out of this despair arises the sense that revolution is an urgent, if impossible, necessity, that the movement must transcend its social base, that it must make common cause with other enemies of the empire around the world.

## Co-optation

Given this new consciousness, what can be said about the future of the movement? It seems to me that one can envision several possibilities. First, any student and youth movement has the potential of becoming a relatively insulated expression of generational revolt. This is not the explicit intention of very many spokesmen for the New Left, but it certainly appears to be the implicit expectation of many agencies of social control. A generational movement may be understood as a movement of cultural and social innovation whose impact has been contained within the framework of existing society. For agencies of social control, the ideal circumstance would be the opportunity to eliminate those elements in the movement that are most disruptive and destructive, while putting into effect some of the cultural, social and political innovations and reforms the movement advocates.

Accordingly, you put Yippies in jail but work out some means to legalize the use of marijuana. You put draft-resisters in jail or into exile while abolishing conscription. You expel SDS from the campus while admitting student representatives to the board of trustees. You deride and derogate the women's liberation movement while liberalizing abortion laws. You break up and harass hippie urban communities while providing fame and fortune to some rock music groups. This is all done with the aid of ideological perspectives that emphasize that what is going on is a generational revolt, that there is a generation gap, that the big problem is one of communication between the old and the young. The hope is that if reforms can be made that will liberalize the cultural and social atmosphere, particularly in relation to sex, drug use, art, music, censorship and so forth, the mass of youth will not become tempted by the message of the radical vanguard.

If the new political and cultural radicalism were to become channeled more fully in the direction of generational revolt, it would then be serving stabilizing and modernizing functions for the going system, and it would not be the first time that a radical movement in the United States ended up functioning this way. But from the point of view of New Left activists, such an outcome for the movement would represent profound failure, particularly if it meant, as it does now seem to mean, that the most active and militant of the participants of the movement would suffer, rather than benefit, from any social change that might be forthcoming.

There is a substantial likelihood, however, that the student movement and the New Left of the sixties will move in the direction we have just outlined. The most important fact supporting this outcome is that the movement has, in the ten years of its existence, failed very largely to break out of its isolation as a movement of the young, and particularly of the relatively advantaged young. There are reasons to think that this isolation could be broken in the near future, and we shall suggest some of these shortly, but it is important to recognize that most of the public understanding of what is happening has revolved around the generational problem, rather than the substantive political and social questions that the movement has raised. Most of the expressed sympathy for the movement on the part of the elders has been couched in

terms of solving the problems of youth and liberalizing the cultural atmosphere, rather than in joining in the making of a social revolution.

At the same time, however, despite the very large-scale public discussion of
the need for reform and innovation, the prevailing tendencies of the state and
other dominant institutions do not seem to be primarily in this direction.
Even such apparently unthreatening changes as liberalization of laws governing drug use, the 18-year-old vote, the involvement of students in direct
participation in university government or the abolition of the draft meet very
strong resistance and do not now seem to be on the agenda. Instead, what is
in prospect is further tightening of drug laws, further restrictions and harassment of the communal outcroppings of the youth culture, further efforts at
censorship, a continuation of the draft and a generally more hostile climate
with respect to even the modest aspirations for change of most young people
today. All of this, of course, could change in a relatively short period of time
as those who are now young move into full citizenship and have the opportunity directly to influence public and institutional policies. But what happens
in the intervening years is likely to be crucial.

Another reason for believing that the New Left has considerable capacity
for resisting this kind of incorporation into the culture is that the movement
is profoundly suspicious of and sensitive to the dangers of co-optation. Most
movement participants are aware at one level or another that the classic
American pattern for controlling revolutionary and quasi-revolutionary
movements is to destroy or isolate the most militant sections while implement-
ing, at least on paper, the programmatic thrust of the movement. This is what
happened in the labor movement. It is what is happening in the black liberation movement, and it is certainly what is being advocated for the student
movement. In this way the American political system has served to contain
the revolutionary thrust of movements that develop within it, while keeping
these movements fragmented, preventing their outreach into sectors of the
population beyond those that form the original constituency of the movement.

As I say, new leftists wish to avoid at all costs the buying off of the movement
through piecemeal reform. This is one reason why the movement is so hesi-
tant to propose concrete reforms and to proclaim its interest in short-range
goals. A greater danger, however, is that the movement has been unable to
offset pressures, both internal and external, that maintain it as a movement
of youth.

The future of the New Left depends now on its ability to break out of its
isolation and to persuade the majority of Americans that their interests
depend on the dismantling of imperialism and the replacement of capitalism
with a fully democratized social order. The movement cannot afford to be
encapsulated as a generational revolt. It cannot wait until the present young
"take over." It cannot survive in a climate of repression and polarization

unless large numbers of people are moving in a similar political direction. It cannot survive and ought not survive if it conceives itself to be an elite band of professional revolutionaries, aiming to "seize power" in the midst of social chaos and breakdown.

What are the structural conditions that might open up the possibility of the New Left transcending its present age and class base? Here are at least some:

☐ The class base of the movement is rapidly changing as the "youth culture" spreads to the high schools and junior colleges, to army bases and young workers. Along with this cultural diffusion, the mood of resistance spreads— protest is now endemic in high schools, it is evident in the armed forces, it is growing in the junior colleges.

☐ Inflation and high taxes have led to a decline in real wages. Current fiscal policies generate rising unemployment. A new period of labor militance may have already begun. This situation converges with the influx of postwar youth into the labor force, with the militant organization of black caucuses in unions, with intensifying organization and militance among public employees and with the first efforts by former student radicals to "reach" workers. It may be that in spite of the Wallace phenomenon, racism and the alleged conservatism of the American working class a new radicalism is about to become visible among factory, government and other workers.

☐ The impoverishment and disintegration of public services, the systematic destruction of the natural environment, urban squalor, the tax burden—all are deeply felt troubles which are directly traceable to the profit system and the military priority. The sense of crisis and frustration that these problems generate throughout society offers the ground for the formulation and promulgation of radical program, action and organization.

☐ Political repression, although obviously dangerous for the survival of radicalism, can have the effect of intensifying rather than weakening insurgency. This would be particularly true if repression is seen as an assault on whole categories of persons, rather than on handfuls of "outside agitators." So, for instance, many participants in the youth culture now connect their own harassment by the police with the Chicago Conspiracy trial and other government attacks on radicals. Repression at this writing seems more likely to stiffen the mood of resistance among young people than it is to end attacks on "law and order."

☐ By 1975 there will be well over 50 million adults born since 1940. Most of these will have achieved political consciousness in the past decade. This fact alone suggests a major transformation of the political landscape by the second half of the seventies.

☐ In the next five years the proportion of the labor force definable as "intelligentsia" will have substantially increased. Current Bureau of Labor

113

Statistics manpower projections for "professional, technical and kindred workers" are for a 40 percent increase in this category between 1966 and 1975, reaching a total of about 13 million in 1975. If my analysis in this essay is correct, this group should be a major source of radicalism in the coming period. The situation of these workers is now dramatically changing from one of high opportunity to relative job scarcity due to current federal and state budgetary policies. Thus one can expect that the radicalization of the intelligentsia will continue to intensify in the years ahead.

One might suggest that these conditions provide the opportunity for a large-scale and successful "new politics" of liberal reform to assert itself. But the current exhaustion of political liberalism may well mean that a new "center-Left" coalition cannot be formed—that we have finally arrived in this country at the point where reformism is no longer viable.

An alternative possibility would be the emergence of a popular socialist party oriented to both "parliamentary" and "extraparliamentary" activity. Although this would certainly facilitate the transcendence of the New Left, there are as yet no signs that such a development is even incipient. In any case, the most important insight of the New Left is that political organization is not enough—the heart of revolution is the reconstruction of civil society and culture.

## "The Long March"

It may well be that the singular mission of the new mass intelligentsia is to catalyze just such a tranformation—to undertake what Rudi Dutschke called "the long march through the institutions of society." This march began in the universities. In coming years it may well continue through all significant cultural, educational, public service and professional institutions. It would have a double aim: to force these institutions to serve the people rather than the corporate system and the state and to engage cultural workers and professionals in struggles to control their work and govern the institutions that coordinate it and determine its use.

It is possible that such struggle by the intelligentsia could stimulate similar struggles in the primary economic institutions—to build a basis for workers' control and for the abolition of technologically unnecessary labor.

In addition to such institutional struggle, the reconstruction of civil society and culture requires the further development of self-organization of communities and especially of exploited and oppressed minorities. Such self-organization—of racial and ethnic minorities and of women—is necessary for any general cultural transformation. Struggle by communities for control of their own development and services prepares the basis for a decentralized and democratized civil society. It is obvious that all such developments have profound need for the services of professional, intellectual, cultural and scientific workers.

It is natural to assume that the development of political, civil and cultural struggle requires central, disciplined organization. My own feeling is that it requires something prior to, and perhaps instead of, the classical revolutionary party. What is really crucial is the organization of local "collectives," "affinity groups," "communes," "cells" of people who share a revolutionary perspective, a common locale of activity, a sense of fraternity, a willingness to bind their fates together. Each such group can be free to work out its priorities, projects and work style. What is necessary is that these groups generally conceive of themselves as catalysts of mass action rather than as utopian communities or elite terrorists. Most of the dramatic movements of the sixties occurred because small groups of friends undertook action that was catalytic or exemplary to larger masses. Most of the exciting cultural development in this period occurred in a similar way. Many of the problems the party is supposed to exist to solve can be coped with without centralization. Problems of communication can be handled by the underground media—which up to now have been the expression of a host of small collectives. National action projects can be coordinated by ad hoc coalitions and umbrella organizations. The generation of resources can be managed through movement banks and quasi foundations. There is no reason why collectives in different or similar milieus cannot meet together to exchange experience. If the purpose of a revolutionary movement is not to seize power but to educate the people to take it for themselves, then a maximally decentralized mode of work is appropriate. And in a period of tightening repression, a cellular rather than centralized mode of organization is obviously advantageous.

The revolution in advanced capitalist society is not a single insurrection. It is not a civil war of pitched battles fought by opposing armies. It is a long, continuing struggle—with political, social and cultural aspects inextricably intertwined. It is already underway. It is not simply a socialist revolution— if by that one means the establishment of a new form of state power that will introduce social planning and redistribute income. It is more than that. For it must be a revolution in which the power to make key decisions is placed in the hands of those whose lives are determined by those decisions. It is not, in short, a revolution aimed at seizing power but a revolution aimed at its dispersal.

It is possible that the New Left's current return to Old Left styles and models signifies that the kind of revolution of which I speak is premature, that the classes and groups that would be most active in producing it have not achieved full consciousness. We are not yet in an age of "postscarcity," and consequently the revolutionary visions appropriate to that age will have a difficult time establishing their reality. Perhaps, then, the New Left of the sixties is not destined to be the catalyst of the new revolution. I am personally convinced, however, that whatever the immediate destiny of the movement might be, the social and cultural changes that produced it and were accelerated by it are irreversible and cannot be contained within a capitalist framework. Once the material basis for human liberation exists, men will struggle against the institutions that stand in its way. The rise of the student movement in the United States and other industrial societies is a crucial demonstration of the truth of this proposition. For it is a sign that a revolutionary class consciousness appropriate to the era of monopoly capital, advanced technology and dying imperialism is in existence.

# EPILOGUE

The preceding essay was written during the summer of 1969; it is now May 1970. Two weeks ago President Nixon invaded Cambodia, producing unprecedented mobilization of millions of American students. These events require that a few words be added to supplement the foregoing analysis.

Shortly after the new school year began, it became clear that the organized New Left of the 60s had died. In particular, SDS as a national organization had come to an end, destroyed from within both by irreconcilable factional conflict and by its national leadership's loss of interest in the student movement. The demise of SDS, however, had little effect on the student and youth revolt; indeed, even prior to the Cambodian adventure, this school year had seen more intense and widespread campus protest than any previous one. Many of the most militant confrontations occurred on campuses with little prior history of militance. Fire bombings, street combat with police, and attacks on property became increasingly commonplace on campuses and in the surrounding student quarters, as did the introduction on campus of heavily armed police and national guard forces. At least seven students died in such confrontations during the year; scores of others were wounded by gunfire and bayonetings, as well as by the traditional billy-club-bings. As the post-Cambodian national strikes, mobilizations, and disorders showed, the campus revolt was now a revolt of the campus majority; no organization was needed to create initiatives. It was hard to neatly label the politics of the mobilized student mass. The majority were not revolutionary, but rather opted for a pragmatic, issue-oriented style; a growing minority were clearly revolutionary, rejecting conventional politics and protest in favor of disruption, confrontation, and insurrection. If the majority rejected a single-minded devotion to revolutionary strategy on both moral and practical grounds, it appeared that the most activated students were prepared to be seriously attentive to arguments for revolutionary change and against capitalism and imperialism.

Indeed, what divided the rebelling mass of students was not the critique and analysis of American society (there was a general consensus that the New Left was right), but rather questions of strategy and tactics, (as well as, of course, degree of involvement and dedication to the movement). The continuing, spreading, and intensifying youth-student revolt showed itself this year to be irreversible, no longer requiring political organization or leadership at the national level for its development.

The problem of isolation of the student and youth movement continues to be an urgent one. Although adults of many strata have become increasingly sympathetic as a result of the war and repression, an obvious process of polarization continues to develop. Only today, 150,000 New Yorkers led by construction craft unionists are said to have paraded in support of "the flag, Nixon and Agnew, and law and order." Students, on the other hand, are becoming increasingly energized to move into the community and try to offset such polarization, while growing numbers are attracted to the idea of going into various forms of semi-skilled work to test the possibility of radical organization among the working class. Simultaneously, a period of increased labor strife is impending, as major union contracts expire. The decline in real wages, coupled with rising unemployment, implies growing labor militance and, therefore, the possibility that sectors of the traditional working class may be more open to radical politics and action.

Moreover, it seems likely that revolts of post-student intelligentsia are in the offing. This would be true simply because of the influx of the 60s generation into the educational, service, governmental, and cultural bureaucracies. The likelihood of conflict within such institutions is intensified by the general political climate, by the emergence of women's liberation consciousness among women employees, by the precipitous decline in governmental subsidy of intelligentsia occupations, and by the consequent contraction of the job market for the educated.

It is also important to realize that by 1975, there will be more than 50 million *adults* under 35—an enormous constituency of young adults whose political outlook has been shaped by the movements and events of the past decade. In addition, it is highly likely that the 18-year-old vote will become a reality. As the 70s proceed, it seems clear that a new political majority will emerge—one in which the post-World War II generation predominates, with the mass intelligentsia constituting an increasingly larger proportion. These demographic changes offer considerable hope to liberal reformers for building their political base. But since no liberal reform program seems likely to offer a plausible way out of the American crisis, these facts should also be a source of hope for radical socialist politics.

Despite the perils of the present—the real danger of hard repression, of a mass-based fascism, of nuclear war, and of general social chaos—there is genuine reason for optimism. The sociocultural revolution begun by the young intelligentsia has expanded and deepened, even in a year marked by repression and fragmentation of the left. Many means for its self-transcendence exist. The primary task for political radicals in the coming period appears to be this: to help the struggle of the intelligentsia connect with the aspirations and needs of the people as a whole . . .

# A VIEW FROM THE RIGHT

## 6. Who Killed the Student Revolution?

### ROBERT NISBET

"The student revolution in the United States is dead." When I wrote that sentence last summer,[1] it was in the spirit of prophecy. Now it can only be regarded as a statement of actuality. Nothing that has happened last fall or winter suggests other than that the back of the revolution is broken. A few minor death struggles here and there, a few lashings of the long tail the revolution acquired in its five years. Nothing else. In another year nearly all evidence of the revolution will have been swept from the American campus. Slogans that only a year ago preoccupied faculty meetings from Berkeley to Harvard and that were the subjects of solemn editorials in the American press are now producing only yawns as they make their way to history's capacious dust-bin. Soon it will be hard to remember the names of even the most heroic of principals in the revolution, the most hallowed of sit-ins, building-occupations, archive-spoliations, and millennialist demonstrations on the campus.

Two questions suggest themselves. First, who killed the revolution? Second, who supported the revolution for almost half a decade in a country that must ordinarily be the least revolutionary in character of any in the 20th century? Although my primary concern is with the first of these questions, proper answer to it can be made only by giving some consideration to the second.

Before dealing with either question, it is only fair to make clear that I have had little relish for the revolution from the start. I have not liked the corruption of student and faculty mind that has all too often been manifest. I have been deeply troubled by the impact of the revolution on the subtle

From *Encounter, 34* (February, 1970), pp. 10–18.

[1] In an article under the title "The Death of the Student Revolution" published 13 September in *The Montreal Star.*

but puissant lines of relationship that normally bind students, faculty, and administration into the fragile entity that is the university in our change-swept, anomic, and power-oriented society of the 20th century.

From the time the first shot was fired at Berkeley in late 1964, it has been clear that the chief casualty would be academic freedom, which is, at bottom, no more than the university's proper autonomy in the social order. There is no question in my mind that this too little appreciated foundation of the university has been greviously, perhaps irreparably, damaged. And it is a matter of quite evident fact that the bond between university and society is at its lowest ebb in history.

Where others have seen constructive, if occasionally violent, action proceeding from youthful idealism, I have much more often seen destructive, vandalistic action proceeding from adolescent boredom. Where others have thought they could see a grass-roots student quest for academic community, I have, for the most part, seen simple, stark grabbing for power by a small minority of cynical, if usually bright, delinquents whose objective was, instead of money or automobiles, rule of the campus. Others may be able to look back and see the revived spirit of individualism and liberty. For my part, I see little more than a combination of adolescent power-thrust and colossal permissiveness by faculty and administration.

At their worst the actions of the student rebels—always a very small minority of the student body—resembled nothing so much as the jackboot authoritarianism of Hitler Youth in the 1920s: complete with shouted obscenities, humiliation of teachers and scholars, desecration of buildings, and instigation of various forms of terror.

These are and have been for five years my general reactions to the so-called academic revolution on the American campus. It is only proper that I should set them down clearly before turning to the subject of the article, which is the nature of the revolution, who caused it, who sustained it, and who, finally, killed it.

## By Love Possessed

The most general cause of the five-year disturbance on the American campus and also, it must be emphasised, of the eventual collapse of the disturbance, lies in the character of the student population of the American university and college. This character is almost solidly middle-class.

The American middle class has many virtues. It is not, however, very good at spawning revolutionaries. It produces more than its share of delinquents and adolescent vandals. But something much more is required, on the evidence of history, in the production of revolutionaries. The middle class is not nearly as proficient at this as is either the European aristocracy (which is quite good at it) or the working class. Moreover, the occasional revolutionary that is produced by the American middle class today tends to be rather soft at the centre and flabby around the edges. Of the tiny group that has shown revolutionary inclinations during the past few years, one may confidently predict a high rate of early defection or flight from the issues through either abject retreat or suicidal behaviour, taking that last in the full sense.

Nothing in the family life from which American college students overwhelmingly derive is likely to fit them for the dedicated, disciplined, and demanding life of the hardcore revolutionary. This family life is an amalgam of almost desperate dependence on the marks of affluence and of almost equally desperate dependence on the children in the family. The first tends to produce a considerable burden of guilt—often expiated these days by doctrinaire political radicalism in parents—and the second leads to a magnification of the parent-child tie beyond anything known in the history of the family. The ambience of the present middle-class family in America is love: love, that is, for the children. It is not merely love, it is undiluted, unconditional, unbreakable love by parents of child. There may be many good things to say about this. But, clearly, such a family structure, with its possessions-oriented, children-dominated, guilt-tinged, and boredom-producing values, is less likely to yield revolutionaries than it is juvenile delinquents.

Or else (as is far more common) rather conservative, conformist, and almost infinitely agreeable mass-children. Tocqueville foresaw that the great danger of democracy in the future would be, not its proneness to frequent revolution, but rather its proneness to a homogeneity of type and immobility of structure through which even the most energetic minds would find it difficult to break free. Despite newspaper stories (of all participants in the campus revolution, newspaper reporters were, as I shall stress below, the most credulous), the overwhelming majority of students, even at a Berkeley or Columbia, were not interested in any reform, much less revolution, on the campus. Bystander was their principal role. And those who were driven to action, the relative handful of the revolt-minded, had neither the necessary qualities for revolutionary leadership (delinquency, yes; revolution, no) nor the capacity to stir it up in others. Middle-class background saw to that.

The nearest to an *academically*-revolutionary cry from the leaders of the revolt—and, it must be acknowledged, from a rather substantial group of students not themselves revolt-minded—was the cry for "relevance." The curriculum, it was said, must be made relevant to the interests and needs of students. I would not wish to even guess at the vast number of newspaper editorials and television commentaries that solemnly and dutifully echoed this cry. It was appealing.

It was also appalling. For invariably what the student cry for relevance turned out to be was the all-too-familiar middle-class child's cry to be entertained, to be stimulated, above all, to be *listened to,* no matter what or how complex the subject at hand. Having become accustomed in their homes to get attention to whatever was on their minds, and of course incessant and lavish praise for their "brightness," is it not to be expected that when the children go off to the university the same attention should be given their interests and needs?

At the present time there is a widespread interest in so-called "sensitivity" and "encounter" types of class—even of whole schools and colleges. *Community* is, of course, the talisman of all that is good and just. These departures from curriculum and scholarship are not merely vagrant exercises in irrationalism. More fundamentally, they are efforts on the part of middle-class children to be rescued from loneliness. This parallels efforts to be rescued from boredom through courses that are "relevant."

Being alone is for most middle-class students a deeply disquieting experience. This can make going off to the university a sometimes traumatic experience. For so many years have adolescents known the warmth of parental love, praise, adulation, and instant recognition of every brilliant or profound utterance at the dinner table—not to mention instant forgiveness for all sins and delinquencies—that entering college can be like a plunge into icy waters. The vast burgeoning on American campuses since about 1960 of all the multitudinous and diverse "welfare" offices—concerned foremost with student adjustment and happiness—can only be explained, it seems to me, by desire to provide psychologically-needy students with surrogates of Mom and Dad. Revamping curricula and colleges into student-planned "sensitivity," "great books," and "encounter" groups is little more, I should think, than a kind of final solution for this middle-class sprung ache to be recognised—constantly and everlastingly.

None of this—family background or college environment—is likely to be a sufficient context for appearance of either revolutionary masses or revolutionary leaders. Still, no one would wish to deny the fact that very real disturbances took place or that a large share of American attention—and apprehension and hostility—was given to these disturbances. I turn to them now.

## The Romance of Politics

Among the active and precipitating causes of the campus disturbances, academic and curricular issues had very little influence or staying power. I want to emphasise this fact. For almost beyond count are the editorials and commentaries by American news media, the articles in alumni magazines, the agenda of faculty meetings, and the guilt-stricken, soul-searching articles by intellectuals, academic and other, in which the central point is the *supposed academic roots* of the "revolution" in the American university.

Overwhelmingly, the objectives of the Mario Savios and the Jerry Rubins and the Mark Rudds were, in the beginning at least (until substantial segments of the faculty chose to endow these objectives with academic essence), not academic at all but political. The objectives were not reform of the university in the first—or last—instances; they were, preposterous as it may today seem, objectives of overthrow of the surrounding social order. It was political romanticism, not academic, that provided the motivating circumstances.

In some ways this is the strangest of all aspects of the revolution: the fact that its roots were not at all in academic deprivation but that, from the very beginning, they were widely supposed to be. I am not forgetting the skill with which leaders of the revolts occasionally seized upon academic slogans and rallying-cries. The photograph of the student with a sign across his chest reading "DO NOT FOLD, BEND, OR MUTILATE" got a great deal of mileage in the American press. So did a good many other gimmicks and subterfuges. If there is any real lesson emerging from the past five years it is, I think, the case with which supposedly tough, intellectually sophisticated newspaper and television reporters can be captured by youth.

The American university student is, and has been for many years, one of the freest—and, at the same time, most carefully nurtured and cherished—beings in Western history. Nevertheless, it proved astonishingly easy to convince a great many newspaper reporters and editorial writers that he was in fact some variant of an Asiatic peasant, even, as one highly successful piece of Left publicity had it, a "nigger." (Of all the trivialisations of the black cause in the United States, the most farcical was this one: the likening of the pampered American student's role to that of the Negro in the Deep South. But a lot of people, including faculty members, were for a time convinced.)

The point is, the student revolution was never genuinely interested in academic reforms. Its leaders were far more interested in the extra-mural issues of Negro civil rights, Viet Nam, and in broadcasting ideas of world revolution drawn from their reading of Mao, Fanon, Marcuse, and other millennialists—writers who, it must be confessed, had had something more substantial in mind when they issued the call for revolution than the position of the American middle-class student in college—than they were in achieving any actual academic reforms.

It is well to remember that the first great episode of the student revolution, which was at Berkeley in late 1964, began with not even a pretence of academic objectives. The revolutionary forays into classroom and community led by Mario Savio and his fellows had nothing to do at first with *academic* issues, with the plight of the student, the irrelevance of courses and curricula, and the research relationships between university and Federal government. The Berkeley phase of the revolution had nothing to do with these; and it had everything to do with the right claimed by a small number of students, fresh from recent (and decidedly strenuous, sometimes bloody) engagements in rural Mississippi and on Automobile Row in San Francisco, to be free to mount attack on the social order with the campus as their base and also sanctuary. They were refused this claimed right, and thus began, in overt form, the student revolution.

Since this essential point has been so widely missed by other commentators, I again stress it. *The so-called academic revolution of the students was not academic at all.* It was in fact a misbegotten, preposterously conceived, hopelessly romantic effort to effect a revolution in the social order, in political and economic society, using the campus as launching pad and as refuge. For obvious and inevitable reasons this use of the campus was denied the student insurrectionaries. Only at this point, when, in fury at having been denied such use of the Berkeley campus by Chancellor Edward Strong (who lost his administrative position in due time for his courage and resoluteness), the insurrectionaries turned on the administration at Berkeley, could anything faintly resembling an academic revolution be said to have begun. But even then there were no academic goals and aspirations.

Nor were there any real academic goals during the five years which were to follow the Berkeley uprising. Why should there have been—except as sops to the more moderate faculty and as bait for the media representatives? From Mario Savio to Mark Rudd one finds little but cold hatred in the minds of the student leaders for the university and its purposes. They were not interested, really, in revolutionising the university. Their interest—a projection of adolescent romantic fantasy—was in revolutionising a social order and, with this, in destroying the university utterly.

One can only marvel at the discrepancy between real aims and those aims for which the student revolution was to receive credit. What Mario Savio and his fellow-revolutionists desired was, as I have said, use of the university campus as a base and sanctuary for revolution in the social order. If there is any evidence of their dislike of university courses and curricula (all were excellent students) prior to about January 1966, immediately after the first great Berkeley outburst, I cannot find it. They did not object to university *academic* practices for the simple reason that these, save as opportunities to indulge intellectual reading-interests, did not matter to them. What mattered was—revolution! Revolution on, first, a local, then national, and finally a world scale. *This* was what the reading of Lenin, Trotsky, Fanon, Mao, Che, and Marcuse had helped stimulate. They could not have cared less about the trival things that faculty committees on reform of curricula went frenziedly to work on, starting about the spring of 1965.

I can do nothing but honour the student insurrectionary leaders. Wrong, juvenile, sometimes evil, I am obliged to regard them. But never stupid! They were, and no doubt are to this moment, as bright a crew of predators and pirates as our country has seen in many decades.

But what, in retrospect, is one to say of those faculty committees, student demonstrations, newspaper editorials, alumni meetings, agitated conferences of intellectuals, and others which saw in all this, not the ends which were frankly if cynically proclaimed by the student revolutionists themselves, but instead a noble crusade for reform of the university, its teaching, its curricula, and its relation to humane values? Numberless are the committee reports by faculty, the manifestos by genuinely concerned students, alumni, and public groups, and the columns, news-analyses, and editorials by the media which chose to believe, despite perfectly lucid declarations by the revolutionists, that what was really at stake was the long-needed academic reform of the university. What delicious humour all these must have aroused in the minds of Mario Savio and his successors.

Overnight such places as Berkeley, which for years had known large student bodies, lecture courses, and research-oriented faculty, but which had nevertheless prospered, had withal been immensely attractive year after year to fresh generations of students, were discovered to be impossibly bureaucratic, aloof, impersonal, and guilty of a totalitarianism that might have done honour to the Nazis.

But all good things come to an end in time. I would guess that the events of spring '69, particularly at Harvard and Cornell, were the beginning of the end. The weird discrepancy could not survive—except in a few minds—for much longer; the strain on credulity was becoming too great even for liberal faculty and newspaper reporters. Ivy League intellectuals could look upon the far-off events of Berkeley, San Francisco State, and Wisconsin with that peculiar detachment regarding the academic universe which is their hallmark. But when the insurrection hit, first, Columbia, then Harvard and Cornell, the time for detachment was over. The broad gulf between actuality and pretension could no longer be missed. The time for sympathy, detachment, fine neutrality had clearly come to an end.

This, then, seems to me to be the second, and perhaps most direct reason for the collapse of the "student revolution." *It was not really a student revolution.* It was an insurrection, yes, and one engineered by individuals who happened to be students, off and on at least, but it was not a revolt that arose from any clear interest-orientation of students, or from any visible commitment to the values of the academic world. Revolutions that succeed in history —whether religious (as during the Reformation), political (as in France at the end of the 18th century), economic (as in the liberation of peasantry and working class), or racial (as in the contemporary American Negro social movement)—are revolutions in which there is reasonably close and persisting relation between aims and actual interest-roots. No such relation existed in the so-called student revolution of 1964–69.

Something must be said about the participation of Negro students. The disturbances could not have lasted more than a few weeks had it not been for the very substantial—if utterly non-academic—themes provided by, first, the Negro civil rights movement and, second, the curse of American engagement in Viet Nam. I shall come to the second a little later. The blacks deserve prior attention.

Of all participants in the campus revolution, Negro students alone, it seems to me, had any *functional* relation to the events of the revolution. But this comes overwhelmingly from the fact that they were in action not as black *students* but as *black* students. The difference is, of course, major. There was thus very commonly a much clearer sense of objective and of strategy on the part of the blacks than of the whites. Whereas white students, accustomed to unconditional love in their rearing, had essentially unconditional (certainly unformed ) attitudes, black students did not. The blacks increasingly manifested a sense of concrete goal, of victory seen in the mature terms of specific gains for blacks. For blacks the campus was a valuable place in which to continue, even widen, a revolutionary struggle in the United States that was also taking place in the ghetto, in industries, in labour unions, and in government halls. Theirs was, in short, a revolution in substance as well as aspiration. It proceeded directly from the historic role of the Negro in American society: subjugation as nearly total as any that can easily be imagined.

But this, while bound to keep the flame of black revolution alight, and also to make for goals capable of reasonable clarity, of at least theoretical attainment, could not help but lead to an ever-widening division between black and white revolutionists. For, as I have noted, the latter being by nurture and temperament almost incapable of seeing goals concretely and conditionally, could hardly help but become in due time an embarrassment to the black cause. The disturbances at Columbia University highlighted this division between blacks—generally, a tightly disciplined group with clear-cut objectives—and whites.

It would not do, of course, to carry this analysis too far—yet. But the division I speak of is nonetheless important in understanding the collapse of the campus revolution. From now on, it seems clear, the black revolution on the campus will be simply a campaign in the wider revolution that is the whole Negro movement in our time. It will tend to be ever more deeply rooted in aspirations peculiar to *black* students and intellectuals. There will be, especially given the intense cultural nationalism of blacks now developing at fast rate, very little room in the black revolution, whether on campus or off, for the guilt-seized, obeisant, but largely ineffectual white. Blacks no longer need whites to conduct the revolution. Whatever may be black revolutionary dislike for white members of the *Establishment*, it is as nothing compared with black dislike of white *revolutionists*. This last is, I believe, a vital point. It is also a corollary of one of the most vital points in the understanding of all revolutions in history: that intensities of hatred within revolutionary ranks tend in a short time to become much greater than those of revolutionaries towards the common enemy.

Few will have failed to note the conspicuous deterioration within the past year or two of white leadership of the student revolution. Whereas some fairly impressive (from a purely technical point of view) figures were produced by white students in the very early stages, chiefly at Berkeley, the more recent types, at Columbia, Harvard, and Cornell, have been rather pathetic. They are so obviously wallowing in guilt-driven desire to serve black intellectuals that the results range from the distasteful to the comical. Overwhelmingly the products, as I have emphasised, of affluent, ever-loving, ever-tender, ever-permissive—and generally leftist—parents, one often had the impression that the white students were more interested, through their depredations, in pleasing Mom and Dad, in giving their parents something to boast about at cocktail parties, than in much else. And, as has become widely evident within recent months, such white students, like left-leaning white intellectuals generally, have become figures of contempt and derision in black intellectual and revolutionary circles.

The Negro rights struggle has a long way to go yet: in the nation's schools (especially in Northern schools where segregation is beyond Supreme Court power and seemingly immovable), in many remaining areas of industry and the professions, in the huge labour unions, and in the final cleaning out of the black ghettos. But, to put the matter bluntly, the blacks today require little help that they cannot themselves provide in what remains of the single most important social movement of the 20th century. After all, there is a Negro on the Supreme Court, another holding Cabinet status in Washington, a considerable number of black mayors in key cities, and, at this moment, some 500 elected black officials in the Southern states themselves. Whatever else the Negro movement requires, help from adolescent whites on the campus who have managed to creep and crawl to the top of, say, *S.D.S.*, is not a part of it.

## Viet Nam

The other extra-mural cause that kept the campus revolts going for more than four years was, of course, Viet Nam. The campus was a place where demonstrations against this war could be conducted with relative impunity. Mobilisations that, four years ago, would have been put down bloodily had they taken place in working-class or suburban areas, or in the heart of a city, went on regularly under the benign and maternal gaze of Alma Mater.

The student Left saw American engagement in Viet Nam as one more evidence of the intolerable corruption of the business-oriented middle class. To be sure, the students were quite incorrect about this relation of the war and the business class. The business-as-usual, money-making, luxury-loving American middle class does not like war any more than it does revolution. Each disrupts, distracts from, and threatens middle-class values. War is, today as always, essentially a product of the military mind working in conjunction with the political intellectual. Serious and nearly irreversible commitment in Viet Nam began only about 1960 when for the first time there was added to the military mind in the Pentagon the extraordinary political intensity of the Bundys, Rostows, and Rusks: not one a product of the business class in America; all of them keenly interested, as political intellectuals invariably are interested, in serving, and in broadening, political power. Moving at first in low gear with small forces, then, increasingly, in high gear under Johnson—with, to be sure, the inevitable and predictable defections of some from both military and intellectual ranks—the United States found itself by 1964 in that classic, textbook position of absolute untenability: fighting a land war in Asia. Once the full implications of this appalling folly were grasped by intellectuals and generals in the government—those, that is, who had not already cut and run—the ultimate objective became that of getting out with the least possible damage to commitments, military forces, and, of course, diplomatic face.

Viet Nam was a natural for the leaders of the revolt on the campus. And they can hardly be blamed for seizing upon it. If no one else would attack the highly esteemed likes of the Kennedys, the Bundys, McNamaras, Rostows, and Rusks, they would. And they did. With impressive success, generally speaking. For there is little question in my mind that had it not been for the passionate attack from the student Left, the curse upon America that began substantially in the early 1960s might well have continued much farther into the future—with who knows what added elements to the curse—than it is now clear will be the case.

The political Left, it has been said, will never forgive Nixon for robbing it of the one substantial cause it had, the one rock on which might have been built a broad-gauged revolution in this country. But Nixon *has* robbed the Left of this issue—and also the related issues of the draft and of arms control with Russia. I do not know when the last American soldier will be evacuated from Viet Nam; no one can know. But this much is clear: the by now overall, deeply committed, irreversible, objective of the United States is to get clear of Viet Nam as quickly as due regard for safety and logistics permits.

Demonstrations will doubtless continue. But, as the very recent mobilisation of some quarter-million people in Washington D.C. made evident, such demonstrations are now respectable. What the student Left began has now been taken over securely and irrevocably by the middle-class moderates, by the churches, and by a substantial fraction of what is being called these days "the silent majority." Jerry Rubin knew exactly what the situation was (lack of brightness, as I have said, is no failing of the student Left) when, in Washington on the occasion of huge and peaceful mobilisation, he spat out disgustedly that "peace has become respectable!"

So it has. And with this major achievement, the last hope of the student Left in continuing their revolt, of making actual their adolescent fantasies of permanent revolution, has fled. Now there is nothing left to base even a major campus building-occupation on, much less a full-blown reign of terror.

## The Professor

In accounting for the death of the so-called revolution on the campus we cannot afford to neglect the role of the faculty. I said at the beginning that we find the causes of the collapse of the revolution closely related to the forces which for nearly five years kept the revolution going. Among these is the university faculty—or, rather, of a substantial and powerful segment of the faculty.

As the faculty gave in the beginning, so it took away in due time. Without faculty stimulus, advice, financial contributions, and other forms of assistance, the student revolt could never really have got off the ground. It will be known to posterity—to the extent that it is remembered at all—as the student revolution. It should be known as the student-faculty revolution.

Not, obviously, all faculty; not even a majority of faculty. The actual number of key figures on the faculty, whether at Berkeley, San Francisco State, Harvard or Columbia would appear to be rather small. But it was, I repeat, a powerful minority, often containing within it Nobel-Prize winners and others of equal stature. We could not possibly understand the early successes at Berkeley—such successes as the humiliation of the Academic Senate, the deposing of President Kerr, Chancellors Strong and Meyerson, as well as a host of lesser fry—except in terms of the very substantial assistance from eminently willing, powerful, internationally renowned, and immensely prestigious faculty members at Berkeley. Most of them have long since fled to other campuses or retreated behind locked Institute doors, but in the beginning they served the student revolutionists well. Granted that they only rarely ventured forth into the open, and that under the iron security of academic tenure they had nothing whatever to fear from administration and Regents, their role in the revolution was a vital one.

In retrospect, I think the major contribution of the faculty to the student revolution was the priceless insistence that all acts of the students, however vandalistic, however destructive of the civil order, be regarded as, not the

128

offences against public law they were in fact, *but as academic-student behaviour*, and hence deserving of the university's full protection. This was an insistence that, having been sold to a large majority of the Berkeley faculty and to high administrative figures, including Regents, proved invaluable to the early life of the revolution. Repeatedly, acts on the part of student revolutionists which would have earned them severe jail sentences had they taken place in most sectors of society, were dealt with as behaviour falling somewhere between the hoary category of student prank and the perhaps regrettable but nonetheless forgivable excesses of profound student idealism.

I am not trying to make the faculty into villains or fools. There is no question but that motives of highest rectitude often actuated faculty members in their support of students long after the justice and wisdom of faculty support of these students had vanished. Faculty members are properly concerned with academic freedom, with freedom of learning and teaching and thinking. There is a very old tradition in the university—going back to the 12th and 13th centuries—whereby students and faculty members protect themselves from the towns-people and other outsiders. There is old and highly honourable support for the view that the university is a sanctuary.

But the university cannot be both sanctuary and staging-ground for revolutionary attack upon society. And the canons of academic order cannot easily be invoked within its walls for acts which are clearly destructive of civil order. I know very well indeed that the more brilliant of the student revolutionists were aware of this from the start. What they could not know, what they would not have dared to guess or even hope for, was the sheer length of time they nevertheless managed to have the best of both worlds.

But they no longer have it. It is increasingly difficult to find even a handful of faculty members that have not become hostile in the extreme to the manifestations of adolescent delinquency that for more than four years passed for revolutionary and progressive ardour. The memory is too galling of buildings occupied and polluted, of library files overturned and damaged, of offices ransacked, of fellow-teachers humiliated in classoom and in public, and of one concession after another being made a fresh base from which to declare war on the authority of the university.

The sight of police called, of student heads clubbed, of tear gas in the air, of militant gatherings dispersed through whatever armed means, all of this was once deeply repugnant to faculty members. It is still repugnant. I hope it will aways be repugnant.

*But it is not as repugnant as it once was.* And this is the key to the matter. Familiarity breeds at least tacit acceptance among even the most fastidiously liberal of faculty minds. What was perceived as revolutionary or reformist action three years ago is now perceived as vandalism. The overwhelming, the nearly total, majority of the American university faculty will regard such action henceforth with undiluted hostility. As I said above, in the American university the faculty giveth and the faculty taketh away.

## The Rise of Power

The final reason for declaring the student revolution in America dead also arises directly from the character of the middle class. It is the fear of a moral void, of anarchy, of authority too long flouted—and, arising directly from this, the almost instinctive turning to power for protection. It may be police power, or the power of the Federal government in matters long left to local government or voluntary association; it may be the power of the state legislature invoked in spheres where it has never before existed, or it may be the power of the trustees or administration in the university over matters traditionally left to ordinary processes of use and wont, to corporate faculty or the students. But power.

The uses of power have multiplied within the past four years. So too have the contexts of acceptance of power. And this last, obviously, is the more frightening circumstance. In some thirty-five years of residence in the University of California, I have never seen any aspect of academic life produce as nearly monolithic a public response as did the Berkeley uprising in 1964. Governor Reagan's popularity in California—higher this year even than last —rests to a large degree on the average citizen's confidence that he is the sworn enemy of student violence. His election three years ago was in vital degree the result of his repeated focusing on what he and millions of others in California regarded as the breakdown of the university's indigenous system of authority. The one college president in recent history whose prestige is national, a prestige that has been fully substantiated by newspaper polls, is President Hayakawa of San Francisco State College. Leaving to one side the very real capabilities Hayakawa manifests as an administrator, not to mention his considerable status as a scholar, the decisive fact is the *image* he has left with, not merely Californians but Americans at large. And this image is one of power: quick, resourceful, unyielding power.

The American people are used to scenes of domestic violence. America is, it has to be confessed, a rather violence-prone nation. It has been since its founding as a national state. Nor are Americans unused to spectacles of student turbulence, which go far back in the history of Harvard, Yale, and other early American colleges. But I can think of no kind of violence—religious, racial, or academic—that has ever produced the national response that the university revolts have since 1964. It may be that the people, with intuitive wisdom, perceived something very different about these revolts; something that went beyond the boundaries of campus and touched upon the very essence of those middle-class values which are the substance of American society.

Power has greatly increased in scope during the past five years in the United States. Police forces have been enlarged; the *technology* of law-enforcement has been immensely improved. Witness only what Mayor Lindsay in New York calls his "war room," a technological marvel that has almost every part of New York City under constant surveillance and that makes effective deployment of police a mere matter of minutes. Power has also become more sophisticated within recent years. It is highly unlikely that the clumsiness of early police responses to campus disturbances will be repeated. There are better, less visible, less troubling (to middle-class conscience), and far more effective ways now at police disposal. Laws have been passed at both national and state level, administrative rulings have been handed down by the innumerable agencies with which the contemporary university deals, university administrations have been decisively toughened. These are real and immediately verifiable consequences of 1964–69.

Far more important than these, however, is the widening popular acceptance of the contexts of power: even power in its more brutal manifestations. Every newspaper poll taken revealed that a substantial majority of the American people approved of the Chicago police actions they saw on television and read about in the newspapers in the summer of 1968. If they could approve the ugly and vicious buffooneries that generally passed for police action in Chicago, it is not difficult to assume their approval of the far more sophisticated techniques of police power that exist today in most cities in the world. And these are techniques of power that have thoroughly permeated the American campus. That is, I think, the single greatest change I have seen in thirty-five years on the university campus.

# SECTION III

# Education

The university once was a community of scholars. That is, it consisted loosely of a group of men who made themselves available to tutor those willing to pay. The class took the form of the dialogue and later, when size increased, the lecture. Only the elites were permitted access, and the opportunity structure was such that only the most wealthy could afford the luxury of "pure thought" or "idle speculation." Today, as we see all around us, the major structural dimensions of education have changed. In the place of close, personal, face-to-face interactions we have literal mob scenes in classrooms where the professor rails at a sea of upturned faces. The university has become massified in terms of attendance, the standards of admission have become widely egalitarian, and access to learned professions has spread to include graduates of the multiversities, state colleges, and schools of wide quality. From a community of scholars, each working closely with students, there are now pockets of a few professors tied to the classroom and their students, while prestige flows to those who publish and who are able, thereby, to escape the confines of academia to research, to write, to travel, and to consult. From a community of scholars, we have now evolved to an aggregate of strangers, people who do not share common goals, interests, and futures, who do not respect the same standards of excellence, and who define the very everyday life of the university in new, ahistorical ways. It is among strangers that conflict occurs.

The structure of the university, however, remains largely unmodified as Nisbet shows. Thus, the same structure, the bureaucratic hierarchy, continues to hold sway while the cultural presuppositions that initially guided the behavior of people in universities have now been eroded. As Nisbet mentions, forces have been at work that undermine the authority of the university, quite

133

apart from the recent protests. Where this emotional and cultural glue weakens, where the underlying sentiments are felt to be disconnected from the structure of human relationships, there are needs to explain, to rationalize, and to innovate with new responses to that set of behavior patterns. In the case of the student activist, we have seen the development of a new ideology, a new set of explanations and beliefs about what is and what ought to be. In addition, the previous commitments that tied people to student roles, obligations to the leisure class, obligations to family, and to the society itself (motivations characterizing the elites) are waning, leading to a new technocratic definition of education itself. There is little interest in idle speculation among students in present universities. Riesman warns against the apparent overwhelming importance that the present may appear to have under those conditions. He reasserts the value of the contemplative life.

However, ideologies themselves do not possess as great an appeal to educated activists as they once did; students tend to reject them as simplifications or as mere rhetoric. Thus, the predominance of issue and situation-oriented confrontations where the demands are patently impossible and, perhaps, unattainable ("Free all political prisoners;" "Stop the war;" for example). These confrontations serve important functions that have been overlooked. Thus, as Lyman and Scott (1970) show, they are fun; they free one from everyday responsibilities: class, home, study. They provide a new and exciting identity ("radical," "demonstrator," "criminal"), and they provide a place for testing one's self against the environment in order to produce (at high cost if need be) a response. They are reassuring in that in number there is *prima facie* evidence that truth and power have been discovered. The poignancy of the Cottle article (at least for me) was his insight into the human, adolescent quality of reactions of the demonstrators after being physically expelled from an occupied building on the Harvard campus. The feelings of hunger, of fear, of concern for others, of a battle lost, of self-doubts, and of courage are all located in the conversations he has captured. This great rage, this eagerness to test self against symbolic fathers, to bring authority down in a most demeaning fashion, is tempered by fear, by guilt, by aimless, boundless, ruminations about the self. Why can Cottle capture this, telling us more about "student demonstrators" than many scholarly and official accounts? What makes his account ring true? It seems to capture the sentiments of the participants, while contrasting them with an obdurant social organization, unyielding courts, harsh faculty, and ambivalent agencies of social control. It is the capacity to move from situations to structures, from mood to constraint, that makes this a moving account of educational experiences.

What of confusion and doubt in the lives of the students studied by Becker? Its apparent absence is perhaps accounted for by the degree to which

134

the interpersonal relationships they experienced in their campus politics, in their dating, and in their campus activities reproduced for them a consistent and meaningful microcosm of the larger social world. For a majority of students there is continuity, a relevance in their education for their later aspirations. But for those where the disjuncture occurs, the disjuncture between self and role, self-expectation and other-imputation grows, only to be temporarily annealed in the heat of protest, display, or demonstration. In Riesman's selection, and in Becker, we see the grounding of life in the meanings of everyday activities, a continuity and plea for the relevance of academic life to later life (for different reasons, of course). In Cottle, there is the hint of what happens when the discrepancy grows to become intolerable, where boundaries seem so blurred that only the quest for immortality in totalistic politics will restore the Humpty Dumpty of thought and feeling.

# 7. Observations on Contemporary College Students— Especially Women[1]

## DAVID RIESMAN

### The Myth of Homogeneity

Among students and faculty in selective colleges one can find a widespread sense of discomfort based on the judgment that there is nothing in all the world so homogeneous as a largely white, upper-middle-class, suburban group of undergraduates, most of them of high academic aptitude. The fear of homogeneity and the mindless conformity that is supposed to accompany it seems to be especially powerful among young women, reflecting the sensitivity many of them have to the charge of overprivilege, a special sensitivity as distinguished from that of young men.

I regard this view as exaggerated and more than a little mythological. Judgments that "the natives" are homogeneous are often made from the outside by undiscerning snobs. But the natives can be equally misled about each other, failing to see the diversities that talent and sensibility enhance, and emphasizing conformities that may be superficial.[2] Similarly, colleges generally considered to be in the same social or academic league can have very different atmospheres. Though some girls apply to both, Smith and Mount

---

[1] This essay is adopted from two different talks I gave recently: a Commencement Address at Pitzer College on June 8, 1969, and a Convocation Address at Chatham College on September 16, 1969.

[2] Cf., e.g., Olmsted's (1957) description of a small study in which a group of Smith College students were asked to say whether they considered themselves more inner-directed" than their parents, their friends of both sexes, and the "average" girl at Smith. Most regarded themselves as more "inner-directed" than other Smith College students but less than their parents or male friends.

Holyoke are quite differentiated; Bryn Mawr, Wellesley, and Vassar are all different; Manhattanville and Barat are not the same although both are run by the Mesdames of the Sacred Heart. Of course these colleges are alike if one compares them with postsecondary institutions in other countries, and judgments of similarity and difference always depend on one's perspective; but my concern here is with the attitudes of students in these women's colleges. One consequence of these attitudes is the large number of transfers out of such colleges by those who claim to feel oppressed by homogeneity even when it is possible they have not begun to explore the resources of the institution they are leaving. At times, this tranfer is part of a bargain with protective parents who want their daughter to attend a woman's college at least at the outset, often under the increasingly mistaken belief that it will act *in loco parentis*, while permitting her to transfer to a co-ed and perhaps less expensive state or urban university at a later stage. Young women are not in any case prisoners of the draft, which holds many men in college or in a particular college. To be sure, women have slightly less social freedom today than men who hitchhike around the country, take jobs in plants or as truck drivers, although in VISTA and the Peace Corps and in protest movements they have won a virtual parity of freedom.

Women's restlessness would seem to be reflected in the almost panicky spread of coeducation in the women's colleges the country over while the former men's colleges have been under only slightly less pressure to abandon their once secure stag status. Yet these pressures are not exactly equal. The men's colleges want women around, not so much to add to diversity (which they are more inclined to seek by increasing the number of black inner-city or Appalachian students ) as to add to the warmth and supposed naturalness of life. The women's colleges seek that warmth and naturalness too, but they also believe that the homogeneity from which they claim to suffer would be less if the place went co-ed.

Smith College recently conducted a poll of both its faculty and student body to inquire about attitudes concerning coeducation, and one of the findings that most struck me was that a number of the student respondents declared that they now regarded having come to Smith as a mistake (see Rose, 1968a, 1968b). Most of these students still regarded Smith as an admirable college, but perhaps these responses reflect their restlessness, the desire for change, and a greater breadth of exposure of which I have spoken. Some of the students said that they would make the same choice again—meaning, I suppose, that they saw no better option. A minority of respondents (more freshmen than upperclassmen) said that they would choose a women's college again, but the majority appeared to feel that coeducation was more "natural," and that the relative isolation and alleged homogeneity of Smith could be in part repaired by coeducation as well as by the continuing effort to recruit more disadvantaged students, black and white. It is not sufficient that Smith is part of a Five-College cooperating network, perhaps a bit like the one set up at Chatham with Carnegie-Mellon, Pittsburgh, Duquesne, Mount Mercy, etc. Nor is it an answer to the craving for naturalness that the students had not been brought up in convents, but, for the most part, had experienced coeducation in secondary school, and also in summer school, or in a junior year abroad, or a term spent at Dartmouth or Wesleyan. One aspect of Smith's current climate may be captured by the fact, reported last spring in an article in *The Washington Post*, that the great majority of the graduating seniors had taken part in anti-Vietnam war demonstrations, and well over half had taken part in some civil rights or student demonstration in addition (Greenfield, 1969a, 1969b).

To some young women inside Smith College, I know that these actions imply homogeneity, since attitudes or at least vocal attitudes differ only as between liberal and various shades of radical. But, viewed from the perspective of the country as a whole, it would be another indication that within the broad spectrum of the suburban upper-middle class there are enormous variations. And I would be inclined to go further and say that the more talented a student body becomes, the more individuated the students will be in their talents and qualities. Correspondingly, while there may be many good reasons in a college such as Smith or Chatham to seek to include students with poor preparation who would not attend a private selective college in the ordinary course of things, I am skeptical about how much diversification such students can provide, in view of the likelihood that they will either overadapt to their perception of the college's norms or aggressively and violently define themselves in opposition to these.

## The Dilemma of Privilege

I stress this matter of homogeneity because of its bearing on the issue of privilege and the attitudes toward it—particularly the ambivalences—that now prevail among many sensitive and socially conscious students—not only students, of course. When my mother entered Bryn Mawr College as a freshman 70 years ago, it was a relatively uncommon choice in an epoch when other young women in similar social strata sat at home, made their debuts, and waited for callers. Young women like my mother were rarely troubled by the fact that Bryn Mawr College would not prepare them to make a living or to reform the shame of the cities or indeed to accomplish any specific goal; it aimed to emancipate their minds, imaginations, and sympathies without committing them to any particular line of work or life. Very few of my mother's classmates worried about being privileged or sheltered; indeed, because they were attending college, they felt less sheltered than most of their peers (cf. Riesman, 1964). Throughout history, privileged groups have felt only intermittent need to justify their favored position. This was simply given in the order of the world, reflected in the fatalism of many of the less privileged, and altogether understandable in societies where good things were scarce and where it was inconceivable, except to mad visionaries, that there would ever be enough to go around. For a minority in the West, Christianity gave pause to the privileged, asking them at least to be responsible for the less fortunate and at the most to give up all and follow Christ. Some of my mother's contemporaries founded settlement houses and helped create the profession of social work; but it may be almost impossible for a young person today to recapture what it must have been like to live at the turn of the century with some moderate feeling of responsibility for the less well-off, but with no great sense of urgency in the matter. Before the First World War shattered the dream of slow, incremental progress in a peaceful Atlantic world, young women in college could develop their private talents with no more than periodic feelings that there might be some contradiction between these and the social good.

Today, in contrast, we live in a time where there is a greater possibility of total destruction of mankind than in any previous period of history. Indeed, it is a time that is overwhelmed by nightmares and fantasies of such total destruction. But at the same time that we have these nightmares, it is also widely believed that it is possible to spread the benefits of affluence and of higher education to everyone almost instantly. The median family income of Americans now stands close $8,000. But this relative abundance has helped dramatize the abysses of both relative and absolute poverty, even while our scientific and technological advances have led many to conclude that we could distribute the social benefits of this power if only we wanted to.

I myself for a long time believed this distribution possible, and in writing *The Lonely Crowd* 20 years ago I helped contribute to the growing belief that the problems of America did not lie on the side of production, but only of distribution; I took for granted that our economy would continue under its own momentum, and that the skill and equipment of our work force were not major problems for the future. I am now persuaded that this was a vast over-statement and have come to believe that no economy can be taken for granted and that its continuation, let alone improvement, demands unremitting intelligence and effort (cf. Riesman, 1969).

Yet many students in our colleges and universities have become persuaded that science and technology are at best boring and at worst positively harmful. To be sure, conventional sex-role definitions in America have meant that very few women have gone into the hard sciences or engineering at any time, and today this older convention is supplemented by the new intensity of elite hostility toward any careers that are thought to be boring, commercial, and uncreative. The intellectual and emotional challenges in scientific and technical fields are today often underestimated. And whatever the neo-feminist implications of the women's liberation movements, they are not sufficient inducement for a college-educated woman to enter a field that has previously discriminated against women and may still make entry difficult. Biology and bio-medical careers may be something of an exception here, since these seem to promise some connection with nature, life, and service.

One way of putting all this is to say that elite attitudes in America are post-industrial before we can afford such attitudes. In the elite colleges an aristocratic disdain for those consumer goods that are valued by people of less cultivation is widespread. It seems to me a social advance that many well-educated young people from college-educated families should have moved away from the greed and the mindless rivalry of earlier generations of American students. As the hunger for possession abates, there is much less showing off of one's physical accoutrements. But perhaps this asceticism is too recent to be accompanied by tolerance for those who have not yet attained it. Among many young people, there is a fervent desire to show off one's lack of showiness, one's moral purity, and one's sincerity. Many of you, no doubt, recall the movie *The Graduate*. The "graduate's" floundering is portrayed as more attractive than the trivial or decadent purposes pursued by the adults around him. By withdrawal from these, he expresses his harsh judgment upon the nouveaux riches adults among his parents' friends, even though he himself has an addiction to sports cars and almost certainly has a hi-fi set. (He blithely disregards as a philistine jock the medical student who marries the girl he himself runs away with.) However one may feel about the moral and aesthetic aspects of these judgments, it seems clear to me that their political consequences can be damaging. Moderately well-off but unsophisticated Americans are the great majority. Their affluence is still too new to have created its own antibodies, and they feel insecure in the face of social scorn from the liberally educated, and in the face of envy and hostility from the really deprived.

The combined threats from above and below to white-collar and blue-collar strata have intensified the political dilemmas of how to cope with the uneven spread of affluence in America and the world. Mass production and mass consumption put pressures on the ecological balance of which we are only now becoming fully aware and they also put pressures on the psychological balance of individuals. To feed the desires of the semi-affluent will not inevitably make them more generous toward the truly poor, and will do nothing to decrease the relative deprivation of the latter. Yet it seems to me clear that the risks of social advance in a democracy must be spread in such a way as not to fall unevenly on such insecure groups, for example, as defense plant workers who should be provided with something like a G.I. Bill of Rights in case we reorder national priorities to move away from dependence on a war economy. And whatever the technical and political obstacles to such movement, it seems evident that moralistic attacks on the vulgarities of other people of lesser enlightenment is self-defeating. Students can easily turn this vigilantism onto each other.

It can in fact be heightened by the sense of guilt of the privileged vis-à-vis the less well-off at home and abroad; at this point aristocratic disdain merges into noblesse oblige. I believe that this early acceptance of responsibility for the fate of others has been intensified by the spread far beyond small circles of visionaries of the belief that justice and dignity for all are in principle within reach, not in some distant future, but now. I am inclined to think, although I know no studies that would establish it, that television has done a good deal to intensify awareness of the gap between American ideals and realities. Some children discover quite young that Wheaties do not always make champions. But television does not only contribute to an already widespread cynicism. It diminishes the sense of distance that once separated us from the occurrence of an atrocity or the existence of an injustice and the slowly spreading news or recognition of these. Now we are able to see in our living rooms that our B-52 bombers make a lunar landscape of much of Vietnam. In the early years of the civil rights movement, TV helped white and Negro activists succeed in making many Americans dramatically aware of arbitrary authority, as in the encounters between nonviolent Negroes and Southern sheriffs. Similarly, poverty has been brought visibly and dramatically to our attention through the mass media. And as I have said, the old legitimations for these evils have also disappeared.

The emotion of guilt can have all sorts of consequences for particular individuals. For some, it may be a way of reminding them of unused capacities, of obligations for their own further development. For others, it may be a restraint against the excesses of narcissism. But I am skeptical of the uses of guilt in the political arena, and would argue that the political victories won through playing on people's guilts are apt to be shortrun.

## The Dilemma of Action Deferred

The vicissitudes of the draft have engendered complicated feelings of guilt in many young men who believe that it is unjust for them to be sheltered even temporarily by educational deferments, who are also aware that their vocational and even marital choices may be influenced by the draft. Their protests against the war may have a special edge on account of these feelings. But a good many young women in college have come to feel that they also are sheltered from the fate of the harsh underside of society and that they must in some fashion compensate. It may be that the exceptional fierceness of a few young women in recent protests reflects among other things their anger that they do not face a direct antagonist like General Hershey, but must create one, even if it has to take the form of their own college dean. Like those vigorous Southern white women who have always resented being put on a pedestal, some young women in our Northern colleges today are rebelling against the privileges allowed their sex in return for a certain degree of subordination.

For the woman who is a college student, these four years can be a very special sort of moratorium in terms of relative freedom from subordination. Yet, during the four years that in my mother's generation allowed some lee-way for the privileged to learn new intellectual skills, to read books, to learn how to play an instrument and a life-long sport, to read as well as to write poetry—in these four years it seems that today some of our most intensely involved young people cannot postpone immersion in the political and parliamentary practices of adulthood. In part, this development reflects a general precocity in which the nineteenth century slogan of the labor movement, namely, "a childhood for every child," seems to become less and less attainable. The age of puberty is actually dropping physiologically, thanks to better nutrition (and, possibly, greater stimulation). The age of sexual, social, and political consent is dropping too. Often young people by the time they arrive in college have held jobs that widened their experience of life, have experimented with drugs and with sexual commitments, and have become immersed in politics within their educational institutions, if not in the larger society.

In college and university, young people have aggressively resisted adult authority while immersing themselves in the committee work that will often occupy them as adults throughout all their lives. Sometimes the university becomes a kind of second family against which one struggles to establish independence and to test the limits of permissible constraint. It also becomes a second family in the search for small enclaves of intimacy such as the co-ops and communes to be found in or off many of the leading college and university campuses. It is difficult to persuade students to mute or postpone the major toils of politics and the not always minor ones of housekeeping when the fear of nuclear or other disasters makes it difficult to imagine a future at all.

Furthermore, it seems to me especially difficult for idealistic young women to defend themselves by fatalism or cynicism against their own idealism. They want to express their deep concern and to show that they are not callous. On some campuses, this can make them vulnerable to coercion by militant and usually male activists, who ironically may succeed in subordinating college women to a cause in the very act of rejecting subordination. (It may be that this paradox is an element in the formation of chapters of the Women's Liberation Movement on some of the more activist campuses.)

142

Young people are often tempted today to suppose that the war against war and against injustice requires only will and courage, and not also trained intelligence. One can see this attitude most poignantly if one talks with black students in the best colleges and universities today. I have sometimes said in such statements that I believed in a division of labor not only among individuals and society at any one time, but also in terms of chronological time. Thus, there is every justification for young blacks taking advantage of college just as young whites might do, recognizing that they would make a contribution to their less privileged fellows later on, according to their developed and mature talents, without sacrificing their education to their civic sense of responsibility. Collectively, black students almost uniformly reject this viewpoint: they refuse to believe that they can wait even a year, let alone four or more years. A promise of later service does not free them for what they would regard as present self-indulgence. Privately, it is sometimes another story. I have talked to a few such students, especially graduate students, who have asked whether there are colleges where they would be under less fierce pressure to be angry and active—pressure that comes as often from whites as from fellow blacks. Some have talked with me about going overseas to study in countries where the race problem is less exigent, where they could have a hiatus or moratorium against continuous commitment, the continuous need to prove that they are purer, braver, angrier, more black, and less Negro than others. I myself feel that it is not only an individual but a social tragedy that, in many places, there is such monolithic pressure on black students today. It is a way of destroying the seed corn when the famine may last a long time.

I am of course generalizing here, both about black and about white students; the country over, one can find great differences in the balances between detachment and involvement, passivity and intensity, from year to year and from place to place. There are black students today in major universities who are studying Renaissance literature or theoretical physics or many other subjects that a provincial and patronizing judgment would not consider relevant. The Peace Corps and similar overseas tasks continue to attract some women and a small number of black students in spite of the paradoxical ethnocentrism of the judgment that problems within the United States are so grave that people cannot be spared for other problems elsewhere.[3]

---

[3] There is of course also the objection to the Peace Corps that it represents American cultural imperialism vis-à-vis indigenous populations although it could as easily be argued that Peace Corps Volunteers are more sympathetic to the native cultures than are the natives themselves. (See Fuchs, 1967).

## The Decline of Personal Ambition

The changing attitudes in elite colleges I have been discussing look to many observers like a decline in personal ambition. Yet it is not entirely clear that such a decline is a concomitant of the greater preoccupation of students with the evils of contemporary society. Students are always talking about their own or each other's ego trips, and accusing each other of ambitions for sainthood or at least for political eminence. What is clear is that in many schools student government is disintegrating, to be replaced either by hit-and-run groups or by plebiscitary democracy or by instant chaos or by all of these together. Whatever desire a student has to be a leader or to be thought a leader has to be repressed. Indeed ambition itself is often seen as an evil, equated with greed or with personal rivalry and striving for mere status. Placing the value of "meaningful" work and personal relations above all else, many young men eschew careers in large organizations or in any situations where competitive skills may be demanded of them. A visible although not perhaps a very large number become dropouts from prevailing career patterns, supporting themselves by part-time jobs, by work as artisans, by remittances from home—upper-class mimics of lower-class casualness.

The consequences for college women of the slowly changing attitudes of college men are hard to assess. Men who are themselves less competitive may feel less threatened by active career-minded women, and they may no longer care to monopolize certain kinds of prestigeful positions. However, since men still set the cultural pace and style, the current tendency to reject careers and ambition catches women at that point in their development as an oppressed group when they have not yet quite made it in terms of careers and ambition. They are a little in the position of the upwardly mobile person who is suddenly told, in a good college that he has striven to reach, that ambition is a hang-up, that striving is a sign of inauthenticity, and that it is more important to *be* than to *do*.

As these remarks suggest, I believe it is important to distinguish between competition with others in its rivalrous aspects and competition with one's own capacities to discover and stretch these to the utmost. The line here in practice is sometimes hard to draw. A woman learning to play the violin is at the same time seeking to play it better than others in her circle or as well as her teacher, and to master the stubborn instrument—the damned or exquisite thingmanship of it. It is the same with writing a poem or conducting a research project or allowing one's charm and beauty to shine rather than feeling that these unequal qualities should be disguised in the name of sincerity and equality.

Since 1946, I have taught at high-powered undergraduate colleges at Chicago, Johns Hopkins, and Harvard. For most of this period my concern

144

was often to prevent the deflation of students as they looked around in their freshman year and noticed 500 other valedictorians, or as they suffered their first B rather than their taken-for-granted A in the very field in which they had thought to specialize. I felt it my job to help such students recognize that in terms of world norms they were still extremely bright even if they had the disgraceful grade of C in a particular field that interested them. I would try to persuade them that they could make a contribution even if they were not as articulate or arrogant as some of their fellow students.

In the last few years the situation has been somewhat reversed. A newly liberated generation of students is less competitive and in a way more inclined to coast. Yet, underlying their humility there may be a certain covert grandiosity. For, where at one time hunger for the trappings of success and lack of modesty were the problem for young men and women, now I sometimes feel it is another kind of narcissism, that is, their belief that if they really extended themselves and were not so concerned with social injustice, then they could be distinguished medievalists or novelists or whatever else. While this belief is often so, it is still a defense and a problem. Both of these attitudes—of inflation and deflation—inhibit learning. Both make curiosity difficult. The inflated person already knows; the deflated person despairs of ever knowing. Both are apt to suffer from boredom and then to try to compensate for this by excitement.

## Careers and Marriage

Since I am myself an academic person with an interest in what women can contribute to the quality of academic life as students, as faculty, and as administrators, some readers may take my remarks thus far as a plea for careers and as a polemic against marriage, home, and motherhood. Such polarizations are common among educated women themselves who, whatever road they take among the dilemmas and opportunities they face, are subject to voices within and without insisting that they should have taken another road. The woman who feels she has left her education down and become a "mere housewife" feels defensive in the presence of an active career woman, while the latter may feel in the more traditional American idiom that she has let her husband and children down, or perhaps has become hard and unfeminine in fighting against discrimination. Even the most emancipated young women who have perhaps been experimenting with communal living or other temporary relationships are somewhat more likely to be seeking a stable relationship and an eventual marriage than has been the case traditionally among young men.[4] As insurance against hasty and overdependent decisions, young

[4] See, however, Weiss, 1969, arguing that both sexes need intimacy but that men are more dependent on the convenience as homemaker that women provide than many

women today need to graduate from college with a skill or a profession that gives them confidence. Hence I would be inclined to argue that the elite liberal arts colleges that in the past prided themselves on their nonvocational outlook need to reconsider their programs. Most young women coming out of such colleges probably eventually want what might be termed marriage-plus, and not career-minus.

I have some fragmentary evidence for this view in a recently completed study by the National Merit Scholarship Corporation of the career progress and plans of women Merit Scholarship winners who entered college between 1956 and 1960 (see Watley, 1969). Something like 80% of this group believed that they could manage both a family and a career. Some of these, understandably, felt pulled and hauled in different directions, and a few thought they were discriminated against on grounds of sex. But these highly talented women, on the whole, had confidence that they would be resilient enough to reconcile competing demands and that they had managed it so far.

Although women outperform men in school, men enrolled in college outnumber women by three to two, reflecting among other things the feeling in many families that a daughter's education matters less than a son's—a verdict many young women of less than outstanding talent, energy, or money seem inclined to accept. Even so, the number of women attending college has grown enormously, along with rising enrollments generally. But this increase has not been reflected in the proportion of women pursuing postbaccalaureate degrees, which may in fact have declined. It is arguable to what extent discrimination enters the picture here. Many departments have felt that a woman is not as apt as a man to do them credit, even if she does pursue her studies through to a doctorate; and having to choose among scarce resources, departments have felt it better to bestow these on a man. Such a judgment seems to me in some respects too individualistic, and in others insufficiently so. It is too individualistic in not taking account of the contributions of a catalytic sort that I believe women can make in helping institutions become less dehydrated for both sexes. (See the excellent discussion of women at the Woodrow Wilson School by Proctor, 1969.) It assumes that each student will be completely self-reliant, a Lone Ranger of the academic plains, without any need of support from a humane intellectual community. But on the other hand, the discrimination against women is anti-individualistic in treating them as a cadre among whom there is a high statistical probability that either before or after the PhD they will drop out of professional work as men define it. It means discriminating against a particular woman because of the record other women have made, something that today would be regarded as indefensible

---

women now are on men as wage-earners; he envisages some women, especially among the very large number of divorced women, preferring boyfriends to marriage because they are less obligated to provide the customary services in the household.

vis-à-vis black or other minority applicants. Furthermore, I think it is important to take chances on women graduate students because women look at people, at concepts, at materials in general, in perspectives different from those of men. For present purposes it is not important to argue about why these differences exist, whether they have any pan-human aspects or are merely the legacy of historical traditions and of the different socialization of the sexes in the United States. As with any such gross comparison, there are many men who have learned to be as adaptable and responsive as most women, and many women who have rejected the sex roles assigned to them in order to play what are generally men's games better than most men do. These differences persist in spite of today's blurring of sex boundaries. If women enter a field in sufficient numbers, they may not merely be molded by it but may also help mold it. The changes will be subtle and we would need extensive longitudinal research before we could begin to understand these issues.[5]

And yet, as I have already implied, I think the overt discrimination against women is much less important than their own attitudes in explaining the career choices many make. Census data show that a higher proportion of women is married today than at any previous time in our history, and a higher proportion also is at work. Given all the problems men face and families face in the United States, it is understandable and often admirable that many women conclude that on marriage they will hold down a *job* but not try to pursue a *career*, leaving that to their spouses. That minority of college women who decide on a two-career family face many obstacles. They must find a sufficiently unanxious and unthreatened man—and even then it would be hard. There are very few young women today, including those from wealthy families, who believe it legitimate to have servants and nurses or anything more than periodic amateur babysitters (see Chaplin, 1968). They dare not exploit their privilege in this way, and they rationalize this attitude by saying that it would be bad for the baby to be taken care of by a stranger, or that it is impossible to get help anyway. Also, menfolk do not want that help either—they want the pleasure of helping bring up the children and they are sometimes willing to share in the housework and even to go beyond gastronomic showmanship in the kitchen.

However, there are certain kinds of professions that I believe women could continue even while taking care of small children. Certain kinds of technical work and teaching, for example, certain kinds of research, certain fields

[5] What changes would be required in our society before women's situation could become more equal are outlined by Rossi (1964). In a more recent essay (1969), Mrs. Rossi distinguishes among pluralist, assimilationist, and what she terms hybrid models of equality between the sexes in which only the hybrid model offers women the chance to be equal to men on independent terms of individuals rather than the previously given cultural definitions.

within medicine (and dentistry) or in the law, some of them lacking in glamor perhaps but of enormous social usefulness. However, women seldom choose professions with such thoughts in mind. Although they reject behaving like princesses and having others take care of their children and housework, they are inclined to feel that they and the society can afford their working at a level well below their potential talents. As already noted, many bright college women enter the labor force insufficiently trained, and they frequently have a series of more or less temporary jobs. It would be a mistake to see this situation as an entirely negative phenomenon. Some are seeking to build lives in which their occupational commitment is only an aspect of a larger commitment to their own personal development, their families, and their civic responsibilities. Others, however, like some young men of hippie or radical leanings, may make believe that all careers are in some measure stultifying, and that since they cannot be truly creative in so corrupt and over-organized a society, they might as well take any odd job that brings them into contact with human beings who are not totally disagreeable. This mode of thinking, though it seems to me a vast overgeneralization, allows many people to find fulfillment in work without high status or visibility, work that can draw on talents for nurturance and support of others and that in a more competitive era would have been suppressed.

Indeed, my quarrel is less with the actual decisions young women make than with the lack of thought and planning during college concerning what one needs to learn now in order to be free to make choices later. Some may not even be able to look ahead to their immediate post-college years when certain choices may be closed to them in or out of marriage because they have not had sufficient training to earn enough to make either themselves or their potential spouses independent of short-run necessities. Still more is it difficult for young women while in college to look ahead to the time when the last child of their not-yet-existent family will have been grown and flown and when they will have many years of energetic usefulness left but insufficient preparation in terms of a skill or a profession for reentering the work-force in an interesting way.[6] My own judgment is that a young woman who in college has mastered a subject with passionate intensity, almost irrespective of what it is, is prepared by that very fact to immerse herself in another subject when she wants to become again fully employed—it is like learning a new language after she has already learned one or two. But I see many young people of both sexes who drift through college hoping that they will

[6] Alice Rossi's (1969) essay cogently critizes this empty-nest view of women's careers as a concession to prevailing masculine requirements for domestic caretakers. She argues that more flexible men would make possible more simultaneous two-career families but that this situation would in turn require great changes both in social institutions to care for children and in the values by which men and women both live.

fall into a subject that interests them much as they hope they will fall in love, not realizing that one has to work at it a bit and that it does not come through waiting.

## Educating Women

Yet it is also true that, at every level of schooling, women are on the whole more responsive and responsible than are men. As infants and children they have been raised and taught by people of the same sex, against whom they do not feel they must establish a separate identity in the way that many boys feel they must vis-à-vis mothers and female elementary school teachers. Huck Finn had to "light out for the Territory." A study by Michael Maccoby (1960) of sixth grade boys and girls in a Brookline, Massachusetts public school concluded that the relation of girls to what they learn was less contaminated or blocked by struggles over authority and the role of the sexes than it was with boys; the girls could respond both to the teacher and to the subject matter without feeling that they were being sissies or subordinated. Whether this situation is in the educational interest of girls or not depends on many factors. Sometimes in the past I have felt that college women, being far less likely to bluff than boys, have a harder time focusing on the one exciting course they are taking while at the same time protecting their standing in all their other courses.

Let me put this matter another way. I would hypothesize that young women respond to the instructor as a person; they hate to let him down—and paradoxically this feeling sometimes leads young women to be reluctant about getting deeply involved in their majors, lest they do let their professor down if they drop the field for marriage or a less demanding career. (I make this statement in the face of our folklore and novels that are full of sexy college girls who beguile their professors into giving them good grades and recommendations.)

These marginal differences in the way the two sexes approach teachers and learning led me to suggest in the commencement address that I gave at Bennington College (Riesman, 1964) that for a certain number of young women it made sense to have a period in their education, perhaps before college or perhaps in college, when they were not thrown with men inside the classroom. This idea seemed to me especially true for certain kinds of rather shy young women, not eager or self-confident enough to compete with domineering young men, particularly since male students are quite free about talking in discussions whether they have done the reading for class or not, and perhaps especially if they have not. Furthermore, since even in our emancipated day men matter slightly more to women than vice versa, college women have in general fewer defenses against being preoccupied with men;

they have fewer hobbies and same-sex diversions. Women are not able even in a womens' college to create the solidarity that is at least adumbrated or hoped for among other disadvantaged groups such as blacks. This situation is understandable, since women are tied as daughters, sisters, girlfriends or spouses to men, whether they like it or not; they cannot create an autonomous subculture of women, except perhaps in a convent (and seldom happily there). Women must live in the enemy camp, perhaps one reason why the tone of the Women's Liberation Movement at times has become so shrill. Correspondingly, a women's college may provide a few islands of temporary solidarity among women, and some intense friendships (although because we live in a less innocent time today, same-sex friendships are often viewed with a certain apprehension, just as cross-sex friendships without sex may be difficult to sustain.) [7]

What I am talking about is a matter of degree and emphasis. It reflects my experience as a teacher in coeducational institutions and as a visitor to women's colleges. It used to be that women in the non-co-ed college could be more scholarly than in the co-ed one, since they did not have to prove to men by their fluttering eyelids and inability to do math that they were truly feminine and properly humble. In this connection, one finding of the Smith survey on attitudes toward coeducation is striking. Girls majoring in the sciences or mathematics were most apt to have come to Smith originally because it was not co-ed, and were most apt to prefer that Smith not go co-ed now. For a girl in a field still defined as masculine by our culture, a college where she can do her own thing without exposure to the daily slights of men or the daily awareness of other girls making much of their femininity and quantitative incompetence may have a certain appeal.

The point in their lives at which young women have the opportunity to develop aspects of themselves that they would not reveal to men in what today is regarded as the artificial setting of a weekend or a date changes with place, social class, and circumstance. Some might profit best from a single-sex setting in junior high school, whereas many others might not need or want such an enclave at any point. In good colleges men are somewhat less defensive about having bright girls around, although the time of emotional and intellectual maturation is still not synchronized and both sexes may be more emancipated in their ideology than they can live up to in practice. Even if they come from one of the first families of America, American women lack the protections of aristocratic status in defining an independent position for themselves on the boundary between the sexes. They are subject to peer

[7] Robert Weiss' (1969) essay on the future of the family, cited earlier, speculates about the problems of sustaining intimacy outside marriage or proto-marital arrangements even in the face of the contemporary ideology that jealously is a mere hang-up, a legacy of sexual chauvinism or capitalist possessiveness.

definitions of sex role from which upper-class position cannot liberate them.[8]

In our chapter, "Feminism, masculinism, and coeducation," in *The Academic Revolution*, Christopher Jencks and I (Jencks & Riesman, 1968) concluded that the women's colleges did very little to protect women's opportunities to confront their specific problems of identity and vocation, and were at best a feeble hedge against the larger dilemmas confronting all American women. Nevertheless, I regret the stampede of virtually all single-sex colleges toward coeducation, just as I regret all other monopolistic definitions of the forms post-secondary education might take. I am inclined to think that those women's colleges that can hold out against the rush may have a future—if they can live so long. For one thing, in spite of the turbulence caused by black students at Vassar and white students at Sarah Lawrence, none of the women's colleges have seen the kinds of disruption and even violence that some of the leading co-ed colleges have endured. Indeed, I have seen it argued that men in co-ed settings become more violent when women taunt them for lacking courage and honor and compete with them, much as white and black students sometimes compete to demonstrate militancy. Even so, a young woman who in the future decides to attend one of the residual colleges that out of inertia or tradition or whatever else has remained non-co-ed may fear that she is getting in with a group of other women as queer as herself. Faculties may not want to teach in such places—and a good deal of the rush toward coeducation on the women's side reflects the problem of recruiting male faculty who prefer the stimulation and combativeness of male students—and distrust those women students who go through the sound barrier, putting them down as bitchy or castrating—women today are often damned if they are docile and damned if they are not. Furthermore, quiet responsive listening is often mistakenly interpreted as docility by faculty members used to the norm of male aggressiveness.

## Coda

In what I have said, I recognize that there are many idiosyncratic elements and individual choices that lead up to a collective decision. For example, some Smith College students of science may have already decided in high school that men were a bore and that the less they had to do with them, the better. Science may have been for them a way of putting men off, or at least postponing them, in the way a number of young women I know have preferred horses to men while in secondary school.

---

[8] One can think of many analogies here. In Great Britain an Earl who is also a Communist is regarded by the society as another one of those lordly eccentrics, whereas in America a scion who is a Communist has no protection from hierarchial values against egalitarian attacks.

However, when students talk about what is a more natural setting, these subtle questions about the timing and phasing of the stages of life get lost. We are, of course, the products of our culture, including not only our larger national or world culture, but even our most immediate culture of the hearth, the family culture in which we grew up. All human activities are refracted through the medium of culture, and the very notion that some activities are more natural than others has itself a cultural history and represents an ideological or fashionable view, intended to build up some activities and people and to denigrate others. The argument for coeducation, that it is more natural for boys and girls to work and live together now since they will live together later, seems to me feeble. What matters is how one best prepares for living together later and this preparation may not necessarily mean living together now. As I need not tell most of you, thoughtful adults today are extremely unsure of themselves when it comes to deciding such matters for young people and, hence, often leave it to the young people themselves. But the result of this indecision may be only to leave the young people to each other's not always tender mercies without the opportunity for a dialectic between detachment and involvement that in some measure the women's colleges provided in the past.

Whether that dialectic has a future, I do not know. In our selective colleges, young men and women face analogous dilemmas of privilege. Both face the impulse to sacrifice the future on behalf of the burning present. Both may be taunted and tempted to sacrifice what is elite or precious or special by the argument that doing so will help the less privileged—although I myself would contend that to pull down the heights of culture will not help fill its abysses. Both sexes face the problem of living at a time when many people doubt whether our institutions are viable or can be redeemed through the ordinary processes of democracy and incremental reform. Such desperate waves of feeling have occurred before in American history, in the great movements of religious revival and in the crusading fervor that spent itself in the Civil War. Thus it is hard to know whether American women have come to claim their inheritance at a moment in history when the society is on the verge of disaster or not. Surely we are living at a time when the old American boosterism and complacency have vanished or become nearly attenuated, not only among the educated, but quite generally. Some soured idealists have responded by an indiscriminate nihilism. Others, more patient, are experimenting with new lifestyles in the hope that these will spread. Still others are spreading the alarm not only about war and racial (and sometimes sexual) oppression, but about a whole congeries of problems such as environmental pollution that are in a sense the legacy of earlier advances. Some prophecies of disaster prove themselves true; others serve to spread the alarm. Yet even if our society is desperate, I would like to defend students who postpone political involvement and get other sorts of education first; and even if I am mistaken about that aspect, I am more certain that they should not be coerced into such involvement before they are ready for it, and that they should have the right to choose its timing, as of their marital involvement. Some of you may well regard these views as overprotective. Perhaps others of you will conclude that, precisely because the future is so cloudy and uncertain, it may be worth your while to prepare for a distant future; and by doing so you may possibly help create that future.

## REFERENCES

CHAPLIN, D.
Domestic service and the rationalization of household economy: Outline for a comparative study.
Unpublished paper, Department of Sociology, University of Wisconsin, 1968.

FUCHS, L. H.
"Those peculiar Americans": The Peace Corps and the American national character.
New York: Meredith Press, 1967.

GREENFIELD, M.
Smith Revisited (I).
The Washington Post, May 12, 1969. (a)

GREENFIELD, M.
Smith Revisited (II).
The Washington Post, May 17, 1969. (b)

JENCKS, C., AND RIESMAN, D.
The academic revolution.
Garden City, N.Y.: Doubleday, 1968.

MACCOBY, M.
The game attitude.
Doctoral dissertation, Harvard University, 1960.

OLMSTED, M. S.
Character and social role.
American Journal of Sociology, 1957, 43, 49–57.

PROCTOR, M. E.
Why a (Princeton) woman can't be more like a man.
Princeton Alumni Bulletin, May 13, 1969, pp. 10–12.

RIESMAN, D.
Constraint and variety in American education.
Magnolia, Mass.: Peter Smith, 1954.

RIESMAN, D.
Some continuities and discontinuities in the education of women.
In D. Riesman, Abundance for what? Garden City, N.Y.: Doubleday, 1964. Pp. 320–344. (a)

RIESMAN, D.
Two generations.
In R. J. Lifton (Ed.), The woman in America.
Boston: Beacon Press, 1964. Pp. 72–97. (b)

RIESMAN, D.
The lonely crowd, 20 years after.
Encounter, October, 1969, pp. 1–5.

RIESMAN, D., GUSFIELD, J. AND
GAMSON, Z.
*Academic values and mass education.*
Garden City, N.Y.: Doubleday, 1970.

ROSE, P. I.
The pulse of the campus.
Smith College and the issue of coeducation. Report No. 1.
Northampton, Mass., April, 1968.
(Mimeo.) (a)

ROSE, P. I.
The views of the faculty.
Smith College and the issue of coeducation. Report No. 2.
Northampton, Mass., May, 1968.
(Mimeo.) (b)

ROSSI, A. S.
Equality between the sexes: An immodest proposal.
In R. J. Lifton (Ed.), *The woman in America.*
Boston: Beacon Press, 1964. Pp. 98–143.

ROSSI, A. S.
The beginning of ideology: Alternative models of sex equality.
*The Humanist,* 1969 (Sep./Oct.).

WATLEY, D. J.
Career or marriage?: A longitudinal study of able young women.
National Merit Scholarship Corporation, 1969.

WEISS, R. S.
Marriage and the family in the next generations.
Unpublished paper, 1969.

# 8. Voices in the Yard

## THOMAS J. COTTLE

Even if perfect social justice and complete freedom from want were to prevail in a world at peace, rebels would still be needed wherever the world is out of joint, which now means everywhere. Rebellion permeates all aspects of human life. It originates from the subconscious will of mankind not to surrender to destructive forces.

René Dubos, *So Human an Animal*

Eternal youth is impossible, for even if there were no other obstacles, introspection would make it impossible.

Franz Kafka, *Diaries II*[1]

The rain, which had threatened for hours the morning of the bust, finally came about eleven o'clock. Being inside the courthouse, no one could tell, but the straggly hair and soggy clothing of the people who ran inside into the ugly safety of the giant lobby made it clear that the sky finally had opened.

There's always a feeling in a courthouse that all the people bustling about, disappearing behind and reappearing through the padded swinging doors with the oval window, are all involved in and deeply committed to your case, even if it's just a parking violation. Certainly, that morning, everyone must have been concerned with the Harvard and Radcliffe students locked up somewhere in the iron and concrete basement of the East Cambridge, Massachusetts, Courthouse. Certainly everyone knew of the SDS take-over of University Hall on April 9, 1969, and the Harvard University administrations' decision and the bust in the stillness of the early hours of the 10th. Certainly, too, everyone has a clearcut and distinct political knowledge and position from which he

From *Time's Children: Impressions of Youth* (Boston: Little Brown, 1971), pp. 255–271; 279.

155

cannot be budged, a sense of camaraderie, and a definition of the enemy from which his very life takes meaning. And everything and everyone and all the words and rhetoric, expectations and deeds are sweetly and undeniably political or legal. Certainly that's all true.

In the courtroom itself at about nine-thirty, amidst the steam and mugginess of a saddened weather and ritualized order of the law, a tall man spoke of the car accident he had sustained at the intersection of two nearby streets. Arresting police officers listened along with a judge and bailiff and the others. The important case had not yet come up.

"Where are the kids? I want to speak with the kids."

"They'll be up in due time."

Somewhere behind a thick, black metal door, young people waited for arraignment proceedings. Only one's fantasies spoke of their condition: if only you could get to them.

"Why can't we see them? I've got brothers in there."

A bevy of lawyers hustled around before the judge as four young men were led upstairs at the back of the courtroom and took their places on hard benches. The proceedings had begun. Those in attendance strained to see them and hear even a word of the rehearsed and linear mutterings of functionaries. The pattern was soon evident. The students would ascend from the jail by fours, men first, women to follow, in alphabetical order. Each case, each human being would be arraigned for criminal trespassing and put into the care of his own recognizance or issued a bail fee if assault and battery charges had been tacked on. Then, in a staggered line of people, they would be set free to find rides back to Harvard and to their homes, temporary and permanent. It seemed a reasonable procedure, the only one, perhaps, allowing each case to be assessed individually, but, as one student explained, it also had the effect of preventing a mass disorder or demonstration. For him it was in effect a neutralizing and dispersal strategy.

So they ascended by fours and were released one by one. For the most part, none had friends in the courtroom. A few, however, would emerge from behind the low balustrades to be greeted by someone. They would shake hands, embrace, clasp arms, run their fingers through someone's hair. A few times a teacher would put his arm around a boy and pull the boy's head down to his shoulder. The students were in fact like soldiers back from some inexplicable and foreign war, and the people waiting behind, at home, equally brave, were saying, as best they could, be proud of your tears and your efforts.

The reports from students of the events were varied save for one detail, the violent horror of the bust and the total unfairness of the act. "There was so much hatred in that building," a freshman boy had said. "You could see it in their eyes. They hated us. They hated." Another commented on the size of the state troopers. "They were so large. So damned large. So enormous. We locked arms and were willing to go peacefully, really, you know, but they were swinging everywhere, breaking anything." Still another young man told of the noise, the shouting and screaming, the mace, the wet cloths in case of tear gas, and the thumping and clubbing, the people falling, dragging each other down, being yanked by the hair, and being shoved viciously into a dean's office, a desk or cabinet slamming against someone's spine. And always the noise.

One by one they came out of the courtroom, a slow process, seemingly unending. One hundred eighty-four people seems so many, so few. Every once in a while one saw fresh head wounds and the swollen welts of purple and red flesh and jagged stitch marks and the blood on the back of their necks and on their shirts or dresses. There were rumors of someone having sustained a broken back after falling through or being pushed out of a window. The students wondered about this. Some offered help. But the faces of these people seemed so active, so pure, even as the sullen fatigue and fury of the night flushed all color deeper, deeper inside. Within the courtroom, in the rear, some older people, the audience, looked on, some laughing, totally amused at the sight of frizzy-haired boys and girls in an array of grotesque costumes. Two postmen came in to watch, rested awhile, then returned to their East Cambridge routes.

Outside the courtroom at the edge of the circular lobby a young man and woman sat facing each other, their legs pulled up under their chins, their heads buried together in and among their entangled arms and legs and hair. They were weeping. They explained to me that they had not been in the bust, but they refused my offer of help. Now they simply couldn't take it anymore and so in their love and friendship together they cried.

When finally some of us could make arrangements to bring in food on the pretext that we had brothers and sisters inside, the jail scene was disclosed to us. All of the girls were penned together. Some sat on the cold floor along the walls, their legs either stretched out, touching the girl on the opposite wall, or tucked under them. Many asked for cigarettes. Then a chant erupted: "We want food. We want food. We want food." Their energy spent, they soon were quiet again. The boys were located in three or four cells, all very crowded. One cell was nothing more than the receiving garage where presumably all the students were dumped on their arrival. The back of this area had a metal door which kept these prisoners from the outside. A flat light stretched along the bottom of the door permitting two boys to read a newspaper. There was no place for them to sit except the floor. I spoke with a friend here. His tired face lit up. "They want cigarettes. Can you get some cigarettes?"

"Have you got any food on you? You know, like a candy bar?"

"What's happening on campus? I'm all right."

"Hey, where's Bill?"

"I heard you had been hospitalized?"

"He ran away before the cops came."

"No," he laughed.

The girls, behind criss-cross metal grating, watched us. The jailors walked around behind, peering into the cells. Clutching slips of paper they lined up the next foursome at the dor where the stairs leading up to the courtroom began.

"Are all the kids from the hospital back?"

"Yeah. Everyone's fine. I think, though, one girl broke her back."

They were leaning in, our faces now inches apart, all of our hands wrapped around the base of the window opening between the anteroom and this garage-type chamber.

In another cell I spoke to some SDS leaders. One was almost completely hoarse, an ugly bump appeared high on his nose. "We're all right. What's happening on campus?"

"Who is that? Is he on the faculty or a dean?"

"They're meeting. The students are meeeting in the church. They're angry and something's happening."

"What the hell are you doing here?"

"Good."

Around the edges of this cell other boys sat, utterly exhausted. I knew many of them as indefatigable workers and talkers. Now, however, without strength they looked thin, hideously weary but not yet beaten. It was nothing short of bizarre to see students from Lowell and Adams Houses, Sever, Emerson and William James Halls in jail. But their sentencing this morning was just the beginning. This was but the first strategy. They had to get out now, to meet again. To organize.

"The students aren't going to help. They're going to be seduced by the bust and not be aware of the issues. We've got to get back and speak in all the houses. Is Alex here?"

"No, he wasn't busted."

"Any food yet?"

"Oh, wow. What's Afro doing?"

"Tell that guy you'll bring in the food. He's O.K. He'll let you."

"I don't know."

"Are there deans and teachers upstairs?"

"Hey, officer. Sir. This guy says he'll get us some food. O.K.?"

"A couple."

"Yeah, I'll bet. Do we have enough bail money? You know what they did? They hid drugs on someone and got him on a narcotics rap."

"I'd give my arm for a peanut butter sandwich."

"No, that's not exactly right. I heard someone had tranquilizers and when the cops came in he threw the bottle away and someone picked it up. Why the hell is it taking so long?"

"Are we next? Where are they now?"

"They're up to the L's."

Upstairs in the business office opposite the courtroom a young blond woman stood hour after hour arranging for bail money. The students required to post bail came in, gave the information asked of them and lifted their right hands as they recited some words. A few were so exhausted they could barely repeat the oaths. Their right hands raised just above their hips, they dragged at cigarettes or shoved chocolate bars into their mouths with their left hands. Everyone about looked at their hair or clothes or partook of some bizarre prattle. It all was as if it wasn't happening. "Well, honey, if I had to be locked up, I'd like to be locked up with you." And she would smile and drag out some more bail money.

Early in the afternoon the women started coming out. The bail money was holding up and a transportation service back to campus had formed. Over and over again the procedure of bail was explained and the many rumors were clarified. Still stunned, one girl could speak only of how handsome the police had seemed. "They were tall, with slim aquiline noses. I remember their freshly pressed uniforms, baby blue. They looked like movie star extras." Another girl, relieved to get out, told of her impatience for many of her colleagues who had worried only about themselves. Frightened, they had lost the sense of company and the spirit of locked arms. But now, even as they signed release papers, everyone's intentions clearly were to return to resume and fight for their demands. "We've got to get organized. People have got to regroup." Before half of them had departed a meeting was scheduled for that night.

I, too, returned to the yard for a meeting, in Sever Hall, where the very next morning SDS pickets would circle the entrance arch, urging students to boycott classes. The meeting in Sever had been in session for some time when I arrived and I entered the room as, quite literally, a "point of grammar" was being raised. For an instant, a group of faculty members were stuck on the proper wording of a statement, and though they laughed their tension and concern were evident. Indeed, it was all evident now: the occupation of the building, the bust, the demands by these certain students that Harvard stop its expansion into Cambridge and abolish ROTC, that amnesty be granted to the sitters-in, that the faculty stay united, and that everyone respond to the ignominious fact that campus unrest, turmoil, violence, or whatever it's called had like thunder pounded down upon Harvard.

Not so very many years ago, I drove my father down Memorial Drive; that's the drive on the "Harvard side" of the river. He wanted to be shown the boundaries of Harvard and the Massachusetts Institute of Technology. I recall the power I felt showing him the long riverbank expanse of our campus and bragging of Harvard's capacity to purchase, to eat up, really, the property it needed so that it could huff and puff its way toward MIT. Almost as great, MIT, presumably, was doing the same thing, so that soon, I reasoned, Cambridge for all intents and purposes would be one incredible university. Nowadays they are called multiversities. The two schools seemed like marvelous giant machines, chewing up houses and people and spitting them out over their shoulders, and I and my whispering generation were all a hungry part of it, watching the destruction and construction, loving every new inch of Harvard and its gorgeous expanding brain, and hoping that someday Harvard might own it all. It was like playing Monopoly and having those unfortunate losers land right smack on your hotels on Boardwalk and Park Place.

God, it was great! All those little shacks and houses falling down would all be shoved aside for the monster brain eating its way to Boston, Somerville and Watertown. If only MIT wouldn't beat us to it. But they couldn't; how could they match our money and power and brains? Soon it would all be ours, and in those drives I would just about believe that it would be mine as well. My father used to ask questions about relocation or dislocation, but those terms, I used to think, had to do with higher economic strategies and no freshman or sophomore could be expected to deal with that. These were issues for my father's friends. It was adult talk.

But there are new respresentatives in this generation. The whisperers, dreamers and entrepreneurs remain, of course, but of the many voices within one single human being, some now are screaming. The prideful Monopoly game we used to observe, its tin markers trespassing on our own and other's real estate, have been thrown in our faces by a growing few, a noisy, knowing few. Then, when these voices are momentarily stilled, more voices are heard until a chorus of almost ten thousand persons fills a stadium to vote for demands and for the legitimacy of making demands so that they might whack their own blow at society's skull with the force of thousands shooting a right arm obliquely upward and outward toward some great marvelous plan, and screaming one word, STRIKE! STRIKE! STRIKE! STRIKE! STRIKE!

Somewhere in childhood each of us learns what essentially is the concept of *simultaneity*. We learn that many things happen in the world at precisely the same instant, so that while we eat or read or study, others are sleeping or fighting or dying. We learn that while young persons sweat out the hours before an arraignment, grocers whose valuable goods will refurbish these persons haven't yet read about a bust or maybe don't care that much about the whole thing. We learn that while a totally unprecedented political convention meets in a football stadium, lacrosse-playing colleagues of the conventioneers run through their warmup drills, and that while a faculty's liberal caucus meets on the second floor of a building, it barely hears itself above the unrecognizable score of a college musical comedy in dress rehearsal on the floor below.

To comprehend simultaneity means also to comprehend ambivalence. For apart from any choir or chorus or convention to which we have committed our voice for even a week, we alone possess innumerable voices: defiance along with doubt, concentrated anger along with exquisite fright, movement toward radical reform along with a prayer to keep things exactly as they are forever. It means fabrics of death wishes trimmed in hopes for immortality, and discrete strikes yielding diffuse guilts and a fluid shame. It means certainty and uncertainty, cogency and ambiguity, pleasure and pain. To one boy it meant occupying Harvard's University Hall, then moving out and walking about Cambridge, occupying the hall again, moving out again, this time so that he might telephone his parents. When they could not be reached, it meant returning. Then, wrapped with three others in the warmth of a blanket, a moist cloth in hand should tear gas be used, it meant bedding down to wait out a sordid and ugly night.

How often during those days did students speak of their phone conversations with parents. "Three thousand dollars a year and you're striking." "Go to it, son. Get yourself involved. I never did. And congratulations." "How could it happen at Harvard?" These were the phone calls, but the letters of alumni to their modern representatives and scion in the yard which the *Harvard Crimson* and *Alumni Bulletin* reprinted came to much the same thing.

Not surprisingly, messages of this sort made the sense and burden of the ambivalence even more exasperating: "I would have felt better if my father had opposed me right out. His siding with me only confused me more. Maybe someday I'll be free of them (my parents). I kept hoping that the strike wasn't going to be the thing that would drive us apart. They made me decide between studying, going back to work, or striking. No, that's not right. They made me decide between them and politics. I've never been involved this way. I can't go to the library when SDS is meeting. There's too much going on, and, you know, there's more here than books and lectures. They don't undersatnd this . . . maybe they do . . . I don't know."

Much has been written about student revolutionaries, their seemingly inevitable upper middle class permissive parents, their superior intelligence, etcetera. But the often conflicting data from these studies only underscore the themes of ambivalence and simultaneity. For no human law prevents young people from manifesting the special warmth toward fathers Kenneth Keniston found in his study *The Young Radicals*, or the especially intense hostility toward fathers which a college senior recently reported in a thesis about his own political colleagues. If students in fact are preserving the politics forsaken by their parents, there may well be feelings of resentment, first, for having been psychologically coopted into this "profession," and, second, because their parents failed in it and chose instead business as usual. (All the same, the time seems right to "study" administrators and faculties, who by their actions or inactivities, that is by their own ambivalence almost make strikes and busts required courses of action.)

Faculty members, too, during these special "Harvard months," knew the ambivalence. The more they dug into the politics and meetings the more they sought ways of climbing out. "If the university's changing, what the students don't know is that the faculty may want out and have already found better places, different places to live and work." More than ever, there was mumbling of being around physically but pulling out spiritually.

But most poignant of all, perhaps, is the need to understand, to have the "whole mess figured out," analyzed—analyzed in the language of law, history, sociology or psychology, but somehow analyzed and thereby settled. A few days after the bust, with the buildings of Harvard veritably cracking under the force of meetings, caucuses, planning sessions, leaflet writing, multilithing and all the rest, a letter had been printed in the *Crimson* offering, ever so succinctly, the Oedipal interpretation of building take-overs and letter box pilfering. This represented, presumably, the reasonable and assiduous action for some. For others, the events seemed absolutely incomprehensible except for two issues: first, there was a pernicious evil in the world, actualized by the imperialistic invasion of Southeast Asia and maybe of Cambridge as well; and, second, Harvard was implicated. Whether it was through the corporation's investment of money, ROTC, the administration's irresponsibility, the faculty's posture of business as usual, Afro-American studies, or expansionism, Harvard itself seemed to be reeling from its own crude but effective arraignment and brutalizing day and night in court. Just who exactly, they asked, trespassed on whom or on what?

Does it not seem like trespassing when one heaps his values and philosophies of education upon us as if they were heavy burlap sacks of onions? And isn't it only natural, only human that we should reach back blindly for some feel or, better yet, handful of precedent upon which to lean? Isn't this after all where religion starts and where the very concept of history derives its life force? But why can't the young take our precedent, our history, our time, as immoral as they may be, as their own, and be thankful and done with it? Have they rejected our precedents and time? Do they now see in history only the efficacy of events like those occurring at Columbia, Nanterre, Berkeley and Chicago? Perhaps their sense of time implies the setting of new precedent rather than the acceptance of it, or the wish to prestructure the future rather than worship the stillness of a literary past. Theirs, after all, is the time of the now and the "us," not the inauthenticity of all the rest of "them" and last night, most especially last night and early this morning.

Well, apart from these magnificent schemes of time and space, it seemed as though the yard would be rippled by the contradictory tugs of the students toward a disjunctive relevance and, if necessary, disengagement, and of the faculty toward reasonableness, unity and, above all, continuity and grace.

Nonetheless, from the moment University Hall was "liberated," each of us not only sought an understanding and workable strategy for settlement, we also resorted to a new and strange vocabulary. Perhaps it is "back-room" political talk left over from high school government days, or "Parliamentese," perhaps "intellectualese." Whatever it is, as it comes to be employed replete with marvelous but overused terms like "negotiable," "legitimacy of demands," and "friendly amendment" and its rules of a special and sacred social grammar, one feels the chill of an exhilarating, fresh, maybe omnipotent involvement only to discover that so much and so many have been dehumanized. Is this the purpose of such a language? Even the students, as direct and honest as they have been, as clever or injudicious as they may seem, have a way of lapsing into dehumanizing language which makes it seem that from time to time they, too, forget that at the root of any violent or nonviolent political demonstration are people: administrators, deans, teachers, students, peasants, workers, policemen, people.

Two of these people, policemen in fact, who several nights before had liberated University Hall in their own way, spoke of the sitters-in as good people, "doing their job as we do ours, I suppose." Neither had been inside Harvard before. One couldn't remember ever before being in Cambridge for that long a time. Quite easily they recalled their anger and sense of a part pride in, part embarrassment over their action. They were put off by the girls, and as they spoke I tried to put together in that inevitable hunt for analysis their feelings of the erotic nature of the arrests with the not quite carnival, but ocean-liner-about-to-depart eroticism some of us had felt in the building that night. Touching bodies even in the course of sitting-in or making arrests is a not so simple part of anyone's job. Funny, the police, even in their street clothes, were handsome men, movie star extras maybe. They hated anarchists, resented rich kids, but not as much as violence. They hoped that "a small minority wouldn't ruin one of the really good places left in the commonwealth." In but a few moments with them, I thought they seemed confused, somewhat washed out by the arrests, and thoroughly ingenuous. I was uncomfortable speaking with them. They knew it and helped as best they could to put me at ease.

Like many others, I am always impressed by how gentle these "central figures of violence" seem, both the "cops" and the "kids." Surely many of the students are. Almost despite their layers of battle plans and divisions of the world into us and them, a forthrightness and sweet gentleness slips through. On the evening following the faculty's decision to defer debate on the Afro-American studies program, I saw and spoke with angry, bitter and hurt students. Single file they stalked out of a closed meeting like a professional football team retuning to the field, while the rest of us stood around seeing how many we knew by name or would even speak with us. Having pledged themselves to the sacredness of their program and of their very destiny, these people were out to do battle. They had spoken a bit, in private, naturally, of a little history they too thought worthwhile preserving.

Yet with all the battle readiness of this handsome cadre, I couldn't help but think of the young women who that afternoon, hours before, had stood watching their tall, white faculty emerge from the Loeb Drama Center. Patiently the women had waited through discussions about a Committee of Fifteen, ROTC and university expansion only to learn that fatigue and mysterious pressures would win out over the urgency of their demands for a Black Studies department and with it, as they say, a new day. The women had just stood there on that Brattle Street curb crying. And how many centuries of ritualized order and precedent kept us from touching and comforting them? Couldn't someone just have arisen to proclaim, finally, what was at stake and what after all has worth? Were all the genuine heroes gone forever?

Even without them, a change in the conception of the Harvard family had occurred. What had worked in the maintenance of an elite and rather awesome kinship group seemed as if it wasn't going to work any longer. Children who once seemed "illegitimate" now were climbing into rather central roles, while distant elderly relatives, the ones who visit once a year at graduation, had come under a most unbecoming attack. They had been advised to stay around all the time or cease visiting. The outside was inside and the inside had everted itself. "We're right at the center of everything," a student mused. "You remember when you're a child and your older brother is the big star, or your big sister is doing all the things? Now it's us, we're right in the center reading about ourselves in the newspaper. It's youth. Everything is youth and us."

How ironic it seems that the occupation, such as it was, took place in the very center of Harvard, and that the bust meant an invasion by foreign police and other guardians of the law like deans. There was, furthermore, all the talk by parents like If Harvard doesn't throw you out, we'll reach in and pull you out. But expulsion meant leaving, whereas sitting in meant staying. With this, not so incidentally, came the justifiable fear that expulsion decrees might be leveled when students were out for the summer. There was also talk of the incoming freshmen and how future admissions policies would be altered. Tomorrow's Harvard, someone quipped, will be comprised of Atlanta Jews, Scarsdale blacks and various, assorted but ever innocuous gentiles.

The outside was inside, the inside had everted itself, and the elite family structure of Harvard just shook. One corporation member, anyway, sat right up alongside SDS "rebels" under the hot lights of educational television. This spontaneous debate, which went on for hours, by its very form symbolized the sloshy fluctuations and realignments within the Harvard family, as every so often new people would come, and new facts, new issues, new political perspectives and new interactions doused in the juices of antipathy would be born. Then there would be a time out for an explication by members of the press.

One faculty member had said that in his early years at Harvard he saw the institution somewhat like a hotel, the faculty as resident hosts and the students as honorable guests, but guests nevertheless. Now he saw that it was really one large family.

But if it was that to him, it was more an expansive block party or budding commune to many of the students. For in their attempt to rap their elders they very explicitly registered votes for keeping the university open to the entire community, to the family of (elite) man, if you will. Their unanimous stadium vote to repudiate the corporation's right to close their university testified to this, as well as to many other things.

It hardly need be said that the occupation, the bust, the strike and the meetings of various sorts and duration didn't all go smoothly. In fact it's a little difficult to determine where exactly they were supposed to go. So many people were and remain bewildered. Decisions and ensuing political positions, predicated on carefully selected and measured bodies of data, collapsed like houses of cards or block towers erected by little boys when a better or brighter, louder or older person came along. Wednesday's dogma dissolved into the weekend's immaturity. Yesterday's satisfaction with reading *Crimson* and New York *Times* editorials was burned out in the conflagration of SDS, stadium and student residence house meetings. Boys living in the luxury of riverside towers sang evenly structured chorales about rent control, subsidy rates and negative income taxes. And a larger group than ever before spoke of the war. Over and over again, not just out of fear of the draft, they spoke of the war.

Saddest of all is not that while the strike went on athletes ran and played and Radcliffe honor students lay sunning half naked on the roofs of their dormitories; saddest of all, perhaps, is the fear among gifted people, among all people, that their dread of war, anger at the poverty in Appalachia, or the starvation in America, Biafra and India, or their disbelief of the expansion in Cambridge may be clichés. Saddest of all is that because Cronkite or Huntley-Brinkley portray so many scenes of a real war and real deaths and real misery that to "reiterate" these facts is "corny," "unoriginal," or "trivial." Suddenly, without cognitive warning, these events belong to the category "Well, I mean, you know." "It's just a cliché," one Harvard senior said in referring to his generation having grown up in the shadow of an atomic war. Despite the essays of Arendt and Keniston and the speeches by Wald, Spock and Chomsky, it's just a cliché.

But the A-bomb drills in third, fourth and fifth grades, the recollection of giggling children burrowing together under desks in the basement of the school and tittering about missing class minutes and what they would do if a war, whatever that meant, broke out on the hockey field or in the front hall or gymnasium has stayed with a certain group of students exactly like their shadows. And the gloom and inexplicable horror of it all, the fuzziness of the future and the commotion of the present have grown, just as the cliché says, like their very own shadows. Waiting for the cops to come as one crowds under a desk or rests his head on the angular frame of a file cabinet may, after all, symbolize a more contemporary form of A-bomb drill.

So, by God, the war broke out right in the middle of the yard, and before the Harvard faculty could even meet, the self-consciousness born of the various media's slogans and clichés choked off some people's feelings to the point where literally they could not budge, they could not take a step, they could not work. Or may be the feelings simply overwhelmed them and they cried, as they had cried some six years before when their President had been slain.

As the clichés reinforced the depersonalization of events like revolution and war, the impression of having seen unadulterated fear on the faces of policemen over six feet tall, on the faces of grown men masked in clear and shiny white plastic, made it all seem very human and frightening again, especially to those who waited through the night on the outside. Even weeks after the bust at least one form of the fright remained. It is terribly difficult to describe, much less explain, but it has to do, somehow, with feelings of the university being "brought down" or being no more, and a sense, I suppose, of the dissolution of the entire world and all human groups. It has to do with attacking authority, seen and unseen, then being repulsed and not being sure anymore what in fact constitutes honorable, decent authority or how it feels when one is manipulating someone or being manipulated.

It is not uncommon for persons in the throes of such actual battles to reaffirm their belief in an ultimate power which is intended mechanistically to control all behavior and action everywhere. It's a power almost in the guise of a fabulous secret or colossal master plan, hidden somewhere, who knows, maybe locked in a dungeon or in a University Hall file. It is spoken of often when violent transitions like beginnings or endings are about to take place or when the movement of the clouds suggests that a storm is moving in upon us. It's a manipulating power of sorts upon which one works out his feelings of dependence and independence, trust and mistrust. Usually it comes into play precisely when one publicly seeks personal autonomy or challenges for a right to control his fate. It takes the form of presidents, faculties, corporations, boards of trustees, and perhaps even God. But one thing is clear: there remains at Harvard College, and presumably elsewhere, a population which, although it may not be large, has not yet made either peace or war with this power and even today, years later, confesses to feelings of naughtiness if not guilt about its political urges as well as confusion if not despair.

Some students actually clapped at the news that soon after the bust a Harvard dean was striken and lay ill in a Boston hospital. Others, horrified and nauseated by the announcement, discovered that a certain strength they had employed and counted on for political action had died away. This just wasn't supposed to happen. This wasn't part of the bargain. But then again, neither were those forty cracked heads with the jagged stitches supposed to happen. So they were right back where they started, and nothing yet had been resolved.

Still, even with the naughtiness and confusion, a sense of prideful commitment to something has taken root in the lives of many students and faculty members. Although they may never have been revolutionaries, and although they probably have stopped attending SDS meetings, where they used to sit around the edges and in the balconies, they have changed. They have become "radicalized," as the saying goes; they have changed in a big way, and it has not been due simply to the fact that they saw their brothers abandoned by authority and clobbered in the middle of the Harvard Yard. More likely it is due to the fact that for all kinds of reasons, even with all of the ambivalence, they have become politicized. And when young bright minds imbibe facts and strategies while learning of the hypocrisy and immortality extant on their campuses, in their communities, and in their country, there's going to be trouble and there's going to be change. Only the tempo of this change seems incalculable.

One change, not of great proportion but of interest nevertheless, is the frequent description nowadays of "good people's" politics as radical. Only a few years ago among the middle class we used to hear (and say), "You'll like them. They're really bright, sensitive, liberal people." Now the same sentiment for the same people goes, "You'll really like them. They're involved, active, radical, good people." Or "They're just not the same now. They've been radicalized."

Of greater significance is the change in fighting back against unjust, insensitive authority. It is not, I feel, mere games or "acting out" of power that students display. Their strikes, boycotts, demonstrations of all sorts inevitably point to something horrible in their world, and in our world too. Their tactics and language may seem violent, unreasoned, unresonable, impetuous, angry, or whatever, but even their own ambivalence and our depersonalizing language cannot hide these horrible things. In their very actions, the students inform all powers how to stop campus revolts. Every day of their lives students point, however clumsily, to the problems and the exact geographical regions where these problems reside. And they just may be telling us, with their many voices, with their rage as well as their love, their intrusiveness as well as their reticence, their anarchy as well as their supreme rationalism, what we may have to do in order to survive. Although they so often are at the political scene before us, we both face embarrassment, severe costs and quite a unique danger.

Toward the end of the Harvard spring of 1969, as Harvard tried to get itself and its people and followers together, I received a letter from a Radcliffe College senior named Deborah Komaiko. The year before she had written me of her plan to do community work rather than honors academic work during her senior year. She felt simply that the former offered greater worth. Then, soon after the strike and the bust and the days of rain and brilliant sunshine, she wrote to me again:

"First, I abhor both sides for using the police as a universal punching bag in what amounts to an intra-class struggle. I did not approve of the tactics of taking the building. But I approved less of calling the police. Still, the frustration with this society has reached a point of no return for many. (It strikes me at this level: we can find ample justification for spending ten billion dollars a year to murder the Vietnamese, but we can't dig up two billion extra dollars to feed our own malnourished people!) This is my inheritance. This is the 'justice,' 'love,' and 'brotherhood' which I can claim a full adult right to! . . .

"How is a twenty-one year old woman supposed to be decent, humane, loving, committed, intelligent while still absorbing the myths of 'justice,' 'love,' and 'brotherhood' (not to mention 'academic freedom'). . . . Is poetry to be the solace, the escape, or the elitist corruption in my adulthood? Not that I expect you or anyone else to answer these questions. It will be agonizing enough looking for your own answers."

# 9. What Do They Really Learn at College?

## HOWARD S. BECKER

When we talk of education, we ordinarily refer to the conventional institutions in which it is carried on: elementary schools, secondary schools, colleges and universities, graduate and professional schools. When we talk of what students learn at school, we usually refer to the things adults want them to learn there. What do people learn as they grow up in our society? Where do they learn it? It may be that the important things that happen to students in college do not happen in the library, the laboratory, or in the classroom.

Most middle-class boys and girls graduate from high school and go on to college. Many, perhaps most, college-goers learn in college precisely what they need to know to get along as adults in a middle-class world. The middle-class worlds of business and the professions demand a number of specific skills and abilities and the experience of college is such as to provide college students with training in precisely those skill and abilities. I shall discuss a number of the demands made by the adult middle-class world, indicating in each case how the world of the college is organized to provide relevant training. Most of what I will talk about is not conventionally regarded as an important part of the college curriculum; nevertheless, these are matters which are important for college students while they are in school and afterward. They know it and they act accordingly.

## Independence from Home

Ours is one of the most mobile societies ever known. People move frequently and they move great distances. Unlike nomadic groups, they do not

From *Trans-action* I, no. 4 (May, 1964), 14–17.

move together, taking their families and communities with them. They move because opportunity beckons elsewhere and it beckons to individuals, not groups. Moving for the sake of opportunity is very common in the middle class. As more and more people enter itinerant professions or go to work for one of the national organizations which ships its men around from city to city, more and more members of the middle class find themselves, as young adults, leaving their homes, neighborhoods, and families behind and setting out for new territory. Friends, instead of being furnished almost automatically by family connections and neighborhood contiguity, must be made without that help. To make the break from family and community requires an independence of spirit that does not come naturally.

Going away to college provides a rehearsal for the real thing, an opportunity to be away from home and friends, to make a new life among strangers, while still retaining the possibilities of affiliation with the old. In the dormitory, and even more so in the fraternity and sorority, one finds himself on his own but at the same time surrounded by strangers who may become friends. One has the experience of learning to shift for oneself and making friends among strangers.

Further, all the little chores that one's family did for you now have to be taken care of in some other way. You get your own meals, take care of your own room, make your own bed, clean your own clothes. These are small things but difficult until one has learned to do them. They are a kind of training for the passage from home, whether it is geographical or simply the making of a new home upon marriage. Going away to college provides an opportunity to play at moving away from home for good and it prepares the youngster for the world in which he will have to live.

## Dating, Marriage, and Poise

We normally expect young people to achieve some kind of workable relationship with members of the opposite sex, to learn how to get along with them and eventually to choose or be chosen for marriage. For middle-class youth, the problem is complicated by the requirement of the adult work world that he choose a wife who will be "culturally adequate" for the circles his business or profession will require him to move in. He must acquire the ability to attract and marry the kind of woman who can run a proper house for him and entertain for him. And for women, this means that they must learn how to perform these functions in an adequate middle-class way. It means for both men and women that they must learn the kind of manners, poise, and cultural skills necessary to move in such a world and to attract such a mate.

Again, the college (and particularly the large state university) provides the proper kind of training. Although it is not part of the curriculum, training in manners, poise, and cultural skills is given in a wide variety of places on the campus. Fraternities and sororities specialize in it. Pledges are taught in formal classes how to introduce themselves to strangers, how to ask for a date or accept one, how to behave on a date, how to handle silverware at a formal dinner, and so on. The need for this training is obvious if one watches incoming freshmen during orientation week. The people who prepare dinners for these students know that, in order to avoid embarrassments, they had better not serve any strange dishes which require more than rudimentary skill with silver. The formal training is reinforced by constant practice. A stranger who walks into a fraternity house finds himself assaulted by a stream of young men rushing up to introduce themselves, fearing that if they do not one of the active members will punish them.

## The Marriage-Hunting Ground

The dating system and the round of formal and informal social functions provided by both the Greek system and the university proper provide a fine training ground for meeting the opposite sex and finding a proper mate. Some pledges are required to have a certain minimum number of dates per month; most students feel some vague pressure to date, even though they find it anxiety-provoking. By participating in a round of parties and social functions, students learn the kind of manners and poise necessary for the social functions, students learn the kind of manners and poise necessary for the social life of the country club or civic organization, skills that will stand them in good stead in their later middle-class lives.

In addition, many, though by no means all, students receive training in dealing socially with "important people." Fraternities, dormitories, and other kinds of student groups make a practice of inviting important people, both campus personages and visitors, to meet with them. Students may have experience socializing with the governor of the state, the chancellor of the university, national political figures, or important visitors from overseas.

## Work Skills

The middle-class occupational world demands a number of generalized work skills from its recruits. They must, first of all, acquire some skills needed for their prospective occupations which the university is set up to teach. It may be that they need to learn the analytic techniques of chemistry or engineering; they may need to learn the skills of reading, writing, and the use of a library. Whatever it is, the university has courses which teach them some of the knowledge and technique necessary to hold a job.

We must not overstate this. Many businesses, industries and professional and graduate schools feel that an undergraduate college cannot, or at least does not, teach the required skills in the proper way. They prefer to train their recruits from scratch. To this end, many firms have in-service training programs which provide the specific knowledge recruits need.

More important than the specific knowledge and techniques necessary for entrance into an occupation is a more generalized kind of work skill, one that in older days was referred to as "stick-to-it-iveness." The entrant into the middle-class occupational world must have the ability to see a job through from beginning to end, to start a projcet and keep his attention and energy focused on it until it is completed.

The ability to get things done does not come naturally to young people; it is a hard-won skill. In acquiring it, the middle-class youth must learn to defer immediate gratifications for those that are longer in coming; he must learn to give up the pleasures of the moment for the larger rewards that await a big job well done. Most students have not had to learn this in high school, where the parade of daily requirements and assignments places the emphasis on receiving the immediate gratification of having done this day's job well.

## College . . .

For many students, it is only when one reaches college that one is required to plan ahead in units of four or five months, keeping attention focused on the long-range goal of passing the course without the constant prodding of the daily assignment. In learning to organize himself well enough to get a good grade in a college course, in learning to keep his mind on one job that long, the college student learns the middle-class skill of getting things done, so important in business and industry.

Finally, the middle-class world demands of those who enter it that they be able to juggle several things at once, that they be able to handle more than one job at a time and to keep them straight. He must learn to manage his time successfully and not fritter it away in actions that produce no reward. At least some college students get magnificent training in how to budget time and energy. The kind of student, of whom there are many, who does well in his courses and at the same time is, let us say, a high-ranking officer in several campus-wide organizations and an officer of his fraternity or dormitory, learns that he cannot waste his time if he is to achieve anything. He learns to set aside particular times for study and not to allow anything to intervene; he learns to handle organizational matters with dispatch; he learns to give up or strictly ration the joys of watching television and drinking beer with the boys. He learns, in short, how to have a time for everything and to do everything in its time.

## Organizational Skills

The typical middle-class career now takes place in a bureaucratic organization. Even the professions, which used to be the stronghold of the individual practitioner, now tend increasingly to find the locus of their activities in a complex organization rather than a professional office; the doctor spends more of his time in the hospital and is responsive to the social control of the bureaucratically organized hospital, rather than practicing independently in his own office. The recruit to the middle-class occupational world requires, if he is to operate successfully in it, the ability to get along in a mass of organization and bureaucracy. If the rules and constraints of large organizations frighten or anger him, he will not be able to achieve what he wants nor will he be an effective member of the organization.

Among the specific things an effective member of a large organization must know and be able to do we can include the following: He must be willing and able to take the consequences for his own actions, to see ahead far enough to realize how what he does will affect others and the organization. He must have some skill in manipulating other people, in getting them to do what he wants without the use of force or coercion; he must learn to be persuasive. He must have the ability to compromise, to give up some of what he wants in order to gain the rest; he must not be a narrow-minded fanatic, who either has his way or not at all. And he must, finally, be knowledgeable and skillful in manipulating the rules and impersonal procedures of bureaucratic organizations to his own advantage, rather than being stymied and buffaloed by them.

## Rehearsal for Management

The network of extracurricular organizations characteristic of the large state university provides a perfect context in which to learn these skills. The student can participate in student politics, either as an active candidate or as a behind-the-scenes organizer. He can become an officer of one of the organizations that helps run campus activities. He can work on the student newspaper. He may be an officer of his fraternity or dormitory. A large number of students have experiences in one or more such organizations during their four years in college.

Melville Dalton, in tracing the antecedents of successful industrial managerial careers, argues that experience in this realm of campus life is a perfect background for success in industry.

Our observations at the University of Kansas corroborate Dalton's findings. Let me point out some sources of experience, important for the recruit to the middle-class occupational world. Many officers of campus organizations find themselves exercising responsibility for large amounts of money; they may administer budgets running as high as $50,000 a year. Some of them administer programs of activity in which it is necessary to coordinate the efforts of several hundred or more of their fellow students. You have only to think, for an example, of the effort and organization necessary for the traditional Homecoming Weekend at any big university.

Some students even have the experience of discovering that the important people with whom they come in contact have feet of clay. As they deal with officers of the university in the course of their organizational work, they discover that these officers may ask them to do things they regard as improper. A typical case, which occurs in many universities, arises when some university officer requests or attempts to coerce the student newspaper into not publishing matter he believes harmful to the university. The student reporters and editors discover, in such a situation, that university officials are, after all, only human too; it is a shocking and educational discovery for a nineteen-year-old to make.

## Motivation

The recruit to the middle-class world must, finally, learn to attach his own desires to the requirements of the organizations he becomes involved in. He must learn to have what we might call *institutional motivation*. He must learn to want things simply and only because the institution in which he participates says these are the things to want.

College provides practice at this linking of personal and institutional desires. The student learns that he requires, at the least, a degree and that he must do whatever it is the college asks of him in order to get that degree. This attachment to the long-range goal furnishes him with the motivation to continue in classes that bore or confound him, to meet requirements that seem to him foolish or childish. The college student learns to want to surmount the obstacles posed for him by the college, simply because they are there. He learns to regard these external obstacles as marks of his own ability and maturity, and because he interprets the obstacles that way, sees his success in college as a sign of his own personal worth. The ability to link institutional and personal desires is an important prerequisite for occupational success in adult life.

Through participation in the college community, the student comes to define himself as the kind of person who ought to have the skills of the middle-class occupational world. He pins his self-respect, his sense of personal worth, on acquiring them. He feels that he will have properly become an adult only when he has all these qualities and skills. He directs his effort and organizes his life in such a way as to achieve them and thus to prove to himself and others that he has grown up. It may be that these are the really important things he learns at college.

It is too bad that convention requires the college studiously to ignore what it really teaches students.

# SECTION IV

# Generational Ties

Although our everyday lives are lived in the present, unlike animals, we are capable of transcending that present. Through the use of language, the pre-eminent symbol system, we are able to communicate experience, to symbolize it, and to pass it on. Literary critics and film makers, with directors and writers, are most concerned with the nature of *images*: how the things of life are abstracted and represented in communication. Writers such as Daniel Boorstin (1964) and Murray Edelman (1966) have argued that the "shadow is the substance," that the symbolic representation of events can take precedence over the actual event itself. Boorstin suggests that this occurs because the abstraction can be created with all the built-in drama necessary to attract attention whereas reality may be diffuse, amorphous, long-standing, and distant.

We are often "victims of imagery." One of the most powerful discussions of role image was Betty Friedan's analysis of the image of women in the "women's magazines" (1963). She discovered that the working assumptions of the journalists who produced the magazines was that women were stupid, that they were incapable of grasping the implications of a complicated argument, and that they only read and comprehended articles with a "woman's slant." Further, when she content analyzed the magazines themselves, she found that the fiction stories portrayed the conventional housewife-hero, bound by children and home. Fewer and fewer women, when contrasted with stories in the 1930s, were portrayed as career women. In this analysis, Friedan discovered the potential power of an image of the family and the home to become *the* reality for many women. She argued that it precluded options for them, limited their horizons, and created a false picture of home life that suggested that dissatisfaction with it was mere carping.

177

Presentation of the images of family in magazines perpetuate the myth of the happy family: white, middle class, and suburban. As Bennett Berger has so nicely shown (1970), this myth of suburbia persists because it has important functions in American life. It suggests that success is still available to all, and that comfort and carefree life are lodged at the foot of the rainbow in a homogeneous suburbia. The family reigns supreme, while the pains of crime, racial tensions, and the like recede happily into the smoke of the central city.

But the split between image and reality may grow apace. As one groupie said about Mick Jagger, "I had dreamed so long of balling him, thinking that each sexual experience was O.K., but not Mick Jagger, that when I finally did ball him, I couldn't keep from thinking that it was O.K., but not Mick Jagger." As Cottle shows in the second excerpt from his book, *Time's Children* (1970), the imagery of roles may have the same quality—they lose their attractiveness as the reality becomes closer. Reality, being that which is real at a given time, that which is affirmed by significant others, can become discordant and detached, so that the self and the role played become only pale representations of each other. When the sense of reality impinges on the image, when the role of father, of mother, becomes more threatening than appealing, or simply a neutral phenomenon, the images eschew their socializing function.

In many respects, the image and the reality of the family is coming under heavy seige from all sides. But as Margaret Mead points out, there are as yet no institutionalized forms that can create the conditions for raising children found in the family. The future family may not be radically different in function (1971) (as analysts of the kibbutz have already pointed out), however, they may take new forms.

It is this adjustment and neutralization of the images of life that, as we have already argued, sets people adrift on their own resources and on their own attempts to make sense of the world. The search for alternatives to the family, as seen in the communes, in cohabitation, in group sex and wife swapping, may not indicate a disaffection with the functional requirements of marriage (other than the child-rearing functions), but more an alienation from the moral rules and cultural meanings that have traditionally surrounded and embedded family life. However, as Lifton suggests (below), the very openness to experience characteristics of the young, their quest for experience, can be a source of new and more viable alternatives for living together. This theme is echoed in Margaret Mead's selection in this book from her *Culture and Commitment* (1970). She argues that a new worldwide culture is evolving, and that the child-rearing and socialization processes that this new society requires are so new, that those most sensitive and able to learn will be the young. For they are entering an age where no other's experience can be a truly adequate guide. They must, with adult guidance and counsel, create their own images of life, and of family and home. The previous mold may have been irreparably cracked in the violent years of the 1960s.

# 10. Time's Children

### THOMAS J. COTTLE

On my last birthday I was ninety-three years old. That is not young of course. In fact it is older than ninety! But age is a relative matter. If you continue to work and to absorb the beauty in the world about you, you find that age does not necessarily mean getting older.

Pablo Casals, *Joys and Sorrows*

I have nothing to do, but watch the days draw out,
Now that I sit in the house from October to June,
And the swallow comes too soon and the spring will be over
And the cuckoo will be gone before I am out again.
A sun, that was once warm, O light that was taken for granted
When I was young and strong, and sun and light unsought for
And the night unfeared and the day expected
And clocks could be trusted, tomorrow assured
And time would not stop in the dark!

T. S. Eliot, *The Family Reunion*

Perhaps, too, it means examining one's priorities. Anyone who lives or works with young people knows that to look out across at them must be to look back at them, in a way, though not down at them. It is to look back at them across the grain and purpose of time. Often it seems so right being with people much younger; it "works," as the artist might say, since our times and life-styles seem to move together, cautiously but successfully. At other hours, however, as for example during the first few days of school each autumn, when we see the new crop and feel them to be so unjustly young, our

From *Time's Children: Impressions of Youth* (Boston: Little, Brown, 1971), pp. 311–318; 341–349.

respective times seem disjointed and the space between us seems unbridgeable. The feeling is like what parents feel when, in a moment of endless duration, they turn swiftly about only to discover that their children are no longer children, that they are no longer young and no longer wholly together as part of a family. The parents turn about and realize that their children have vanished, leaving as an after image a swirling glow in a suddenly sorrowful room. Parents and some of us who teach discover, too, that the children who depart take a chunk of time with them, an irretrievable chunk which makes us feel that we may never again get close to young people or, even worse, to the remnants of our own childhoods.

Sadly perhaps, gratefully perhaps we find that *the motion of young people everywhere is in a sense the motion of ourselves*. It is a reminder of the passing of our own private and unshared years as well as a conclusion to the public and social years we spend with children or as children. The motion of youth and the passage of years imprint time upon all of us, or at least upon those of us belonging to that generation now feeling its age. Children, certainly the very youngest people, it often seems to me, are time itself; not its embodiment, really, but its flame and reality. The future seems to them, or ought to seem, so open and endless, complicated, to be sure, but ultimately possible. And their past, I imagine, is unusually pure, even with all the errors and impertinences it contains. The hours of their past become friends with the present, and the present remains each second changed, barely altered by a culture and civilization which crash into the environments of the famous and the disenfranchised, the young and the old.

Time in these years of youth moved, as I recall, at its appropriate and appointed tempo, a tempo marked somewhere at the head of a logically computed but still artistic score. The moments of speeding advance and trudging retreat were all part of a plan for youth, all part of a temporal mechanics for living. The moments constituted a tempo that gave direction and motion to us even though our actions and sentiments must have seemed and maybe still seem like random notes and random rests to those who observed us and cared for us. These were the people, of course, who taught us constraint and promulgated the values that ultimately held us and our culture barely together. And so we keep in our memory those special and particular experiences and those particular people who in their way tie us to a tradition, a convention, a family and a name. And later on we reason that it must have been the constraints on psychic and social action which preserved the tonalities not just of ourselves but of entire generations.

Time and youth were once somehow together, the one being the other, both enduring for themselves, both enduring for the other and presenting to us spans of splashing aliveness and testimonies of achievement, excitement and critical pain; presenting to us as well the fibers of expectation and inference and every taste that can be had of death. We grew up to learn that a measured flow of time had been bequeathed to us for as long as, well, for as long as our spidery tenure might last. A peculiar word, "last." It gives promise of endurance and pronouncement of finality. So do the words "youth and time."

We matured, changed, displayed before ourselves some bit of what was being transacted behind our own eyes. And we all believed, even truthfully reported that a mutual understanding, a truce made in and of time had been completed, and that we had resolved all that life and death and being young and old might mean. But of course no truce existed, for in our aging we were soon enough obliged to look again, not upward this time but backward to where we had been. Like time itself, youth was again appearing to engulf us.

Then, in maybe the single discovery we made apart from the younger ones, apart from our own youth that is, they became us and we them. Or so it seemed. The young surround us so naturally, their bodies and chants pushing, urging, punishing us; they lead and follow us. As though in battalions, they order us to march in the footsteps of their pride and diffidence or gallop amidst their sexuality and adventure. How is it possible that they arrive before us and after us, smaller and larger, more amusing and urbane, more naïve and unexposed?

To examine youth, therefore, means either to walk in their tempo for those instants when the tempi of the generations may be contiguous, or to settle in among the years which accumulate for us, confront head-on the clashing of the present and the past, and hear the explosion of regrets and life plans made so long ago they hardly seem to carry our name anymore. But so much time had accumulated that our examination seems false and uncertain. We have passed into what we all call adolescence and early adulthood only to find that photographs of our childhood have become crusty through our own disbelief. They seem foreign and unfriendly. The space of the photograph is reminiscent of something: the high school room, the smell of lockers or hideaways, the feel of streets, beaches and stony concrete. But the faces must be identified through an act of inference normally reserved for dealing with the future; hence it is hard to believe that we are recalling and not prophesying. Isn't this the case? We look at the picture and say, yes, I remember that schoolroom. I used to sit next to Bobby and Henry. And that teacher, Miss Marshall, and . . . and . . . is that what I looked like then? I guess so. It must be. That must be the past.

It seems ironic, though, that these self-conceptions linger this way in the past and that they must be guessed at or reasoned out. It seems impossible, even a trifle unjust. How can there be such displacements and discontinuities in time when at most all we can admit to feeling are the slight but delectable interruptions of sleep and dreams? If the days follow along in line, we argue, like children well behaved on their way to a fresh, green park, why is last year or five years ago, why is our youth so separated from us now, and at times so incongruous? Why is it that the children at the head of the line have already disappeared? Very small children have similar reactions when they in turn undertake their examinations of youth. We see the sentiment in a three-year-old's expression as he sees a photograph of himself of two years before: "Baby. See the baby! What's the baby's name? Who is that?"

Everyone, presumably, protects his own notions and treasures of the past and of youth, extending or limiting their boundaries and seasons. And everyone of a certain age, an age which institutions and cultures help to compute, eventually decides he is no longer young. When one becomes that age, whole measures of time seem to be dismissed, dropped from the repertoire of habits, and the years and months, the congeries of time undergo a preparation and are put into storage. But they are stored, these years of the past, in peculiar fashion, for often we feel that we have continued on in the identical modes and styles of our youth, in the ways, that is, of our parents, so that the past doesn't seem dead at all.

Yet often, too, we find ourselves performing actions which bespeak what seem to us a historic urgency and dazzling spontaneity. Suddenly nothing has to do with yesterday's styles or childhood or our parents. Everything is new and totally recast as if our lives were made of clay hardening in society's molds and emerging finally in the forms of single days. These particular actions do not necessarily appear genuine or reasonable to us, but they come about, so we imagine, without preparation or rehearsal. Somehow we just do them. They just happen. We may even wonder where such actions and response came from. Where was the action waiting? Was it pausing, perhaps, in some interior anteroom? Some of us wonder too where actions live after they have been sent from us, presumably to return to time. Are they retrievable or but bolts of quicksilver showing us their face a mere once and no more?

Youth has this uncertain way about it, for in one sense we as young people did not contemplate time the same way we did only moments after our departure from the buildings and persons we associate with being young and hence come to define as our younger years. The flow of time is gradual, as the buildup of a conception of the past grows in proper and tolerable duration. But then miraculously, often violently, we recognize that while most assuredly we are with people our own age we are no longer with young people, no longer with people young as young meant before. We begin to think about age in a new way, especially on our birthdays, and in the beginning of this series of recognitions and required reconciliations it is first the past which closes itself off to us. Exhibiting an antipathy and haughtiness, the past turns a heavy shoulder toward us and bids us in unbending fashion to move ahead, although there remains a voice somewhere daring us to seek impossible replications of prior years.

Do we not know an uneasy feeling when we think of how the play and freedom of childhood (and for some of us college as well) have been altered by the constraints and opportunities of adulthood? The constraints are like iron edges pricking our personalities and somehow destroying the smooth and linear flow of sweet time. Time, too, so it seems, possesses these edges, angularity amidst its unequivocal forms. For we learn that no one returns to the past, no matter what.

Before we truly understood this, however, time seemed to have played a casual game with us, offering freedom and caprice. One might even say that time played jokes on us and on itself. For the long and magical moments of childhood the years meant so little, and maturation for the most part went unfelt. Life was adventure and defeat, trial and setback, but it was encased in a resiliency sanctioned by a usually stern but frequently mischievous sense of history. One could come back and try something again, repeat a day of fun or a whole year in school perhaps. One could pass as a young man or young woman, and a culture fragmented into chips from the cracking of social reordering on its surface let it all happen. At least some of the culture's chips, the richer ones probably, permitted these youthful gambles and lines of failures. Let them have their fun now, we used to hear, for soon they won't be able to get away with this kind of light foolishness and aimless leisure. Soon their interminable dance will be stilled.

Yet in other parts of our culture it seemed as though water had seeped in between the cracks of the years and had frozen to a thick, crusty shell. It seemed as though water had trapped those persons whose simple measured destinies precluded free and capricious movement and some final hopeful liberation. Large groups of young people and old people stayed right where they were, frozen in the houses where their parents and grandparents lived what some have felt to be lives deprived of a substance and a joy that come from sleight of hand tricks with time, like rearranging the flow of preordained histories or shocking everyone with absolutely audacious expectations. We don't always think of it this way, but not becoming what your father was, living better than he did, more enlightened and more dramatically, is, after all, reordering history and, hence, performing rather nifty sleight of hand magic with time's sense of direction.

We have names, however, for those unable to perform such magic, just as we have names for the cultures, states and forgotten, monochromatic towns where their children march to school and then, cerebrally, march among their day-by-day lessons, abiding by the social and educational currents, honoring the brittle habits of teachers and bosses, and then march home. We say about these towns, or about the poor parts of our own cities where the

184

people stamped for avoidance were dumped and remain penned, that only the day matters, that only the single beat matters, presenting its force and slim royalty once every turn of the world. One by one, one by one. We say this and much more about the places we see from the trains entering or leaving the smokey, smelly stations of enormous cities where concrete platforms hold the very world upright and stand bracing the black iron beams, old and tired, sweating their rust and decay. The beams are themselves like the men who brought them there and lifted them into a position and posture so that others might be kept safe before their own departures for better times and better places.

We say about these rotting places that some of us study from time to time that they offer a special glory in their day-by-day, beat-by-beat theater. But we also say the children there lack a drive to become all that they might, that the years have frozen them solid, and that they actually prefer the meager tonalities of their own compositions, their own flamboyant street styles and the lugubrious architecture of their own craftsmen and fathers. We say these children do not speak aloud to themselves or dream too much or even wish. And we say that because of an evil accumulation of years discolored by the blackness of the mines, or the frazzled whiteness of cotton fields owned by the good but still the very richest, or by the coldness of the brown earth surrounding the falling fences, or the forests that literally upped and moved just to stay out of sight of their churches, stores, latrines, and grave sites, the genes which no man has yet begun to comprehend have been disabled or discredited and made malignant.

There is, then, something called our time, the time we inherit from our own and bequeath to our own, and something called their time, the time of *them*, and the time of their youth. The two times coexist, of course, which is to say little more than that they hack their rhythms, their periodicities all they like, just as long as nobody gets hurt. But does this mean that a truly universal youth exists, a youthfulness that everyone shares? Or is there instead a segregated youth, a time divided so that now youth has reassessed itself and chosen to open its time only to those of the same color or of the same demanded style? Does youth now stand begging to hold together its isolated strength and greatness, or are the disparities of culture so great that we continue to think first of our own youth belonging to all the others?

An anger has arisen in this land, a momentous rage with a force almost as great as life itself. Its smell is sweet, its heat is delicious, its voices are assuredly young. One result of this anger is that time has been made groggy by this youth force and has found itself scarred so that it may just contemplate throwing off the capes of its own original laws and begin anew, as "they" do when buildings are razed on dusty lots where moments before people lived. Time has been urged by youth to contemplate starting fresh, from scratch, or pay a cataclysmic consequence. Thus we live in a time where there will be more and more thorny discontinuities and entire redefinitions of what it means to be young; what it means precisely to be twelve or eighteen.

To move about the dungeons and palaces where youth is kept and where the images of youth become institutionalized as schools, clubs or political fraternities is to recognize that the anger of youth accompanies the compassion of youth just as the hate accompanies love and the impulse to care for someone accompanies the impulse to hurt him. It is not merely, then, that some schools or teachers or administrators, that some of us, are good and some bad, or that some educational philosophies seem genuinely custodial or murderous whereas others seem more imaginative or, as they still say, "progressive." Dichotomies of this sort are usually cognitive conveniences, rarely gauges of the truth.

It is rather the antinomies and ambivalence, the intense feelings of such extraordinarily discrepant meaning and emotion and conflictual push to action and then away from action that cause us to wonder about ourselves and our institutions and then turn us into immobilized fools, distraught and humiliated right in the middle of personal and political revolutions. It is the ambivalence and confusion that attracts us to youth's expressions like "identity crisis," "copping out," and "getting it together." And if we are immobilized, struck down by two competing drives or wants, then most probably there are four, eight, sixteen drives pinning us to the tracks where moments ago we glided so easily into healthy life, that is into love and work. In these times we just cannot "get it together" no matter how intense our rage, for we have been stilled by the antinomies and the ambivalence.

What a profound conceptual contribution Freud made in the notion of the Oedipal configuration, not only because of the social psychological relationships it describes, but because of its inherent insistence that portions of a man's imagination simultaneously hold secret packages of feeling sometimes so discrepant, so foreign from one another it would seem that he would burst into hundreds of swollen pieces. It is the reverence for the parent and the impulse to kill him, not separated, not one in each hand, but both in one reality, both clutched in one fist, both stored in one mind. Assuming an almost religious magnitude, the respect and adoration become united with a hate and brutality supposedly known only to prehistoric monsters. Behind the ambivalence are masked demons dancing a curious and chaotic commotion in our souls.

Parents, teachers and the companions of the young breathe that life and death and dance that demonic dance. The young and the small at times wish that the old and tall might flop over dead. The old and powerful wish that the young and insignificant might recede or wander away or maybe find another country. Love it or leave it. The number of these kinds of murders committed each day must be fantastic! But at the same time, adulation and unquestioned obedience to much authority also stand high. Pride is swallowed one second, hate the next, the wish for love and the wish for death the next. So it is that we almost can see the signs of life and death flickering on and off the surfaces of authorities appointed to oversee youth's daily and nightly routines.

What complicates these matters even more is that our customs and rituals often cannot keep up with or comprehend the consequences of our changing sensations and private trials. Society seems to have no place for ambivalence and the indecision it yields. Often it is as if the social casings, the social roles into which we are obliged to fit our personal intrusiveness, our "real" selves, perhaps, cannot accommodate the presence of all of our feelings, especially the anger. And how unfair this is, not just for youth, since all these other feelings have as much right to be seen and heard as the ones for which the social customs and rituals were originally conceived.

More generally, societies and psyches have developed ingenious procedures for honing conscious and unconscious materials, patterns and processes that change and rearrange themselves as much in sleep as in action, as much in death as in life. Dangerous experiments with drugs are undertaken, flirtations with lunacy are repeated, and undeniable self-destruction is sustained partly as a reaction to the realities of our societies, partly as a reaction to anger and loss, but partly as well to find and demonstrate that these marvelous and frightening experiences exist not as bizarre extensions of our world, not as cantilevered perches, but as hunks of the same substantial structure that houses language, rudimentary perception and pedestrian reasoning. What frightens us, I think, is that at times reality itself seems to overhang a valley entirely unsupported in a way that would make the most daring architects gasp. The young help to erect this new reality of political actions, ideologies, and life-styles. They build it, behold it, then, just as we believed we were adapting to it, they tear it all down and start in again constructing still a newer reality and a fresher definition of social order and peace.

By their hopes for the young and in their prayers that the young may liberate the world if only because they are young, the old seek a liberation of their own lives of increasing constraint and incapacities. On these prayers and the efforts they initiate glistens the love being transferred between the generations. But often, too, the old wish for the obliteration of the young, and in this curse they covet a paradoxical liberation, a liberation turned on its head with time running backward, for we just cannot be young again like the young. We must instead be young like the middle-aged, or young like the old. When care for and trust in the young are entertained, succeeding futures, also paradoxically, are preserved and the histories of prior generations finally safeguarded. But when enduring antipathies toward the young dominate the transactions between generations, a false freedom is born, a freedom conceived in the belief that if one liquidates another's future, one's own past is cured and one's own future is rendered limitless. Among so many inherited rights, aging confers the power of potential rejector on all who survive. Soon the son will become the father who leaves. Still, rejection is no new business, as the young practice it among their peers, often reaching a precision and dexterity with its weapons that make us think they have been advised of its lifelong utility. Quite possibly, they have been. It's funny and sad to think what we teach children in the name of "preparing" them for adulthood and for the time when we are no longer here.

It's also funny and sad to think of the number of false liberation movements attempted each day as parents and children wrestle with and among themselves in the hopes of "getting together" and moving apart all at the same time. In these moments, which seem to make up so much of our present society, the faces of the rejectors and the rejected are so frequently seen close together. But this is part of what "they" call maturation and ambivalence, love and hate.

It is also part of what "they" call "rapid social change." The place, resting and moving, of each person who lives or has lived has become so fragile today, so evanescent. Once we were taught to believe in the permanent sanctity of the dead. Surely *their* reputations were finalized, sealed and delivered and their skeletons left untouched to rot deeper and deeper into the ground. But no more. Dead men have been lifted and carted away as the bare scent of their posthumous spirits have come into disfavor and their corpses made the recipients of national animus. More recently, the racially segregated status of cemeteries has been violated in ways that make churchgoers tremble in their appeals to paradisic courts. For when a black man is allowed to lie alongside a white man, the time has finally come to alter the most grotesque of written histories and to rearrange the substance of individual memory. The time has come to mature, resolve or at least recognize ambivalence and find a place for it in society. The time has come, in other words, for social change.

To some extent, these are but a few of the demands that youth outlines, some of the supposed crimes that youth allegedly commits: the tearing down of saints, the ripping open of tradition, the denial and desecration of memory and custom; and the obliteration of authority. Our impression is that youth's many and often capricious philosophies teach that no man knows such worth that he cannot be expended and that no man maintains such control over his energies that he can be expected to embrace all of fidelity's covenants. Through their boisterous sexuality, for example, the young are said to every day chew away at the fibers not "merely" of society but of the realities it labors so hard to contain. It is said that the young rip the fibers of realities and throw them in the faces of generations they know planted them and nourished them.

But it isn't so. It just isn't so that they alone are the guilty ones. We know this by the intensity of our own urges to run to the books and movies, drawings, music, poetry and life-styles which in their gaudy and flavorful way reenact the same fantasies we now project onto youth, rightly or wrongly, the true owners of these particular products. We know it, too, by the actions we somehow cannot help ourselves from taking that fortunately remain private and unsuspected. Yet even with our most impeccable constraints, the products of the young, or of what Philip Slater has called the "counter culture," kindle reminiscences of our own timorous advances and almost comical regrets: "When I was young and used to listen to the sixteen-year-old boys in the high school locker room," the young man recalled, "I used to dream about growing up, so that one day I too could do what these older boys did. Lie!"

To write about youth means confronting one's prior and future selves and generations and, even more, one's single self properly bound, trapped and free, in the single glowing point of now. It means confronting not just one child, one day, one dream, or one event, but all days, all dreams, all events, all the best friends, the few lovers and the ancestors too, and all according to the sequences and antisequences these people and these events dictate and underwrite. It means a confrontation in which no one is left out as well as an understanding that the physics governing our psychologies recognizes that an expenditure of energy is required in the movement we make toward generations and objects identical to that required in the movement made away from them. The physics, therefore, describes a logic in the sometimes violent separations from parents that occur at precisely the same instant as the sometimes violent couplings with new friends and in the same way, probably, with a new sex, the other sex. Strange how that special unit of time circumscribing psychic transactions can seem so small and yet retain so much. It seems less strange if we recall that enclosed in this unit of time are all the remains, all that so far has been constructed of a unique identity. All eternity, perhaps, as some philosophers have taught, recurs in that one unit.

The escape from home, for example, and the sniping at family values and peculiar social structures are not exactly the precursors of attachments to people and institutions outside the family. In the beginning, they are part of one single action disguised as fragments by a seemingly long extension in time. It is not, therefore, that the engine of sexuality runs only when the engine of generational obedience is turned off. More precisely, the engine of obedience runs its energy into the engine of sexuality. When everything in that first engine is seemingly flat and impotent, the other engine appears to catch. But while it may seem as though the engine of sexuality proceeds under its own power, it remains attached to its parent engine in a single system for quite a while. (Only later on does the child dare examine the possibility that these engines may be separated and thereby gain the health and wisdom that this separation yields.) In the beginning, however, the major source of attraction and attachment to people and the fundamental linkage between people and the autonomy provided by their friendships is still the family, or at least relationships defined by kinship networks and authority.

Although it is true that with each decade aspects of maturity bloom earlier and earlier, the concept of adolescence has not yet lost all its validity. Gradations of psychological and social growth persist which, ironically, seem more and more in evidence as the young increase in what we call sophistication and awarenes. So like a child running away from home to claim a vital independence and a chance to choose and own, the child running into love and sexuality, protest and freedom, the child running, really, toward the border between adulthood and childhood (a border that *does* in fact exist in our minds and in our societies) must pack together and stuff into his pockets the coins, food and mementos of his entire life. For they represent his first social psychological and economic arrangement with the family. With little preparation and even less warning, everything in this all-or-nothing transaction is packed, as if by the act of physically moving the child might lure away the memories of those places and people with such a devastating impact and finality that he might alter the content and rationality of his future and, most especially, of the reveries that future will hold.

The child takes the currency and foodstuff and runs to those he loves, and like a despotic general burns the villages behind him, the bridges, the outposts and the supply depots. Through this militant outburst the past presumably is pillaged and a sparkling new present and future are made to wait for him, his goals, and his greatness. And who's going to stand up and say it isn't so or it doesn't happen this way!

To write about youth and youth's lives of attachments to things and people and work implies a presence of myriad feelings, all the feelings and emotions that human beings can generate, and all at once; feelings generated in varying formulas, in varying proportions and saliences. Perhaps the metaphor of emotional debits and credits has worth, for it does seem that we run some emotional accounts into the red when we absolutely require clean and crisp capital in other accounts. Possibly, too, when we come to know emotions and feelings well, there will emerge a principle of balancing payments and monies received. But the systems of feelings now are so incomprehensible that to call any behavior, or political revolt for that matter, actions of love or hate, actions of guided or misguided purpose, actions of children or adults can be only partially correct. Too few actions will be so clear-cut that they might be assigned merely to one account or another. For there *will* be anger in love; there *will* be bitter regret in vast hope. And, regardless of what the words mean to us, there *will* be adult maturity in childlike expressions and childlike imagination in adult impressions.

To label or diagnose, observe or record, which after all constitute the process of writing about youth, is to select images and language from realities only thinly "in touch" with the magic of one's own conscious and unconscious worlds. In some ways and in some glorious times, we are one with or feel ourselves to be united with this "other reality," this counter culture, joined, that is, with these people and their generation. But, mainly, the source of our impressions, the grist, as it's still called, is our own interiors, interiors that do more than pay homage to materials that once lived outside of us or before us. It is *our* love and hate, *our* feelings of despair and courage plasticity and conservatism, and *our* ambivalences that haunt the pages on which we print and draw a transient, flickering youth. It is unspoken talent and shameless temerity as much as it is insight and sensitivity.

Now, in the "real" sciences we could not exonerate such blasphemously personal thrusts at the truth. But somehow, in the outlandish physics systematizing and ordering social and psychological action, whatever it is that accepts our invitation to be written on a particular morning when the night before we had all but convinced ourselves that we were, finally, written out becomes part of the reality we have chosen to study. It becomes a part here just as much as it explicates a part there, and for a moment we are young like the young. The parts must appertain, moreover, for we have chosen youth, of all things, as this reality. But the parts must also be connected to the currency, food and souvenirs we, too, once stuffed together, hurriedly and without forewarning as we made our plans to pillage a past and thereby create a dazzling present and bountiful future.

But now, writing about youth seems impossible, since everything happens so quickly, pouring forth so rapidly that too little time is left over to catch much of anything anymore. Perhaps it wasn't this way once, in our youth, when resiliency was assured and our bodies were proud and indestructible and maybe our souls immortal. But it all happens so quickly now that no one seems to treasure even the impressions that emerge, unrefined, still dripping with the fluids of unconscious and conscious substance. Everyone demands finished products, all perfectly intelligible. Yet even worse, it all happens so quickly that we have begun to lose people from our land. What really is happening to the poor and the sick, and those who once were strong but whom failure has made frail and scared? Because of the rushing lives of so many people it is essential that we stop absolutely still, that we stop writing and stop talking and through our simple impressions, thoughtful and impure, regain those whom we have before turned away and restore the rare collection of time they have broken and hidden from us.

There is no life that can stand our taking away its fragile estimations of worth, just as there is no life that can come away unharmed from the tensions and deprivations endemic in our contemporary patterns of training, growth, education, bureaucracy, socialization, and career. All of us suffer in our way, the rich and the poor, and no one waits out the time of the temporary well. No one manages perfectly or completely a splintered life of demands heaped on demands. No one knows youth; no one knows aging; no one can adequately speak for another, even in a democracy. But each of us guards impressions of a life space colored and swept by time, and a sense of what it means to have morsels of the world we're able to see change, and what it means to have things resist even our most forceful efforts, singular and collective, to alter them. When the bewilderment of change, of time, really, and the reconciliation of the unchangeable properties of reality come to be internalized, then everything everywhere seems to have "gotten together," and identity arises as a part of that everything. Life now is fat, and death, even to the very young, a bit less terrifying.

The arc of time diminishes; youth waits its turn, then takes its sometimes foolish gambles with predestination and immortality. The rest of us work our narrow work, hoping that the markers separating the generations might move again and that when sophistication, knowledge and anger, style and unbecoming pride are for an instant laid away, each day and each person in that day might repossess a fundamental dignity.

# 11. Prefigurative Cultures and Unknown Children

MARGARET MEAD

Our present crisis has been variously attributed to the overwhelming rapidity of change, the collapse of the family, the decay of capitalism, the triumph of a soulless technology, and in wholesale repudiation, to the final breakdown of the Establishment. Behind these attributions there is a more basic conflict between those for whom the present represents no more than an intensification of our existing cofigurative culture, in which peers are more than ever replacing parents as the significant models of behavior, and those who contend that we are in fact entering a totally new phase of cultural evolution. . . .

It is only when one specifies the nature of the process that the contrast between past and present change becomes clear. One urgent problem, I believe, is the delineation of the nature of change in the modern world, including its speed and dimensions, so that we can better understand the distinctions that must be made between change in the past and that which is now ongoing.

The primary evidence that our present situation is unique, without any parallel in the past, is that the generation gap is world wide. The particular events taking place in any country—China, England, Pakistan, Japan, the United States, New Guinea, or elsewhere—are not enough to explain the

193

unrest that is stirring modern youth everywhere. Recent technological change or the handicaps imposed by its absence, revolution or the suppression of revolutionary activities, the crumbling of faith in ancient creeds or the attraction of new creeds—all these serve only as partial explanations of the particular forms taken by youth revolt in different countries. Undoubtedly, an upsurge of nationalism is more likely in a country like Japan, which is recovering from a recent defeat, or in countries that have newly broken away from their colonial past than it is, for example, in the United States. It is easier for the government of a country as isolated as China to order vast changes by edict than it is for the government of the Soviet Union, acting on a European stage, to subdue Czechoslovakian resistance. The breakdown of the family is more apparent in the West than in the East. The speed of change is more conspicuous and more consciously perceived in the least and in the most industrialized countries than it is in countries occupying an intermediate position. But all this is, in a sense, incidental when the focus of attention is on *youthful dissidence,* which is world wide in its dimensons.

Concentration on particularities can only hinder the search for an explanatory principle. Instead, it is necessary to strip the occurrences in each country of their superficial, national, and immediately temporal aspects. The desire for a liberal form of communism in Czechoslovakia, the search for "racial" equality in the United States, the desire to liberate Japan from American military influence, the support given to excessive conservatism in Northern Ireland and Rhodesia or to the excesses of communism in Cuba—all these are *particularistic forms. Youthful activism is common to them all.*

It was with the hope of turning anthropological analysis to this use that I tried to describe the essential characteristics of the postfigurative model and some of the forms taken by the cofigurative model under certain conditions of rapid change. It is my belief that the delineation of these models, as we have come to understand them through the study of older cultures, can help to clarify what is happening in the contemporary world.

The key question is this: *What are the new conditions that have brought about the revolt of youth right around the world?*

The first of these is the *emergence of a world community.* For the first time human beings throughout the world, in their information about one another and responses to one another, have become a community that is united by shared knowledge and danger. We cannot say for certain now that at any period in the past there was a single community made up of many small societies whose members were aware of one another in such a way that consciousness of what differentiated one small society from another heightened the self-consciousness of each constituent group. But as far as we know, no such single, interacting community has existed within archaeological time.

The largest clusters of interacting human groups were fragments of a still larger unknown whole. The greatest empires pushed their borders outward into regions where there were peoples whose languages, customs and very appearance were unknown. In the very partially charted world of the past the idea that all men were, in the same sense, human beings was either unreal or a mystical belief. Men could think about the fatherhood of God and the brotherhood of man and biologists could argue the issue of monogenesis versus polygenesis; but what all men had in common was a matter of continuing speculation and dispute.

The events of the last twenty-five years changed this drastically. Exploration has been complete enough to convince us that there are no humanoid types on the planet except our own species. World-wide rapid air travel and globe-encircling television satellites have turned us into one community in which events taking place on one side of the earth become immediately and simultaneously available to peoples everywhere else. No artist or political censor has time to intervene and edit as a leader is shot or a flag planted on the moon. The world is a community though it lacks as yet the forms of organization and the sanctions by which a political community can be governed.

The nineteenth-century industrial revolution replaced the cruder forms of energy. The twentieth-century scientific revolution has made it possible to *multiply agricultural production* manyfold but also drastically and dangerously to modify the ecology of the entire planet and destroy all living things. Science has made possible, through the use of computers, a new concentration of intellectual efforts that allows men to begin the exploration of the solar system, and opens the way to simulations by means of which men, especially men working in organized groups, can transcend earlier intellectual accomplishments.

The revolution in the development of food resources is on a world-wide scale. Up to the present, in many parts of the world, the medical revolution has so increased the population that the major effect of increased, efficient food production has been to stave off famine. But if we are able to bring the human population into a new balance, all of humanity can be, for the first time, well nourished. The medical revolution by reducing the pressure for population increase has begun, in turn, to release women from the age-old necessity of devoting themselves almost completely to reproductivity and, thus, will profoundly alter women's future and the future rearing of children.

Most importantly, these changes have taken place almost simultaneously—within the lifetime of one generation—and the impact of knowledge of the change is world wide. Only yesterday, a New Guinea native's only contact with modern civilization may have been a trade knife that was passed from hand to hand into his village or an airplane seen in the sky; today, as soon as he enters the smallest frontier settlement, he meets the transistor radio. Until yesterday, the village dwellers everywhere were cut off from the urban life of their own country; today radio and television bring them sounds and sights of cities all over the world.

Men who are the carriers of vastly different cultural traditions are entering the present at the same point in time. It is as if, all around the world, men were converging on identical immigration posts, each with its identifying sign: "You are now about to enter the post-World War II world at Gate 1 (or Gate 23 or Gate 2003, etc.)." Whoever they are and wherever their particular point of entry may be, all men are equally immigrant into the new era—some come as refugees and some as castaways.

*They are like the immigrants who came as pioneers to a new land, lacking all knowledge of what demands the new conditions of life would make upon them.* Those who came later could take their peer groups as models. But among the first comers, the young adults had as models only their own tentative adaptations and innovations. Their past, the culture that had shaped their understanding—their thoughts, their feelings, and their conceptions of the world—was no sure guide to the present. And the elders among them, bound to the past, could provide no models for the future.

Today, everyone born and bred before World War II is such an immigrant in time—as his forebears were in space—struggling to grapple with the unfamiliar conditions of life in a new era. Like all immigrants and pioneers, these immigrants in time are the bearers of older cultures. The difference today is that they represent all the cultures of the world. And all of them, whether they are sophisticated French intellectuals or members of a remote New Guinea tribe, land-bound peasants in Haiti or nuclear physicists, *have certain characteristics in common.*

Whoever they are, these immigrants grew up under skies across which no satellite had ever flashed. Their perception of the past was an edited version of what had happened. Whether they were wholly dependent on oral memory, art, and drama or also had access to print and still photography and film, what they could know had been altered by the very act of preservation. Their perception of the immediate present was limited to what they could take in through their own eyes and ears to the edited versions of other men's sensory experience and memories. Their conception of the future was essentially one in which change was incorporated into a deeper changelessness. The New Guinea native, entering the complex modern world, followed cultural models provided by Europeans and expected in some way to share their future. The industrialist or military planner, envisaging what a computer, not yet constructed, might make possible, treated it as another addition to the repertoire of inventions that have enhanced man's skills. It expanded what men could do, but did not change the future.

It is significant that mid-twentieth-century science fiction, written by young writers with little experience of human life, rang untrue to the sophisticated and experienced ear and was less interesting to most well-educated men than such myths as those of Icarus and Daedalus, which include men and gods as well as the mechanisms of flight. Most scientists shared the lack of prescience of other members of their generation and failed to share the dreams of modern science fiction writers.

When the first atom bomb was exploded at the end of World War II, only a few individuals realized that all humanity was entering a new age. And to this day the majority of those over twenty-five have failed to grasp emotionally, however well they may grasp intellectually, the difference between any war in which, no matter how terrible the casualties, mankind will survive, and one in which there will be no survivors. They continue to think that a war, fought with more lethal weapons, would just be a worse war; they still do not grasp the implications of scientific weapons of extinction. Even scientists, when they form committees, are apt to have as their goal not the total abolition of war, but the prevention of the particular kinds of warfare for which they themselves feel an uncomfortable special responsibility—such as the use of pesticides in Vietnam.

In this sense, then, of having moved into a present for which none of us was prepared by our understanding of the past, our interpretations of ongoing experience or our expectations about the future, all of us who grew up before World War II are pioneers, immigrants in time who have left behind our familiar worlds to live in a new age under conditions that are different from any we have known. Our thinking still binds us to the past—to the world as it existed in our childhood and youth. Born and bred before the electronic revolution, most of us do not realize what it means.

We still hold the seats of power and command the resources and the skills necessary to keep order and organize the kinds of societies we know about. We control the educational systems, the apprenticeship systems, the career ladders up which the young must climb, step by step. The elders in the advanced countries control the resources needed by the young and less advanced countries for their development. Nevertheless, we have passed the point of no return. We are committed to life in an unfamiliar setting; we are making do with what we know. We are building makeshift dwellings in old patterns with new and better understood materials.

The young generation, however, the articulate young rebels all around the world who are lashing out against the controls to which they are subjected, are like the first generation born into a new country. They are at home in this time. Satellites are familiar in their skies. They have never known a time when war did not threaten annihilation. Those who use computers do not anthropomorphize them; they know that they are programmed by human beings. When they are given the facts, they can understand immediately that continued pollution of the air and water and soil will soon make the planet uninhabitable and that it will be impossible to feed an indefinitely expanding world population. They can see that control of conception is feasible and necessary. As members of one species in an underdeveloped world community, they recognize that invidious distinctions based on race and caste are anachronisms. They insist on the vital necessity of some form of world order.

They live in a world in which events are presented to them in all their complex immediacy; they are no longer bound by the simplified linear sequences dictated by the printed word. In their eyes the killing of an enemy is not qualitatively different from the murder of a neighbor. They cannot reconcile our efforts to save our own children by every known means with our readiness to destroy the children of others with napalm. Old distinctions between peacetime and wartime, friend and foe, "my" group and "theirs"— the outsiders, the aliens—have lost their meaning. They know that the people of one nation alone cannot save their own children; each holds the responsibility for the others' children.

*Although I have said they know these things, perhaps I should say that this is how they feel.* Like the first generation born in a new country, they listen only half-comprehendingly to their parents' talk about the past. For as the children of pioneers had no access to the memories which could still move their parents to tears, the young today cannot share their parents' responses to events that deeply moved them in the past. But this is not all that separates the young from their elders. Watching, they can see that their elders are groping, that they are managing clumsily and often unsuccessfuly the tasks imposed on them by the new conditions. They have no firsthand knowledge of the way their parents lived far across the seas, of how differently wood responded to tools, or land to hoe. They see that their elders are using means that are inappropriate, that their performance is poor, and the outcome very uncertain. *The young do not know what must be done, but they feel that there must be a better way. . . .*

They feel that there must be a better way and that they must find it.

*Today, nowhere in the world are there elders who know what the children know, no matter how remote and simple the societies are in which the children live. In the past there were always some elders who knew more than any children in terms of their experience of having grown up within a cultural system. Today there are none.* It is not only that parents are no longer guides, but that there are no guides, whether one seeks them in one's own country or abroad. There are no elders who know what those who have been reared within the last twenty years know about the world into which they were born.

The elders are separated from them by the fact that they, too, are a strangely isolated generation. No generation has ever known, experienced, and incorporated such rapid changes, watched the sources of power, the means of communications, the definition of humanity, the limits of their explorable universe, the certainties of a known and limited world, the fundamental imperatives of life and death—all change before their eyes. They know more about change than any generation has ever known and so stand, over, against, and vastly alienated, from the young, who by the very nature of their position, have had to reject their elders' past.

Just as the early Americans had to teach themselves not to daydream of the past but concentrate on the present, and so in turn taught their children not to daydream but to act, so today's elders have to treat their own past as incommunicable, and teach their children, even in the midst of lamenting that it is so, not to ask, because they can never understand. We have to realize that no other generation will ever experience what we have experienced. In this sense we must recognize that we have no descendants, as our children have no forebears.

At this breaking point between two radically different and closely related groups, both are inevitably very lonely, as we face each other knowing that they will never experience what we have experienced, and that we can never experience what they have experienced.

The situation that has brought about this radical change will not occur again in any such drastic form in the foreseeable future. Once we have discovered that this planet is inhabited by only one human species this cannot be disavowed. The sense of responsibility for the existence of the entire living world, once laid upon our shoulders, will not be lifted. The young will hopefully be prepared to educate their own children for change. But just because this gap is unique, because nothing like it has ever occurred before, the elders are set apart from any previous generation and from the young. . . .

We are familiar with the problems of communication between speakers of two languages who have been reared in radically different cultures, one, for example, in China and the other in the United States. Not only language, but also the incommensurability of their experience prevents them from understanding each other. Yet a willingness to learn the other's language and to explore the premises of both cultures can open the way to conversation. It can be done, but it is not often done.

The problem becomes more difficult, because it is more subtle, when speakers from two different cultures share what is regarded as a common tongue, such as English for Americans and Englishmen, Spanish for Spaniards and Latin Americans. Then true communication becomes possible only when both realize that they speak not one, but two languages in which the

199

"same" words have divergent, sometimes radically different meanings. Then, if they are willing to listen and to ask, they can begin to talk and talk with delight.

This is also the problem of the two generations. Once the fact of a deep, new, unprecedented world-wide generation gap is firmly established, in the minds of both the young and the old, communication can be established again. But as long as any adult thinks that he, like the parents and teachers of old, can become introspective, invoke his own youth to understand the youth before him, then he is lost.

But this is what most elders are still doing. The fact that they delegate authority—that the father sends his sons away to school to learn new ideas and the older scientist sends his pupils to other laboratories to work on newer problems—changes nothing. It only means that parents and teachers are continuing to use the mechanisms of configuration characteristic of a world in which parents, having given up the right to teach their own children, expect their children to learn from other adults and their more knowledgeable age mates. Even in science, where we have tried to build in the expectation of discovery and innovations, students learn from old models, and normal young scientists work to fill in blank spaces in accepted paradigms. In today's accelerating rate of scientific discovery, the old are outmoded rapidly and replaced by near peers, but still within a framework of authority.

In the deepest sense, now as in the past, the elders are still in control. And partly because they are in control, they do not realize that the conditions for beginning a new dialogue with the young do not yet exist.

Ironically, it is often those who were, as teachers, very close to former generations of students, who now feel that the generation gap cannot be bridged and that their devotion to teaching has been betrayed by the young who cannot learn in the old ways.

From one point of view the situation in which we now find ourselves can be described as a *crisis in faith*, in which men, having lost their faith not only in religion but also in political ideology and in science, feel they have been deprived of every kind of security. I believe this crisis in faith can be attributed, at least in part, to the fact that there are now no elders who know more than the young themselves about what the young are experiencing. C. H. Waddington has hypothesized that one component of human evolution and the capacity for choice is the ability of the human child to accept on authority from elders the criteria for right and wrong. The acceptance of the distinction between right and wrong by the child is a consequence of his dependence on parental figures who are trusted, feared, and loved, who hold the child's very life in their hands. But today the elders can no longer present with certainty moral imperatives to the young.

True, in many parts of the world the parental generation still lives by a postfigurative set of values. From parents in such cultures children may learn that there have been unquestioned absolutes, and this learning may carry over into later experience as an expectation that absolute values can and should be reestablished. Nativistic cults, dogmatic religious and political movements flourish most vigorously at the point of recent breakdown of postfigurative cultures and least in those cultures in which orderly change is expected to occur within a set of stable values at higher levels of abstraction.

The older industrialized countries of the West have incorporated in their cultural assumptions the idea of change without revolution through the development of new social techniques to deal with the conditions brought about by economic change and technological advances. In these same countries, obsolescence tends to be treated as survival, loved or deprecated as the case may be. In England, the messenger who carried a dispatch case to France was retained long after the dispatches were sent by post; there, too, the pageantry of the throne exists side by side with the parliamentary government that has long superseded the throne as the source of power. In Sweden the most modern laws about sex behavior coexist with the most uncompromising orthodox religious support of an absolute morality.

Similarly, in the United States there is both a deep commitment to developmental change, which is interpreted as progress, and a continuing resort to absolutism, which takes many forms. There are the religious sects and minor political groups, the principal appeal of which is their dogmatism with regard to right and wrong. There are the Utopian communities that have been a constant feature of our social, political, and intellectual development. And there is the tacit acceptance of a color caste system that exists in violation of our declared belief in the fundamental equality of all men.

Elsewhere in the world where change has been rapid, abrupt and often violent, where the idea of orderly processes of change has not taken hold, there is a continuing possibility of sudden eruptions that may take the form of revolutions and counterrevolutions—as in most Latin American countries —or may bring about, in sudden reversal—even though in a new form—the re-establishment of an archaic orthodoxy in which nonbelievers may be persecuted, tortured, and burned alive. The young people, today, who turn themselves into living torches mirror in very complex ways both the attitudes of orthodox absolutism and reactions to it. They follow the example of Buddhists who responded to the dogmatisms of communism and reactive anticommunism with an extreme violation of their own permissive and unabsolute religious values. But their acts also represent, implicitly, the treatment accorded heretics and nonbelievers by any absolutist system that allows no appeal from its dogmas.

There are still parents who answer a child's questions—why must I go to bed? or eat my vegetables? or stop sucking my thumb? or learn to read?—with simple assertions: Because it is *right* to do so, because *God* says so, or because *I* say so. These parents are preparing the way for the re-establishment of post-figurative elements in the culture. But these elements will be far more rigid and intractable than in the past because they must be defended in a world in which conflicting points of view, rather than orthodoxies, are prevalent and accessible.

Most parents, however, are too uncertain to assert old dogmatisms. They do not know how to teach these children who are so different from what they themselves once were, and most children are unable to learn from parents and elders they will never resemble. In the past, in the United States, the children of immigrant parents pleaded with them not to speak their foreign language in public and not to wear their outlandish, foreign clothes. They knew the burning shame of being, at the same time, unable to repudiate their parents and unable to accept simply and naturally their way of speaking and doing things. But in time they learned to find new teachers as guides, to model their behavior on that of more adapted age mates, and to slip in, unnoticed, among a group whose parents were more bearable.

Today the dissident young discover very rapidly that this solution is no longer possible. The breach between themselves and their parents also exists between their friends and their friends' parents and between their friends and their teachers. There are no bearable answers in the old books or in the brightly colored, superficially livened-up new textbooks they are asked to study.

Some look abroad for models. They are attracted by Camus, who, in his conflict between his Algerian birth and his intellectual allegiance to France, expressed some of the conflict they feel; but he is dead. They try to adapt to their own purposes the words of an aging Marxist, Marcuse, or the writings of the existentialists. They develop cultist attitudes of desperate admiration for the heroes of other young revolutionary groups. White students ally themselves with the black separatists. Black students attempt to restructure the past in their struggle to restructure the present.

These young dissidents realize the critical need for immediate world action on problems that affect the whole world. What they want is, in some way, to begin all over again. The idea of orderly, developmental change is lost for this generation of young, who cannot take over the past from their elders, but can only repudiate what their elders are doing now. The past for them is a colossal, unintelligible failure and the future may hold nothing but the destruction of the planet. Caught between the two, they are ready to make way for something new by a kind of social bulldozing—like the bulldozing in which every tree and feature of the landscape is destroyed to make way for a new community. Awareness of the reality of the crisis (which is, in fact, perceived most accurately not by the young, but by their discerning and prophetic elders) and the sense the young have that their elders do not understand the modern world, because they do not understand rebellion in which planned reformation of the present system is almost inconceivable.

Nevertheless those who have no power also have no routes to power except through those against whom they are rebelling. In the end, it was men who gave the vote to women; and it will be the House of Lords that votes to abolish the House of Lords, and those over eighteen who must agree if those under eighteen are to vote, as also, in the final analysis, nations will act to limit national sovereignty. Effective, rapid evolutionary change, in which no one is guillotined and no one is forced into exile, depends on the co-operation of a large number of those in power with the dispossessed who are seeking power. The innovating idea may come from others, but the initiative for successful action must come from those whose privileges, now regarded as obsolete, are about to be abolished.

There are those among the dissident young who recognize this. Significantly, they want their parents or those who represent their parents—deans and college presidents and editorial writers—to be on their side, to agree with them or at least to give them a blessing. Behind their demands is their hope that, even as they demonstrate against the college administration, the college president will come and talk with them—and bring his children. But there are also some who entertain no such hope.

I have spoken mainly about the most articulate young people, those who want to drop out of the whole system and those who want to take the system apart and start over. But the feeling that nothing out of the past is meaningful and workable is very much more pervasive. Among the less articulate it is expressed in such things as the refusal to learn at school, cooperate at work, or follow normal political paths. Perhaps most noncompliance is of this passive kind. But the periodic massing of students behind their more active peers suggests that even passive noncompliance is highly inflammable.

Resistance among the young is also expressed by an essentially uninvolved and exploitative compliance with rules that are regarded as meaningless. Perhaps those who take this stand are the most frightening. Going through the forms by which men were educated for generations, but which no longer serve to educate those who accept them, can only teach students to regard all social systems in terms of exploitation.

But whatever stand they take, none of the young, neither the most idealistic nor the most cynical, is untouched by the sense that there are no adults anywhere in the world from whom they can learn what the next steps should be.

These, in brief, are the conditions of our time. These are the two generations—pioneers in a new era and their children, who have as yet to find a way of communicating about the world in which both live, though their perceptions of it are so different. No one knows what the next steps should be. Recognizing that this is so is, I submit, the *beginning of an answer*.

For I beileve we are on the verge of developing a new kind of culture, one that is as much a departure in style from cofigurative cultures, as the institutionalization of cofiguration in orderly—and disorderly—change was a departure from the postfigurative style. I call this new style *prefigurative*, because in this new culture it will be the child—and not the parent and grandparent—that represents what is to come. Instead of the erect, white-haired elder who, in postfigurative cultures, stood for the past and the future in all their grandeur and continuity, the unborn child, already conceived but still in the womb, must become the symbol of what life will be like. This is a child whose sex and appearance and capabilities are unknown. This is a child who is a genius or suffers from some deep impairment, who will need imaginative, innovative, and dedicated adult care far beyond any we give today. . . .

The continuity of culture and the incorporation of every innovation depended on the success of the postfigurative system by which the young were taught to replicate the lives of their ancestors. Then, as men learned to live in many different environments and as they traveled and traded with one another, contrasts among different postfigurative cultures began to provide the necessary conditions for change and for the development of cofigurative cultures in which people who had been reared to one form of commitment learned to adapt themselves to other forms but with the same absolute commitment.

Later, as the idea of change became embodied as a postfigurative element in many cultures, the young could learn from their elders that they should go beyond them—achieve more and do different things. But this beyond was always within the informed imagination of their elders; the son might be expected to cross the seas his father never crossed, study nuclear physics when his father had only an elementary school education, fly in the plane which his father watched from the ground. The peasant's son became a scholar; the poor man's son crossed the ocean his father had never seen; the teacher's son became a scientist.

Love and trust, based on dependency and answering care, made it possible for the individual who had been reared in one culture to move into another, transforming without destroying his earlier learning. It is seldom the first generation of voluntary immigrants and pioneers who cannot meet the demands of a new environment. Their previous learning carries them through. But unless they embody what is new postfiguratively, they cannot pass on to children what they themselves had acquired through their own early training —the ability to learn from others the things their parents could not teach them.

Now, in a world in which there are no more knowledgeable others to whom parents can commit the children they themselves cannot teach, parents feel uncertain and helpless. Still believing that there should be answers, parents ask: How can we tell our children what is right? So some parents try to solve the problem by advising their children, very vaguely: You will have to figure that out for yourselves. And some parents ask: What are the others doing? But this resource of a cofigurative culture is becoming meaningless to parents who feel that the "others"—their children's age mates —are moving in ways that are unsafe for their own children to emulate and who find that they do not understand what their children figure out for themselves.

It is the adults who still believe that there is a safe and socially approved road to a kind of life they themselves have not experienced who react with the greatest anger and bitterness to the discovery that what they had hoped for no longer exists for their children. These are the parents, the trustees, the legislators, the columnists, and commentators who denounce most vocally what is happening in schools and colleges and universities in which they had placed their hopes for their children.

Today, as we are coming to understand better the circular processes through which culture is developed and transmitted, we recognize that man's most human characteristic is not his ability to learn, which he shares with many other species, but his ability to teach and store what others have developed and taught him. Learning, which is based on human dependency, is relatively simple. But human capacities for creating elaborate teachable systems, for understanding and utilizing the resources of the natural world, and for governing society and creating imaginary worlds, all these are very complex. In the past, men relied on the least elaborate part of the circular system, the dependent learning by children, for continuity of transmission and for the embodiment of the new. Now, with our greater understanding of the process, we must cultivate the most flexible and complex part of the system—the behavior of adults. We must, in fact, teach ourselves how to alter adult behavior so that we can give up postfigurative upbringing, with its tolerated cofigurative components, and discover prefigurative ways of teaching and learning that will keep the future open. We must create new models for adults who can teach their children not what to learn, but how to learn and not what they should be committed to, but the value of commitment.

Postfigurative cultures, which focused on the elders—those who had learned the most and were able to do the most with what they had learned—were essentially closed systems that continually replicated the past. We must now move toward the creation of open systems that focus on the future—and so on children, those whose capacities are least known and whose choices must be left open.

In doing this we explicitly recognize that the paths by which we came into the present can never be traversed again. The past is the road by which we have arrived where we are. Older forms of culture have provided us with the knowledge, the techniques, and the tools necessary for our contemporary civilization. Coming by different roads out of the past, all the peoples of the earth are now arriving in the new world community. No road into the present need be repudiated and no former way of life forgotten. But all these different pasts, our own and all others, must be treated as precursors. . . .

# 12. The Young and Old—Notes on a New History

ROBERT J. LIFTON

What is a New History? And why do the young seek one? I raise these questions to introduce the idea of a particular New History—ours—and to suggest certain ways in which we can begin to understand it.

Let us define a New History as a radical and widely shared re-creation of the forms of human culture—biological, experiential, institutional, technological, aesthetic, and interpretive. The newness of these cultural forms derives not from their spontaneous generation, but from extensions and transformations of what already exists; that which is most genuinely revolutionary makes psychological use of the past for its plunge into the future. Of special importance is the *reassertion of the symbolic sense of immortality man requires as he struggles to perpetuate himself biologically* and *communally, through his works*, in *his tie to nature*, and through *transcendent forms of psychic experience*.

The shapers of a New History—political revolutionaries, revolutionary thinkers, extreme holocausts, and technological breakthroughs—also express the death of the old. This has been true of the American, French, Russian, and Chinese revolutions; the ideas of Copernicus, Darwin, and Freud; the mutilations of the two World Wars; and, most pertinent to us, the technological revolution which produced Auschwitz and Hiroshima, as well as the post-modern automated and electronic society. Each of these has been associated with "the end of an era," with the devitalization, or symbolic death, of forms and images defining the world-view and life-patterns of large numbers of people over long periods of time.

Great events and new ideas can thus, in different ways, cause, reflect, or symbolize historical shifts. The combination of *Nazi genocide and the American atomic bombings of two Japanese cities terminated man's sense of limits concerning his self-destructive potential, and thereby inaugurated an era in which he is devoid of assurance of living on eternally as a species.* It has taken almost twenty-five years for formulations of the significance of these events to begin to emerge—formulations which cannot be separated from the technological developments of this same quarter-century, or from the increasing sense of a universal world-society that has accompanied them.

The New History, then, is built upon the ultimate paradox of two competing, and closely related, *images*: that of the *extinction of history by technology*, and that of *man's evolving awareness of himself as a single species*. It may be more correct to speak of just one image, extraordinarily divided. And whatever the difficulties in evaluating the human consequences of this image, psychologists and historians who ignore it cease to relate themselves to contemporary experience.

The celebrated 1962 "Port Huron Statement" of the Students for a Democratic Society, which is still something of a manifesto for the American New Left, contains the assertion: "Our work is guided by the sense that we may be the last generation in the experiment with living." I think we should take this seriously, just as many of us took seriously Albert Camus' declaration that, in contrast with every generation's tendency to see itself as "charged with remaking the world," his own had a task "perhaps even greater, for it consists in keeping the world from destroying itself." What I wish to stress is the overriding significance for each generation after Hiroshima (and the SDS leaders, though twenty-five years younger than Camus, made their statement just five years after he made his) of precisely this threat of historical extinction. *In seeking new beginnings, men are now haunted by an image of the end of everything.*

Do the young feel this most strongly? They often say just the opposite. When I discuss Hiroshima with students, they are likely to point to a disparity between my (and Camus') specific concern about nuclear weapons and their generation's feeling that these weapons are just another among the horrors of the world bequeathed to them. Our two "histories" contrast significantly: my (over forty) generation's shocked "survival" of Hiroshima and continuing need to differentiate the pre-Hiroshima world we knew from the world of nuclear weapons in which we now live; their (under twenty-five) generation's experience of growing up in a world in which nuclear weapons have always been part of the landscape. This gradual adaptation, as opposed to original shock, is of great importance. Man is psychologically flexible enough to come to terms with almost anything, so long as it is presented to him as an ordained element of his environment.

But such adaptation is achieved at a price, and achieved only partially at that. The inner knowledge on the part of the young that their world has always been capable of exterminating itself creates an undercurrent of anxiety against which they must constantly defend themselves—anxiety related not so much to death as to a fundamental terror of premature death and unfulfilled life, and to high uncertainty about all forms of human continuity. Their frequent insistence that nuclear weapons are "nothing special" is their form of emotional desensitization, or what I call psychic numbing (as opposed to other forms called forth by their elders). But the young must do a great deal of continuous psychological work to maintain their nuclear "cool." And this in turn may make them unusually responsive to possibilities of breaking out of such numbing, and of altering the world which has imposed it upon them.

All perceptions of theatening historical developments must occur through what Ernst Cassirer called the *"symbolic net"*—that special area of psychic re-creation characteristic of man, the only creature who "instead of dealing with . . . things themselves . . . constantly converses . . . with himself." In these internal (and often unconscious) dialogues, anxieties about technological annihilation merge with various perceptions of more symbolic forms of death. That is, Hiroshima and Auschwitz become inwardly associated with the worldwide sense of profound historical dislocation: with the disintegration of formerly vital and nourishing symbols revolving around family, religion, principles of community, and the life cycle in general; and with the inability of the massive and impersonal postmodern institutions (of government, education, and finance) to replace psychologically that which has been lost. They become associated also with the confusions of the knowledge-revolution, and the unprecedented dissemination of half-knowledge through media whose psychological impact has barely begun to be discerned. There is a very real sense in which the world itself has become a "total environment"—a closed psychic chamber with continuous reverberations, bouncing about chaotically and dangerously. The symbolic death perceived, then, is this combination of formlessness and totality, of the inadequacy of existing forms and imprisonment within them. And the young are exquisitely sensitive to such "historical death," whatever their capacity (which we shall return to later) for resisting an awareness of the biological kind.

The young are struck by the fact that most of mankind simply goes about its business as if these extreme dislocations did not exist—as if there were no such thing as ultimate technological violence or existence rendered absurd. The war in Vietnam did not create these murderous incongruities, but it does epitomize them, and it consumes the American youth in them. No wonder, then, that in their "conversations with themselves," so many of the young everywhere seem to be asking: How can we bring the world—and ourselves —back to life?

In referring to the young and their quests, my examples are drawn mostly from the more radical among them; and what I say refers more to those who are white, educated, and of middle-class origin, than to blacks, uneducated youth, or those of working-class backgrounds. The same is true concerning my references to my own generation. In neither case can the people I describe be anything more than a very small minority within their age group, their country, or, for that matter, their university. But in both cases they seem to me to exemplify certain shared themes, psychological and historical, that in one way or another affect all people in our era and are likely to take on increasing importance over the next few decades and beyond.

**II**

Students of revolution and rebellion have recognized the close relationship of both to death symbolism, and to visions of transcending death by achieving an eternal historical imprint. Hannah Arendt speaks of revolution as containing an "all-pervasive preoccupation with permanence, with a 'perpetual state' . . . for . . . 'posterity.' "[1] And *Albert Camus* describes *insurrection*, "in its exalted and tragic forms," as "*a prolonged protest against death, a violent accusation against the universal death penalty*," and as "*the desire for immortality and for clarity*." But Camus also stressed the rebel's "appeal to the essence of being," his quest "not . . . for life, but for reasons for living."[2] And this brings us to an all-important question concerning mental participation in revolution: What is the place of ideology, and of images and ideas, and of the self in relationship to all three?

*Men have always pursued immortalizing visions.* But most of the revolutionary ideologies of the past two centuries have provided elaborate blueprints for individual and collective immortality—specifications of ultimate cause and ultimate effect, theological in tone and scientific in claim. When present-day revolutionaries reject these Cartesian litanies they are taking seriously some of the important psychological and historical insights of the last few decades. For they are rejecting an oppressive ideological totalism—with its demand for control of all communication within a milieu, its imposed guilt and cult of purity and confession, its loading of the language, and its principles of doctrine over person and even of the dispensing of existence itself (in the sense that sharp lines are drawn between those whose right to exist can be recognized and those who possess no such right). This rejection represents, at its best, a quest by the young for a new kind of revolution—one perhaps no less enduring in historical impact, but devoid of the claim to omniscience and of the catastrophic chain of human manipulations stemming from that claim.

It is, of course, quite possible that the *anti-ideological stance of today's* *young* will turn out to be a transitory phenomenon, a version of the euphoric denial of dogma that so frequently appears during the early moments of revolution, only to be overwhelmed by absolutist doctrine and suffocating organization in the name of revolutionary discipline. Yet there is reason for believing that the present antipathy to ideology is something more, that it is an expression of a powerful and highly appropriate contemporary style. The shift we are witnessing from fixed, all-encompassing forms of ideology to more fluid *ideological fragments* approaches Camus' inspiring vision of continuously decongealing rebellion, as opposed to dogmatically congealed, all-or-none revolution. I would also see it as an expression of contemporary, or what I call *"protean," psychological style*—post-Freudian and post-modern, characterized by interminable exploration and flux, and by relatively easy shifts in identification and belief.* Protean man as rebel, then, seeks to remain open, while in the midst of rebellion, to the extraordinarily rich, confusing, liberating, and threatening array of contemporary historical possibilities.

His specific talent for fluidity greatly enhances his tactical leverage. For instance, Daniel Cohn-Bendit, the leader of the French student uprisings of May, 1968, in an interesting dialogue with Jean-Paul Sartre insisted that the classical Marxist-Leninist principle of the omniscient revolutionary vanguard (the working class, as represented by the Communist Party) be replaced with "a much simpler and more honorable one: the theory of an active minority acting, you might say, as a permanent ferment, pushing forward without trying to control events." Cohn-Bendit went on to characterize this process as "uncontrollable spontaneity" and as "disorder which allows people to speak freely and will later result in some form of 'self-organization.'" He rejected as "the wrong solution" an alternate approach (urged upon him by many among the Old Left) of formulating an attainable program and drawing up realizable demands. While this was "bound to happen at some point," he was convinced it would "have a crippling effect." In the same spirit are the warnings of Tom Hayden, a key figure in the American New Left, to his SDS colleagues and followers, against "fixed leaders"; and his insistence upon "participatory democracy," as well as upon ideology of a kind that is secondary to, and largely achieved through, revolutionary action. So widespread has this approach been that the American New Left has been characterized as more a process than a program.

* Related psychological styles have undoubtedly emerged during such earlier periods of historical dislocation as the Renaissance in the West or the Meiji Restoration in Japan. But the extremity of recent technological change, the contemporary loss of a sense that society is still "there," and the flooding of imagery of limitless choices by the mass media— these have combined to create, if not a world of shape-shifters, one in which rapid shifts in external commitments and inner forms have become part of a functional pattern of living.

I would suggest that the general principle of *"uncontrollable spontaneity"* represents a meeting ground between tactic and deeper psychological inclination. The underlying inclination consists precisely of the protean style of multiple identifications, shifting beliefs, and constant search for new combinations. Whatever its pitfalls, this style of revolutionary behavior is an attempt on the part of the young to mobilize the fluidity of the twentieth century as a weapon against what they perceive to be two kinds of stagnation: the old, unresponsive institutions (universities, governments, families) and newly emerging but fixed technological visions (people "programmed" by computers in a "technetronic society"). A central feature of his attempt is the stress upon the communal spirit and the creation of actual new communities. And here too we observe an alternation between conservative images of stable and intimate group ties, and images of transforming society itself in order to make such ties more possible than is now the case.

The process, and the underlying psychological tendencies, moreover, seem to be universal. Observing the nearly simultaneous student uprisings in America, France, Japan, Brazil, Germany, Italy, Mexico, South Africa, Czechoslovakia, Chile, Yugoslavia, and Spain, one can view them all as parts of a large single tendency, occurring within a single worldwide human and technical system. Here the planet's instant communications network is of enormous importance, as is the process of psychological contagion. To recognize the striking congruence in these rebellions, one need not deny the great differences in say, Czech students rebelling against Stalinism, Spanish students against Falangism, and American, French, and Italian students against the Vietnam war, the consumer society, and academic injustices.

In every case the young seek active involvement in the institutional decisions governing their lives, new alternatives to consuming and being consumed, and liberated styles of individual and community existence. Unspecific and ephemeral as these goals may seem, they are early expressions of a quest for historical rebirth, for reattachment to the Great Chain of Being, for reassertion of symbolic immortality.

The French example is again revealing (though not unique), especially in its extraordinary flowering of graffiti. Here one must take note of the prominence of the genre—of the informal slogan-on-the-wall virtually replacing formal revolutionary doctrine, no less than the content. But one is struck by the stress of many of the slogans, sometimes to the point of intentional absurdity, upon enlarging the individual life space, on saying "yes" to more and "no" to less. Characteristic were "Think of your desires as realities," "Prohibiting is forbidden" (a play on words in which the ubiquitous "Défense d'afficher" is converted to "Défense d'interdire"), and, of course, the two most famous: "Imagination in power" and "Imagination is revolution." Sartre was referring to the over-all spirit of these graffiti, but perhaps most to the revolutionary acts themselves, when he commented (in the same dialogue mentioned before) : "I would like to describe what you have done as extending the field of possibilities."

Precisely such "extending [of] the field of possibilities" is at the heart of the worldwide youth rebellion—for hippies no less than political radicals— and at the heart of the protean insistence upon continuous psychic re-creation of the self. Around this image of unlimited extension and perpetual re-creation, as projected into a dimly imagined future, the young seek to create a new mode of revolutionary immortality.

## III

*Of enormous importance for these rebellions is another basic component of the protean style, the spirit of mockery.* While young rebels are by no means immune from the most pedantic and humorless discourse, they come alive to others and themselves only when giving way to—or seizing upon— their very strong inclination toward mockery. The mocking political rebel merges with the hippie and with a variety of exponents of pop culture to "put on"—that is mislead or deceive by means of some form of mockery or absurdity—his uncomprehending cohorts, his elders, or anyone in authority. (Despite important differences, there has always been a fundamental unity in the rebellions of hippies and young radicals which is perhaps just now becoming fully manifest.) In dress, hair, and general social and sexual style the mocking rebel is not only "extending the field of possibilities," but making telling commentary—teasing, ironic, contemptuous—on the absurd folkways of "the others." The mockery can be gentle and even loving, or it can be bitter and provocative in the extreme.\*

The tone of mockery can be a source of great unifying power. One could argue, for instance, that mockery provided the necessary continuity in the evolution, metaphorically speaking, from hippie (socially withdrawn experiments in feeling) to Yippie (activist assaults upon social institutions) ; as well as the psychological style around which elements of student-radical and hippie cultures could come to coexist within individual minds. In the Columbia rebellion the spirit of mockery was able to unite, if not in political action, at least in a measure of shared feeling, such disparate groups as hippies, Yippies, white student radicals and moderates, and some blacks (the police could also be included, but from across the barricades). And one can add to the list the distinguished professor whose pun I quoted, many of his faculty colleagues, a large number of Columbia students not involved in the strike, the writer of this essay, and probably most of its readers. *For mockery is*

\* A classic example of the mocking put-on was Yippie leader Jerry Rubin's appearance at the House Un-American Activities Committee.

*central to the absurd incongruity in the relationship of self to society, and ultimately of death to life, which we all share.* There are moments when this incongruity can be dealt with only by the combinations of humor, taunt, mimicry, derision, and ridicule contained within the style of mockery. For when historical dislocation is sufficiently profound, mockery can become the only inwardly authentic tone for expressing what people feel about their relationships to the institutions of their world. And in this sense young rebels express what a great many other people—from conservative Wall Street broker to liberal college professor to black militant to anti-black Wallaceite— in one way or another inwardly experience.

On the border of mockery are such slogans of the French students as "We are all undesirables!" and the much more powerful "We are all German Jews!" The slogans refer directly to the origins of Cohn-Bendit, the student leader, but their significance extends much further. They mock not only anti-Semitism and national-racial chauvinism, but the over-all process of victimization itself, and the "old history" for harboring such victimization. The method by which this was done is worth noting: a vast open-air charade with thousands of students who, by shouting in unison, "We are all German Jews!", momentarily became classical European victims, thereby rendering ridiculous the very categories of victim and victimizer. At this affirmative border of mockery, then, and at the far reaches of the protean style, is a call for man to cease his folly in dividing himself into what Erik Erikson has called pseudo-species, and to see himself as the single species he is.

One can observe a related if much more confusing impulse toward inclusiveness, though, in the diversity of ideological fragments young rebels embrace. Thus hippies, for their experiments with the self, draw upon Eastern and Western mysticism, chemically induced ecstasy, and various traditions, new and old, of polymorphous sexuality. Young radicals may incorporate any of these aspects of hippie culture, and combine them with ideas and images drawn from many different revolutionary experiences (pre-Marxist utopians, anarchists, Marx, Trotsky, Lenin, Rosa Luxemburg, Mao, Castro, Guevara, Debray, Ho, Gandhi, Fanon, Malcolm X, Martin Luther King, Stokely Carmichael, and H. Rap Brown); from recent psychological and social theorists (Sartre, Camus, C. Wright Mills, Herbert Marcuse, Norman O. Brown, Erik Erikson, Abraham Maslow, and Paul Goodman); and from just about any kind of evolving cultural style (derived from jazz or black power or "soul," from the small-group movement and the Esalen-type stress upon Joy, or from camp-mockery of Victorian or other retrospectively amusing periods), including all of the revolutionary and intellectual traditions just mentioned.

*Moreover, the emphasis upon the experiential—upon the way a man and his ideas feel to one right now, rather than upon precise theory—encourages inclusivenss and fits in with the focus upon images and fragments.* Details of intellectual history may be neglected, and even revered figures are often greatly misunderstood. But the over-all process can be seen as a revolutionary equivalent to the artist's inclination to borrow freely, selectively, impressionistically, and distortingly from predecessors and contemporaries as a means of finding his own way.

Of enormous importance as *models are heroic images* of men whose lives can be viewed as continuously revolutionary. The extraordinary lives of Mao, Castro, and especially Guevara can combine wih romantic mythology of many kinds, including that of perpetual revolution. In a sense Castro and Guevara are transitional figures between the total ideologies of the past and the more fragmentary and experiential ones of the New History. (I shall comment later upon the particular dilemmas Mao presents for the new rebels.) But heroes and models tend to be easily discarded and replaced, or else retained with a looseness and flexibility that permits the strangest of revolutionary bedfellows. In lives as in ideologies, the young seek not the entire package but those fragments which contribute to their own struggle to formulate and change their world, to their own sense of wholeness. *Their constant search for new forms becomes a form in itself.*

To dismiss all this as a "style revolution" is to miss the point—unless one is aware of the sense in which style is everything. One does better to speak of a *revolution of forms,* of a quest for images of rebirth which reassert feelings of connection and re-establish the sense of immortality; and of a *process revolution,* consistent with the principles of action painting and kinetic sculpture, in which active rebelling both expresses and creates the basic images of rebellion. The novelist Donald Barthelme's statement that "Fragments are the only form I trust" has ramifications far beyond the literary. However severe the problems posed by such a principle for social and especially political revolution, we deceive ourselves unless we learn to focus upon these shifting forms—to recognize new styles of life and new relations to institutions and to ideas. Indeed, we require a little revolutionizing of our psychological assumptions, so that both the young and the old can be understood, not as bound by static behavioral categories, but as in continuous historical motion.

## IV

Let us, for instance, turn to the extremely important *symbolism surrounding fathers and sons.* Here the theme of fatherlessness is prominent—but it does not necessarily include a search for a "substitute father."

In addition to his biological and familial relationship to his children, we may speak of the father as one who mediates between prevailing social images on the one hand and the developmental thrusts of his children (biological or symbolic) on the other. Because the father is clearly not a simple conduit, and imposes a strong personal imprint (his "personality") upon the child, we tend to fall into the lazy psychoanalytic habit of seeing every authoritative man or group coming into subsequent contact with the child from the larger society as a "substitute" for the father, as a "father figure." Yet considering the enormous part played by general historical forces in shaping what the father transmits (or fails to transmit), one might just as well say that he is a "substitute" for history, a "history figure." The analogy is admittedly a bit far-fetched—a flesh-and-blood father, and not "history," conceives the child, teaches him things, and tells him off—but so is the tendency toward indiscriminate labeling of one person as a "substitute" for another. We do better, especially during periods of rapid change, to see fathers and sons as bound up in a shifting psychological equilibrium, each influencing the other, both enmeshed in forms specific to their family and thir historical epoch. (Mothers and daughters are, of course, very much part of all this. But the mother's "mediation," for biological and cultural reasons, tends to be more heavily infused with nurturing; her way of representing forms of social authority tends to be more indirect, complex, and organically rooted. And revolutionary daughters, like their mothers, deserve an evaluation of their own, quite beyond the scope of this essay.) A son's developing image (or images) of the world should not be attributed to a single cause, nor considered a replacement for an earlier imprint.

*Nor is the father by any means a pure representative of the past.* Rather he is a molder of compromise between the history he has known and the newer one in which the life of his family is immersed. During periods like the present he is, psychologically speaking, by no means a clear spokesman for stability and "order." He is more of a troubled negotiator, caught between the relatively orderly images he can retain (or reach back for) from his own experience, and the relatively disorderly ones anticipating the new shape of things. While likely to be more on the side of the former than the latter, in the midst of a revolution of forms his allegiances may not be too clear. He finds himself suspended in time, weakened by the diminishing power of old forms, and by his inability to relate himself significantly to (or even comprehend) the new.

During earlier revolutions (the French Revolution or the social revolution of the Renaissance) the old history under attack, however vulnerable, was still part of a coherent formulation of the world—theological, political, and social. One suspects that this formulation provided the fathers of the time with psychic ammunition sufficient at least to confront, and oppose directly, their rebellious sons. But the old history now being attacked, reflecting as it does more than two hundred years of erosion of traditional forms of every kind, permits fathers no such symbolic strength, no such capacity for confrontation.

Instead we find a characteristic father-son pattern emerging in families in various parts of the world—among young American radicals (as reported by Kenneth Keniston), middle-class Germans (described by Alexander Mitscherlich), Japanese *Zengakuren* student-activists (whom I interviewed), and, very likely, among many young French student-rebels. The pattern is this: The son, fortified and recurrently exhilarated by his radical convictions, and by his sense of being ethically and historically *right*, pities rather than hates his father for the latter's "sellout" to evil social forces. Whether kindly or contemptuous in this judgment, he views his father as one who has erred and been misled, as a man in need of patient re-education (if he is to be salvaged at all) rather than total denunciation. And the father himself, inwardly, cannot help but share many of these judgments, however he may try to attribute them to his son's immaturity and youthful excess. This is the sense in which fathers no longer exercise ethical—or formative—authority over their sons. They have lost their capacity to guide their offspring (rather than be guided by them) through the shifting forms of their common world. They can be fathers but not mentors.

This loss of mentorship is what we generally call "the absence of male authority." Its large-scale occurrence reflects the *historical* absence of a meaningful set of inner images of what one should value, how one should live. But it is experienced by the individual as a profound sense of fatherlessness. Sons feel abandoned by their fathers and perceive the world as devoid of strong men who know how things are and how they sould be. They experience the hunger for new forms—and especially imagery of rebirth—that I have described as characteristic of contemporary man.

But precisely this kind of symbolic fatherlessness, as I have also suggested, makes possible every variety of experiment and innovation. Just as the young lack the nurturing comfort of fixed social forms, so are they free of the restricting demands of these forms. Since nothing is psychologically certain, everything is possible. And there emerges what might be called an "unencumbered generation" (if we may give it still one more name), in politics as well as in everyday life.

Unencumbered rebellion can include every variety of tactical and ideological foray into present-day existence—as expressed in this country's "new politics" (the young radicals' politics of confrontation, the Yippies' "politics of ecstasy," and the more staid but still politically unconventional and youth-influenced campaigns of Eugene McCarthy and Robert Kennedy); and especially in contemporary novels (such as the nightmare version depicted by Sol Yurick in *The Bag*). This potential of innovation is perhaps the least understood dimension of the new rebels. It particularly confuses members of the Old Left, and provokes them either to reassert older judgments about how radicals should behave, or to attempt (often with considerable sympathy) to subsume the new rebellion under a traditional ideological label. "Anarchism" is the most tempting, because of its stress upon human relations in autonomous communities and opposition to centralized power, and because of what George Woodcock has referred to as "its cult of the spontaneous . . . [and] striking protean fluidity in adapting its approach and methods to special historical circumstances." But even Woodcock speaks of "a new manifestation of the idea"; and the young themselves tend to alternate between accepting the anarchist label as one of their ideological fragments, and expressing wariness toward it as still another potential ideological trap. Perhaps Sartre was wiser in his characterization of the phenomenon to Cohn-Bendit: "You have many more ideas than your fathers had. . . . Your imagination is far richer."

The university was perceived throughout as both an arena of fearful dangers (revisionist ideas), and as what might be called an immortalizing agent (for the promulgation at the highest cultural levels of the most complete Maoist thought).

In its own fashion, the Cultural Revolution was a response to the New History, which in China's case includes not only Russian and Eastern European revisionism but early manifestations of proteanism. Chinese universities, however, have been forced to flee from contemporary confusions into what is most simple and pure in that country's Old Revolutionary History; this is in contrast to the more open-ended plunge into a threatening but more openended future being taken by universities throughout the rest of the world. Yet these issues are far from decided. Universities everywhere, China included, are likely to experience powerful pressures from the young for "restructuring." While this hardly guarantees equivalent restructuring of national governments, it may well be a prelude to fundamental changes in almost every aspect of human experience.

# VI

One can hardly speak of definitive conclusions about something just beginning. Nor would I claim a position of omniscient detachment from the events of the New History—I have in no way been immune from the combinations of feelings about them I have described for my generation of Left-intellectuals, and have here and there contributed to dialogues on them. But having earlier in this essay affirmed the significance of the New History, I wish now to suggest some of its pitfalls, and then, finally, present-day potentialities for avoiding them.

From the standpoint of the young, these pitfalls are related to what is best called romantic totalism. I refer to a post-Cartesian absolutism, to a new quest for old feelings. *Its controlling image, at whatever level of consciousness, is that of replacing history with experience.*

This is, to a considerable extent, the romanticism of the "youth movement." I have heard a number of thoughtful European-born intellectuals tell, with some anxiety, how the tone and atmosphere now emanating from young American rebels is reminiscent of that of the German youth movement of the late Weimar Republic (and the Hitler Youth into which it was so readily converted). What they find common to both is a cult of feeling and a disdain for restraint and reason. While I would emphasize the differences between the two groups much more than any similarities, there is a current in contemporary youth movements that is more Nietzschean than Marxist-Leninist. It consists of a stress upon what I call *experiential transcendence, upon the cultivation of states of feeling so intense and so absorbing that time and death cease to exist.* (Drugs are of great importance here but as part of a general quest.) The pattern becomes totalistic when it begins to tamper with history to the extent of victimizing opponents in order to reinforce these feelings, and a danger signal is the *absolute denial of the principle of historical continuity.*

The *replacement of history with experience—* with totally liberated feeling —is by no means a new idea, and has long found expression in classical forms of mysticism and ecstasy. But it has reappeared with considerable force in the present-day drug revolution, and in the writings of a number of articulate contemporary spokesmen such as Norman O. Brown. This general focus upon the transcendent psychic experience would seem to be related to impairments in other modes of symbolic immortality. That is, the modern decline of theological concepts of immortality, on the one hand, and the threat posed by present weapons (nuclear, bacterial, and chemical) to man's biological and cultural continuity, on the other, have radically undermined symbolism of death and transcendence. In the absence of intact images of biological and cultural immortality, man's anxiety about both his death and his manner of life is profoundly intensified. One response to this anxiety, and simultaneous quest for new forms, is the unique contemporary blending of experiential transcendence with social and political revolution.

We have already noted that political revolution has its own *transformationist myth* of making all things new. When this combines with the *experiential myth* (of eliminating time and death), two extreme positions can result. One of these is the condemnation and negation of an entire historical tradition: the attempt by some of the young to sever totally their relationship to the West by means of an impossibly absolute identity replacement, whether the new identity is that of the Oriental mystic or that of the Asian or African victim of colonialism or slavery. And a second consequence of this dismissal of history can be the emergence of a single criterion of judgment: what feels revolutionary is good, what does not is counter-revolutionary.

A related, equally *romantic pitfall might be called "generational totalism."* The problem is not so much the slogan "Don't trust anyone over thirty" as the unconscious assumption that can be behind it: that "youth power" knows no limits because youth equals immortality. To be sure, it is part of being young to believe that one will never die, that such things happen only to other people, old people. But this conviction ordinarily lives side by side with a realization —at first preconscious, but over the years increasingly a matter of awareness— that life is, after all, finite. And a more symbolic sense of immortality, through works and connections outlasting one's individual life span, takes hold and permits one to depend a little less upon the fantasy that one will live forever.

Under *extreme historical conditions*, however, certain groups—in this case, youth groups—feel the need to cling to the omnipotence provided by a more literal image of immortality, which they in turn contrast with the death-tainted lives of others. When this happens, we encounter a version of the victimizing process: the young "victimize" the old (or older) by equating age with individual or historical "exhaustion" and death; and the "victim," under duress, may indeed feel himself to be "as if dead," and collude in his victimization. Conversely, the older generation has its need to victimize, sometimes (but not always) in the form of counterattack, and may feel compelled to view every innovative action of the young as destructive or "deadly." Indeed, *the larger significance and greatest potential danger of what we call the "generation gap" reside in these questions of broken historical connection and impaired sense of immortality.*

The recent slogan of French students, "The young make love, the old make obscene gestures," is patronizing rather than totalistic, and its mocking blend of truth and absurdity permits a chuckle all around. But when the same students refer to older critics as "people who do not exist," or when young American radicals label everyone and everything either "relevant" ("revolutionary") or "irrelevant" ("counter-revolutionary") on the basis of whether or not the person, idea, or event is consistent or inconsistent with their own point of view—then we are dealing with something more potentially malignant, with the drawing of sharp lines between people and nonpeople.

Perhaps the ultimate expression of generational totalism was that of an early group of Russian revolutionaries who advocated the suppression and even annihilation of everyone over the age of twenty-five because they were felt to be too contaminated with that era's old history to be able to absorb the correct principles of the New. I have heard no recent political suggestions of this kind; but there have certainly been indications (aside from the Hollywood version of youth suppressing age in the film *Wild in the Streets*) that young radicals at times have felt a similar impulse; and that some of their antagonists in the older generations have felt a related urge to eliminate or incarcerate everyone *under* twenty-five.

I have stressed the promiscuous use of the word "relevant." Beyond its dictionary meanings, its Latin origin, *relevare*, to raise up, is suggestive of its current meaning. What is considered relevant is that which "raises up" a particular version of the New History—whether that of the young rebels or of the slightly older technocrats (such as Zbigniew Brezinski) who are also fond of the word. Correspondingly, everything else must be "put down"—not only criticized and defeated but denied existence.

Such existential negation is, of course, an old story: one need only recall Trotsky's famous reference to the "dustbin of history." But the young, paradoxically, call it forth in relationship to the very images and fragments we spoke of before as protean alternatives to totalism. An example is the all-encompassing image of the "Establishment": taken over from British rebels, it has come to mean everything from the American (or Russian, or just about any other) political and bureaucratic leadership, to American businessmen (from influential tycoons to salaried executives to storekeepers), to university administrators (whether reactionary or liberal presidents or simple organization men), and even to many of the student and youth leaders who are themselves very much at odds with people in these other categories. And just as Establishment becomes a devil-image, so do other terms—such as (in different ways) "confrontation" and "youth"—become god-images. It is true that these god- and devil-images can illuminate many situations, as did such analogous Old Left expressions as "the proletarian standpoint," "the exploiting classes," and "bourgeois remnants," these last three in association with a more structured ideology. What is at issue, however, is the degree to which a particular image is given a transcendent status and is then uncritically applied to the most complex situations in a way that makes it the start and finish of any ethical judgment or conceptual analysis.

This image-focused totalism enters into the ultimate romanticization, that of death and immortality. While the *sense* of immortality—of unending historical continuity—is central to ordinary psychological experience, *romantic totalism tends to confuse death with immortality, and even to equate them.* Here one recalls Robespierre's famous dictum, "Death is the beginning of immortality," which Hannah Arendt has called "the briefest and most grandiose definition . . . [of] the specifically modern emphasis on politics, evidenced in the revolutions." Robespierre's phrase still resonates for us, partly because it captures an elusive truth about individual death as a *rite de passage* for the community, a transition between a man's biological life and the continuing life of his works. But within the phrase there also lurks the romantic temptation to court death in the service of immortality—to view dying, and in some cases even killing, as the only true avenues to immortality.

The great majority of today's radical young embrace no such imagery—they are in fact intent upon exploring the fullest possibilities of life. But some can at times be prone to a glorification of life-and-death gestures, and to all-or-none "revolutionary tactics," even in petty disputes hardly worthy of these

221

cosmic images. In such situations their sense of mockery, and especially self-mockery, deserts them. For these and the related sense of absurdity can, at least at their most creative, deflate claims to omniscience and provide a contemporary equivalent to the classical mode of tragedy. Like tragedy, mockery conveys man's sense of limitations before death and before the natural universe, but it does so now in a world divested of more "straight" ways to cope with mortality. Those young rebels who reject this dimension, and insist instead upon unwavering militant rectitude, move toward romanticized death and the more destructive quests for immortality.

## VII

Yet precisely the openness of the young may help them to avoid definitive commitments to these self-defeating patterns. They need not be bound by the excesses of either Cartesian rationalism or the contemporary cult of experience which feeds romantic totalism. Indeed, though the latter is a response to and ostensibly a replacement for the former, there is a sense in which each is a one-dimensional mirror-image of the other. Today's young have available for their formulations of self and world the great twentieth-century insights which liberate man from the senseless exclusions of the opposition between emphasis on "experience" and on the "rational." I refer to the principles of symbolic thought, as expressed in the work of such people as Cassirer and Langer, and of Freud and Erikson. One can never know the exact effect of great insights upon the historical process, but it is quite possible that, with the decline of the total ideologies of the old history, ideas as such will become more important than ever in the shaping of the New. Having available an unprecedented variety of ideas and images, the young are likely to attempt more than did previous generations and perhaps make more mistakes, but also to show greater capacity to extricate themselves from a particular course and revise tactics, beliefs, and styles—all in the service of contributing to embryonic social forms.

These forms are likely to be highly fluid, but need not by any means consist exclusively of shape-shifting. Rather, they can come to combine flux with elements of connectedness and consistency, and to do so in new ways and with new kinds of equilibria. Any New History worthy of that name not only pits itself against, but draws actively upon, the old. Only through such continuity can the young bring a measure of sure-footedness to their continuous movement. And to draw upon the old history means to look both ways: to deepen the collective awareness of Auschwitz and Hiroshima and what they signify, and at the same time to carve out a future that remains open rather than bound by absolute assumptions about a "technetronic society" or by equally absolute polarities of "revolution" and "counterrevolution."

222

# EPILOGUE

## PETER K. MANNING

Take a look at a great painting, or Polaroid snapshot. Does it have a message? A song is a picture. You see it; more accurately, you see it, taste it, feel it. . . . Telling a guy to listen to a song is like giving him a dime for the roller coaster. It's an experience. A song is an experience. The guy who writes the song and the guy who sings it each feels something; the idea is to get you to feel the same thing, or something like it. And you can feel it without knowing what it is. (Williams, 1970, p. 63)

This quote suggests that those whose interest is in capturing experience in a systematic fashion have an easy task, for they must only *feel*. Of course, Williams is only speaking here to the listener whose interest is in his own pleasure and enjoyment (why not?), not to be the poet as a craftsman, the working photographer, or the critic who aims to evaluate the extent to which one person captures the feelings of others. The critic's role is analogous to that of the sociologist. The sociologist must root himself in personal experience; he must be able to feel, to taste, to envision alternatives to the here and now even while it enmeshes him, but his mandate demands more of him. He must construct the meaning of his experience in a public, generic, shareable, clear and systematic fashion.

Existential sociology, because of its commitment to the analysis of the place of feelings or sensibilities and their relations to structures in social life, represents a challenge to at least the modal tendencies found in sociology. Let us first not create artificial dichotomies, for existential sociology is evaluated knowledge. The differences may be in matters of style or degree.

This epilogue tries in a brief way to simply delineate these matters of style and degree, and then to tie this perspective to youth, showing that it allows us to appropriately analyze youth and may in addition, allow the young to analyze society. (Those who by this time are convinced of the worth of the perspective, or have decided to the contrary, may wish to skip this section and move to the bibliographic note.)

First, *the existential sociologist is committed to deep immersion in the everyday*

223

*life of the actor.* The role of the sociologist is seen as cutting out or delineating the path that leads to better understanding of the relationships between the individual as he experiences his social world and the structures that are given in that world. That is, he aims to understand the common-sense world of the actor, to see his typifications of events, his readings of others' intentions, his perspectives, his system of relevances, and all within the biographical history of the person. Whereas the traditional sociological approach urges the investigator to adopt a spectatorial or distant stance toward human dilemmas, existential sociology urges that the investigator become involved in a detailed and intimate fashion with the social scene, to understand it from within. Participant observation and its forms is thus an intimate aspect of the existentially oriented research enterprise.

Second, *a connection between the social world of the observed and the observer is fundamental to existential sociology; this role should not be solely that of the disattached, scientific observer.*

Connection between the world and the investigator is initially established in the realm of feelings and intuitions, but it must be conceptualized; that is, abstracted and shaped into a more parsimonious form for communication. The process of abstraction often involves shifting between roles, between psychic closeness and distance, between concrete fact and concept. It is for this reason that sociologists are so concerned about developing and measuring *concepts*, which turns from personal into generic experience. (Schutz argues that we must begin with personal experience, but move to a more abstract version of that experience by creating a typification of the typifications of everyday life.) The concepts that are required by existential sociology are those that capture minute variations in situations rather than global descriptions of events and processes that are beyond comprehension. (How does one "understand" the Viet Nam War? Doesn't Dylan's record "God on Our Side" tell us more sociologically than all the news reports that assault our psyches daily? Short of this sort of understanding, where does one begin?)

Third, *existential sociology aims to increase human awareness and understanding.* This proposition implies that knowledge increases one's freedom of action, one's choices. Although I do not believe that anything is "out there" other than what the person perceives is out there, I do not believe that he is always able to "see" and understand the implications of the social events and processes in which he is implicated. The contrary seems to be the case. In order to increase understanding, the person must see through the fictions on which social life is based and evaluate them afresh. However, it is not just knowledge that is central to change and to increased awareness: what seems to be central is to discover means by which we can jar people into reexamining the problematic nature of their social worlds. Recent events: the flood that in the spring of 1972 killed nearly 200 people in Rapid City, South Dakota; the murder of over 100 people in the Tel Aviv airport; the ordered busing of the entire metropolitan school system of Detroit to commence in 1973; and still another assassination attempt. These events in themselves are no more or less trivial than the music I hear in the background as I type, the color of my shirt today, the noise of the children upstairs, or the cover of the new book I know sits behind me on the table. To be understood, they must be framed within a perspective that assigns relevance to given persons in designated life situations. To do sociology, we must not only experience life (without that experience we have no sensibility and therefore no sociology), we must in addition make it problematic by contrasting it to alternative ways of being and doing, and by presenting these life ways in a coherent fashion.

Fourth, *existential sociology assumes that meaning arises in interaction.* The art object, the Bach sonata, the Beatles record, and the Picasso sketch cannot be assumed to have intrinsic meaning outside of the context in which they are recognized, indicated, named, and classified. We cannot, in other words, dissociate meaning from the language by which it is in large part assigned. On the other hand, the importance of the paralinguistic (voice tone, pitch, and hesitations, for example) and nonverbal forms of communication must not be overlooked. Insofar as existential sociology reacts to the linearity and the nonpoetic nature of sociological analysis, it is likely to include a wider range of concerns with poems, music, nonlinear modes of communication, and experimental ways of making sense of social life. These modes of communication express the position that the observer and observed occupy in the social structure; they are sociological indices of social position, feeling, and social structure. To take a scientific perspective, although being invested in the actor's world, and to try to raise human awareness, involves the stuff of sociology: human interactions. Naming and analysis by the sociologist will ultimately set him apart from the everyday world, and provide him a role that does not exist within the common-sense boundaries of those he observes will give him that distance that is essential to understanding.

In one, two, three fashion, the above guiding concepts provide a sketch of some of the features that distinguish existential sociology from other sociologies. In assembling this book, I was aware of the several sometime contradictory demands that such ideas make. Some of the selections do not illustrate all of the tenets, but the overall flavor is evident. Above all, certain features of the behavior and understandings that we attribute to the youth make the existential *perspective* and the *content*, youth, congruous. They appear to me to provide dramatic opportunities for the exercise of the sociological imagination.

The sociological imagination involves to me something like what Kenneth Keniston describes in his *Young Radicals* (1968, p. 269). "The focal issue for youth is the issue of social role, of the individual's relationship to the established structures of society. . . . The task of youth is to find or create some congruence, in a broad sense, between the individual and existing institutions." The young, because they are trying in many desperate ways to articulate themselves with the myriad of experiences in which they are cast, are given to excess, to extremes, and to passions. At times, they see no boundaries between themselves and the world; at times, they see far too many constraints around them and they seek means of blurring the ties to conventional reality. Sociologists stand in the same relations to society as do the youth: they must learn that between one's self and the world (a boundary around the self, not around feelings), is the first step toward understanding the place of any single image found in that world and its connection to the larger world from which it issues.

The young, on the other hand, may themselves be significant sources of new insights and knowledge. That is, as well as being the objects of social analysis, they may also be the subjects, those who provide new knowledge as a result of their observations. Change affects people in different social segments in different ways, and the position of the youth occupying as they do a marginal location, may facilitate fresh new social knowledge:

> A characteristic of death is conformity; a characteristic of life is the disruption of conformity, the revelation of differences, of a tensed variety that makes every element aware of every other and especially of itself, of its unique and authentic shape. Our society will prosper insofar as it promotes rather than merely allows differences among its parts. Only by the encouragement of eccentricity will it be able to locate, scrutinize, and periodically shift its center . . .
>
> Everyone must study himself in those who otherwise seem alien. All of what we are is what we are (Poirier, 1971, p. 186).

Once we see the division between the self here and the self of others, and we begin to see that these distinctions are not simple commonsense, but the very stuff of sociology, it is possible to build up the images of society from our own proximal experiences that will be a basis for understanding social life. As a result of reading these works on the young, in experiencing their order, content, and the style with which they are presented, perhaps some psychic distance, feelings of alienation and inauthenticity, can be diminished. Like hearing a song that replicates the experience described in the song and then reexperiencing hearing the song and feeling those experiences again, the reading of these works may generate a sense of conceptual clarity and substantive interest in the experiences of the young, and young experiences.

## LIST OF REFERENCES IN SECTION INTRODUCTIONS

Bell, Daniel, 1965 — "The Disjunction of Culture and Social Structure: Some Notes on The Meaning of Social Reality." *Daedalus*, 94 (Winter), 208–222.

Berger, Bennett, 1971 — *Looking For America*. Englewood Cliffs: N.J.: Prentice-Hall.

Boorstin, Daniel, 1964 — *The Image*. New York: Harper Colophon Books.

Cottle, Thomas J., 1971 — *Time's Children*. Boston: Little, Brown and Co.

Davis, Fred, 1967 — "Why We May All Be Hippies Someday." *Trans-action*, 5 (December), 10–18.

Douglas, Jack D., 1967 — *The Social Meanings of Suicide*. Princeton, N.J.: Princeton University Press.

Durkheim, Emile, 1897 — *Suicide*. Paris: Felix Alcan, 1897. English ed., trans. by John A. Spaulding and George Simpson, New York: The Free Press, 1951.

Edelman, Murray, 1966   *The Symbolic Uses of Politics.* Urbana: University of Illinois.

Eisen, Jonathan (ed.), 1969   *The Age of Rock.* New York: Vintage Books.

Feuer, Lewis, 1968   *The Conflict of Generations.* New York: Basic Books.

Freidan, Betty, 1963   *The Feminine Mystique.* New York: Dell.

Goldman, Albert, 1971   *Freakshow.* New York: Atheneum.

Gouldner, Alvin, 1970   *The Coming Crisis in Western Sociology.* N.Y.: Basic Books.

Keniston, Kenneth, 1966   *The Uncommitted.* New York: Harcourt, Brace and Co.

Lifton, Robert J., 1967   *Death in Life: The Survivors of Hiroshima.* New York: Vintage Books.

Lyman, Stanford and Marvin Scott, 1970   *Sociology of the Absurd.* New York: Appleton-Century Crofts.

Manning, Peter K. (ed.), Forthcoming   *Collective Behavior and Change.* Englewood Cliffs, New York: Prentice-Hall.

Mead, Margaret, 1971   "Future Families." *Trans-action,* 8 (September), 50–53.

   , 1970   *Culture and Commitment.* New York: Doubleday.

Melly, George, 1970   *Protest into Style.* New York: Anchor Books.

Neville, R. (ed.), 1971   *Play Power.* New York: Random House.

Nuttall, Jeff, 1968   *Bomb Culture.* London: MacGibbon and Kee, Ltd.

Reich, Charles, 1970   *The Greening of America.* New York: Random House.

Roszak, Theodore, 1969   *Making of a Counter-Culture.* New York: Doubleday.

Rubin, Jerry, 1970   *Do It!* New York: Random House.

Wolfe, Tom, 1966   *The Kandy Kolored Tangerine Flake Streamlined Baby.* New York: Farrar, Straus and Giroux.

# BIBLIOGRAPHIC NOTE

It is my feeling that one of the prime sources for obtaining an understanding of the sensibilities of modern youth is the pop or mass culture, particularly *rock music*. The music seems to supply the moving force behind many of the changes in other areas of mass culture, and it reflects many of the trends and actual events that impinge on the youthful consciousness. As I have argued above, the previous sociological approaches now appear to be excessively concerned with a reified notion of social structure, and too little concerned with the interface of the person as a sensate being in a body within the structure of social relations. (A recent paper attempts to begin this synthesis: "Health Maintenance Among Peruvian Peasants," by Horacio Fabrega Jr., and Peter K. Manning, *Human Organization*, Fall, 1972.) The section on *existential sociology* may instruct the curious. Finally, *youth themselves* have been insightfully discussed, in my opinion, by only a handful of writers: their works are listed below.

## Rock Music

The general reader will find several books of use, in particular, Jonathan Eisen's edited *The Age of Rock* (Vols. I and II) Vintage, 1969 and 1970. There are several general treatments of the emergence of rock: David Amram's *Vibrations*, MacMillan, 1968; Carl Belz's *The Story of Rock*, Oxford, 1969; David Laing's *The Sound of Our Time*, Quadrangle Books, 1970; Charles Gillett's *The Sound of the City*, Outerbridge and Dienstfrey, 1970; Nik Cohn's *Rock from the Beginning*, Stein and Day, 1969; Jeff Nuttall's book, *Bomb Culture*, MacGibbon and Kee, Ltd., 1968, integrates the growth of music with the rise of youthful disaffection after World War II, especially in England (I highly recommend this book); George Melly's *Revolt into Style*, Doubleday Anchor, 1970, is a similar and valuable book with a focus on England. Ralph Gleason's *The Jefferson Airplace and the San Francisco Sound*, Ballantine, 1969 is a good treatment of the San Francisco scene (The Airplane, The Grateful Dead, The Moby Grape, The

Quick Silver Messenger Service) and should be read in conjunction with Tom Wolfe's *The Electric Kool Air Acid Test*, Farrar, Straus, and Giroux, 1968, and Michael Lydon's insightful collective biography of the Grateful Dead in *Rock Folk*, Dial, 1971. Incisive articles on rock stars are found in *Rolling Stone Interviews*.

In the critical vein, Laing's essays are worthwhile, but for the sheer virtuosity read Paul Williams' *Outlaw Blues*, Bantam, 1970; Albert Goldman's brilliant *Freakshow*, Atheneum, 1971, and Richard Goldstein's *Goldstein's Greatest Hits*, Tower Books, 1970. Periodicals with coverage of record releases, reviews, and interviews with figures in the rock scene are *Crawdaddy!* and *Rolling Stone*. A good bibliography and discography is in Gillett, cited above, and in Robinson and Zwerling, *The Rock Scene*, Pyramid, 1971.

Nothing, of course, can supersede the experience of hearing rock, especially while attending a live performance. A listing of recent hits best illustrative of the modern trends, both in "high" and "low" rock art would be virtually useless and dated by the time it appears. Begin, however, with the suggested list in Paul Williams, *Outlaw Blues*, and proceed from there to whatever is exciting. Go into record stores, talk to the sales people, and listen to FM radio, especially late at night.

## Music

I am not a competent music critic, nor do I have an adequate grounding in the fine arts to suggest a pedagogical strategy. I would suggest Roger Sessions' book, *The Experience of Music*, Atheneum, 1968, as a beginning point.

## Existential Sociology

The works of Sartre are a critical beginning, but should be read with Camus, Merleau-Ponty and Husserl (heavy, philosophical reading). Very useful also are the writings of R. D. Laing, the existential psychiatrist; Genet; Robert J. Lifton, especially his *History and Human Survival*, Random House, 1970; and the writing of his colleagues, Robert Coles, Kenneth Keniston (*The Uncommitted*, Harcourt and Brace, 1965 and *Young Radicals*, Harcourt and Brace, 1968), and Erik Erickson. In the sociological tradition, see the works of Peter Berger (begin with *Invitation to Sociology*, Doubleday, 1963), Thomas Luckmann, and E. A. Tiryakian, which build on the important work of Alfred Schultz, Karl Mannheim, and Georges Gurvitch. In the more phenomenological vein, see the collected papers of Harold Garfinkel, *Studies in Ethnomethodology*, Prentice-Hall, 1967; Jack Douglas' *Social Meanings of Suicide*, Princeton, 1967; and Douglas' collections (cited above) *Deviance and Respectability*, Basic Books, 1970, and *Understanding Everyday Life*, Aldine, 1970. See also David Matza's *Becoming Deviant*, Prentice-Hall, 1969. Several recent French writers are also important in this developing perspective: Michael Foucault, *Madness and Civilization*, Pantheon, 1970; also the works of Levi-Strauss (see Edmund Leach's introduction to Levi-Strauss published by Viking Press, 1970). A general introduction is found in Peter K. Manning, "Existential Sociology." *Sociological Quarterly,* forthcoming, 1973.

## Youth

This is an almost ever-extending field. I personally have learned from the following writers, and I therefore recommend them to you: Edgar Z. Friedenberg's, *The Vanishing Adolescent,* Dell, 1962; *Coming of Age in America,* Random House, 1965; *The Dignity of Youth and Other Atavisms,* Beacon, 1965, and his collection of articles in *The Anti-American Generation,* Trans-Action, 1971; Bennett Berger, *Looking for America,* Prentice-Hall, 1971 (a collection of his essays) the aforementioned books by Keniston, Lifton, and the works of David Riesman (who was making sense of youth in 1956—before any one knew there was a "problem"), especially *The Lonely Crowd* (still the best book on American civilization in recent times); Reuel Denney; Tom Wolfe's, *The Electric Kool-Aid Acid Test,* Farrar, Straus and Giroux, 1968; *The Pump House Gang,* Farrar, Straus and Giroux, 1968; and *The Kandy Kolored Tangerine Flake Streamline Baby,* Farrar, Strauss and Giroux, 1966; John Aldridge's *In The Country of The Young,* Harper's 1971; Richard Flack's *Youth and Social Change,* Markham, 1972; Theodore Roszak's *Making of a Counter-Culture,* Doubleday, 1969, and Phillip Slater's *The Pursuit of Loneliness,* Beacon, 1970. A most fascinating book is Thomas Cottle's *Time's Children,* Little, Brown, 1971. As for personal statements, I find them mostly to be a bore, but I liked James Simon Kunen's *The Strawberry Statement,* Random House, 1969. The historically interested should read Lewis Feuer's *Conflict of Generations,* Basic, 1969, with a critical eye to Feuer's biases, and Phillip Aries, *Centuries of Childhood,* Vintage, 1968.

Social relations. (Readers interested in the body-self-social structure interface may find the following papers by Horacio Fabrega, Jr. and myself useful: "Health Maintenance Among Peruvian Peasants" *Human Organization* Fall, 1972; "The Experience of Self and Body: Illness and Disease in the Chiapas Highlands," in George Psathas, ed. *Socology and Phenomenology* Wiley, 1973; "An Integrated theory of Disease: Ladino-Mestizo Views of Disease in the Chiapas Highlands" *Psychosomatic Medicine* forthcoming, 1973; and "On the Activities of Beggars: Accommodations of Marginal Persons" forthcoming.